[redacted]

Business for Intermediate GNVQ

[redacted]

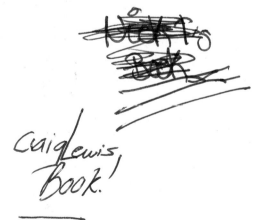

by Chris Nuttall
Tony Pitt
David Knight
Malcolm Meerabux
Barrie Birch

[redacted]

Craig Lewis, Book!

Collins Educational
An imprint of HarperCollins*Publishers*

Chris Nuttall, Tony Pitt, David Knight,
Malcolm Meerabux and Barrie Birch assert the moral
right to be identified as the authors of this work.

Published by
Collins Educational Ltd
An imprint of HarperCollins *Publishers*
77–85 Fulham Palace Road
Hammersmith
London W6 8JB

First published 1996
Reprinted 1998

ISBN 0–00–322375–2

Series commissioned by Richard Jackman.
Designed by DSM Partnership.
Cover designed by Trevor Burrows.
Project managed by Lesley Young.
Production by Mandy Inness.
Typesetting by Derek Lee.
Printed and bound by Scotprint Ltd., Musselburgh,
Scotland.

Contents

INTRODUCTION

Welcome to Business for Intermediate GNVQ. You are probably eager to get started on your new course but, first, let's look at how the course is structured and what you have to do to pass it. This book is specially written to help you to achieve success in the course and, at the same time, to enjoy your studies and get the most out of them.

WHAT IS A GNVQ?

The letters GNVQ stand for General National Vocational Qualification.

A **vocational qualification** is a qualification which is based on skills rather than just knowledge. In other words, to pass Business for Intermediate GNVQ you must show that you can do certain things rather than simply that you know about them. This is where GNVQs differ from conventional qualifications such as GCSEs and A-levels. Of course, to demonstrate the skills you acquire effectively, you also have to know about business. This is called **underpinning knowledge** because it forms a sound foundation for your skills.

GNVQ courses are **general** because they provide a broad-based vocational education which is focused on a particular area of work rather than a specific type of job. So, the course you are taking looks at business in general, rather than specific areas of work in business, such as administration or personnel.

GNVQs are **national** qualifications because they are based on national standards. The actual specifications for GNVQs are drawn up and published by the National Council for Vocational Qualifications (NCVQ). The standard of achievement in gaining a

GNVQ is therefore recognised throughout the UK and even internationally. Although they are drawn up and approved by NCVQ, three awarding bodies actually monitor the individual courses and award a certificate to successful students. The awarding bodies are BTEC, RSA and City and Guilds. One of these will administer the course you are taking.

GNVQs are directly relevant to the world of work and employment. They show that you have the appropriate skills and knowledge that employers are looking for. They will also help you to gain a place in higher education, if that is your aim.

INTERMEDIATE GNVQ IN BUSINESS

WHAT IS BUSINESS?

The term '**business**' covers all forms of activity connected with providing goods and services. It includes the activities of giant companies, such as Marks and Spencer, and the activities of organisations such as leisure centres, the local library and even your dentist. The goods and services provided by business organisations may be intended for private individuals or other business organisations.

THE STRUCTURE OF THE COURSE

The Intermediate GNVQ in Business is designed to help you to develop creative and analytical thinking. During the course you will:

- investigate business and business organisations;
- suggest changes to products and services
- design and produce promotional materials;
- plan for employment;

and lots more.

The course is made up of units, elements and performance criteria. A **unit** brings together major related aspects of the skills and knowledge of the GNVQ area. Each unit is made up of between two and five elements. An **element** is a more specific aspect of the skills and knowledge involved in a unit. The title of an element broadly describes what you are expected to do to achieve that element. **Performance criteria** are the actual activities which you must perform in achieving an element. The portfolio assignments in this book are written so that they fully cover all relevant performance criteria for every element in each unit.

You will study four mandatory units, two optional units and three mandatory core skill units. The **mandatory units** are:

- Unit 1: Business Organisations and Employment;
- Unit 2: People in Business Organisations;
- Unit 3: Consumers and Customers;
- Unit 4: Financial and Administrative Support.

You have to take all four mandatory units to pass the course.

Besides the four mandatory units, you must also take two out of a selection of **optional units**. Unlike the mandatory units, which are specified by NCVQ, each awarding body develops its own optional units, although they must be approved by NCVQ. The optional units you take will depend on which units are offered by your school or college, and your own interests.

The three **mandatory core skills units** are common to all GNVQ areas. You must achieve all three units to pass your GNVQ. The mandatory core skill units are:

- **Application of Number**:
  - collecting and recording data;
  - tackling problems;
  - interpreting and presenting data.
- **Communication**:
  - taking part in discussions;
  - preparing written materials;
  - using images;
  - reading and responding to written materials.
- **Information Technology**:
  - preparing information;
  - processing information;
  - presenting information;
  - evaluating the use of information technology.

The portfolio assignments in this book provide opportunities for you to produce evidence of coverage of some core skill units, and this has been indicated where appropriate. In some cases, however, coverage of specific core skills depends on how you present your evidence. For example, if you produce a written report using a word-processing package, this will provide evidence for the Information Technology core skill. Other forms of evidence will provide coverage of Application of Number and Communication. You should always check with your tutor to find out what core skills evidence you can claim. Don't forget that, as well as the portfolio assignments, many of the activities in this book will provide opportunities for claiming evidence of core skills.

Perhaps the most important thing to remember about core skills is that you should apply them in vocational or work situations. You must show that you have the appropriate skills, that you can use them and that you can do this in the context of the GNVQ area.

How will you be assessed?

You will be assessed on the evidence you provide to show that you have achieved all performance criteria. Each mandatory unit also has a unit test, which is taken under exam conditions. This will assess your knowledge of the unit area.

You will collect your evidence of having achieved the relevant performance criteria in a **Portfolio of Evidence**. Your portfolio must be carefully planned, organised, maintained and indexed. The evidence you collect will take many forms, including:

- **written work**, such as notes on a topic, a detailed plan, a report or a table;
- **witness statements**, such as written evidence provided by your tutor or another person – perhaps an employer – who has witnessed you taking part in a discussion, dealing with a customer or making a presentation;
- **video or audio recordings** of presentations you have made, group discussions, role plays, and so on;
- **other evidence**, such as letters, photographs, leaflets and brochures. These may be your own work, or evidence you have collected in support of other work you have done

The unit tests normally consist of between 25 and 40 questions. Each test takes one hour. You have more than one opportunity to take each test, so if you are unsuccessful at your first attempt, you can resit the test until you are successful.

Grading your GNVQ

A major part of your Portfolio of Evidence will be the portfolio assignments you complete. These will not only provide evidence of coverage of all relevant performance criteria, but also provide opportunities for achieving either a merit or a distinction.

Each assignment you produce may be graded higher than a pass according to your achievement in:

- **planning** – drawing up plans of action and monitoring the progress of your work
- **information seeking and handling** – identifying your information needs, and identifying and using appropriate sources to obtain the information;
- **evaluation** – evaluating the work you produce and justifying the approach you took to complete the assignment;
- **quality of outcomes** – how well your work brings together and demonstrates the relevant knowledge, skills and understanding, and your ability to use the 'language' of business.

How this book will help you

This book is specially written to provide up-to-date coverage of the latest specifications of Business for Intermediate GNVQ. It contains all the underpinning knowledge you will require and provides opportunities for producing evidence of coverage of every performance criterion in the mandatory units. It also provides opportunities for producing evidence of coverage of core skills.

Each chapter of the book covers one unit. The unit is indicated by the title of the chapter. Within each chapter, there are sections covering each element and performance criterion within each element. In this way you can check exactly where you are in the course.

All the underpinning knowledge you need is given in the main text. This is supported by case studies, diagrams and pictures to increase understanding and show how the knowledge you gain is applied in the world of business.

ACTIVITIES

Activities are exercises which will help you to understand what you have been reading and apply it to your own experience. You can complete many of the activities in the classroom, sometimes working with others or analysing case studies, documents and figures given in the book. Some activities, however, involve enquiries or investigations outside the classroom.

PORTFOLIO ASSIGNMENTS

The suggested portfolio assignments in this book are more substantial pieces of work than the activities. If you complete all the portfolio assignments, you will have all the evidence you need to demonstrate coverage of all four mandatory units. The portfolio assignments also provide opportunities for grading and for coverage of core skills.

QUICK response

QUICK RESPONSE QUESTIONS

In addition to the activities in the text, you will find quick response questions in the margins. These are designed for you to answer quickly, without the need for discussion or research. They are intended to test your comprehension of what you have just read, or to encourage you to think critically about a point in the text.

PRODUCING THE EVIDENCE

You will carry out two types of research in order to produce the evidence you need: desk research and field research.

Desk research involves finding and studying sources of information which are already available. These include:

- articles and reports about business in newspapers and magazines: the business pages of 'quality' newspapers such as *The Times* and *The Independent* are particularly useful sources of information about business; general magazines, such as *The Economist*, and professional magazines, such as *Management Today* and *Professional Manager* (both published by the Institute of Management) also contain articles of particular interest;
- books on business and business studies – including this book!

- brochures and leaflets published by commercial organisations, such as banks, and information obtainable from professional and trade associations;
- Government publications, such as *Social Trends* and the *Family Expenditure Survey*, and publications of the Statistical Office of the European Community;
- reports and information published by commercial research organisations such as Mintel.

Many of these books, newspapers, magazines and other publications are available from your school, college or local library. In many larger towns you can also often find a business library which contains a much greater variety of useful sources of published information about business. Get to know your library well. When you need to research a topic, ask the librarian. They are usually able to direct you to the right source. Many college libraries also have access to information on CD-ROM. This may include relevant articles from past issues of newspapers and magazines.

Often, however, you will need to obtain first-hand information not available from published sources. At these times you must carry out your own **field research**. Field research is where you obtain the information you need for yourself. For example, several portfolio assignments in this book ask you to investigate an actual business organisation. Establishing contacts with people in business and finding out about real business organisations form an essential part of your GNVQ course.

There are several ways in which you may become involved with business organisations. Your tutor may arrange a period of work experience for you, or links with businesses may be established through an external organisation, possibly a local Education Business Partnership or Training and Enterprise Council (TEC). You should ask your tutor about arrangements for links with industry.

Whatever links with businesses are arranged for you, however, or even if you have to find and establish links with business organisations for yourself, you must go about it in the right way if you are to get the most out of them.

Before trying to establish contact with someone in a business organisation, ask yourself:

- What do I need to find out?
- Where am I most likely to get the information I need?

When you have considered those questions, you should identify a local business organisation which you think can help you. Try to find out the name of someone in the business organisation who will deal with your enquiry. You can easily do this by telephoning the organisation. Explain to the receptionist or person you speak to the type of information you want to find out, and ask them the name and title of the person you should contact.

Most business organisations are willing to help GNVQ students but you must remember that their time is limited. When you have the name of someone in the organisation, write to them, explaining what you want to find out, and asking for an appointment to see them. Make sure that your letter is neat, with correct spelling and grammar, and set out correctly. If possible, produce your letter on a word processor. Produce a draft first and check this carefully. Only send your final version when you are sure it is the best you can do.

Before you go to see your contact, prepare a list of the questions you are going to ask. Make sure your questions cover all the information you need. Try to ask 'open questions' which call for explanations, rather than 'closed' questions which can be answered simply by 'yes' or 'no'. In this way you will obtain more information.

When you get to the meeting, ask the person you are seeing if you can take notes (make sure you have a notepad and pen ready!). This will help you to remember everything they say. Make sure you ask all your questions – and listen to the answers. Ask further questions if you think these will help you to get more information. Always be punctual, polite, show interest and thank the person for their time and help.

Contacting people in business, arranging appointments and going to meet them for the first time can be daunting. If you go about it in a positive way, however, well prepared and with enthusiasm, it can be one of the most rewarding parts of your GNVQ course.

Studying for a GNVQ will probably be quite different from any type of study you have done before. Most important of all, you will be responsible for a large part of your own learning and will have to do much of your own research. This calls for discipline, commitment – and sometimes just dogged persistence. You must produce your own evidence and make sure it is kept neatly and properly referenced in your Portfolio of Evidence.

We hope that you will find this book a useful and enjoyable guide to Business for Intermediate GNVQ. **Work hard, enjoy yourself – and good luck!**

I

UNIT

Business organisations and employment

CONTENTS

OUTLINE

In this unit you will see that there are many different types of business organisations which all produce goods and services designed to meet the needs and wants of customers. These organisations may be in the primary, secondary or tertiary industrial sector, according to their activities.

Privately owned businesses are in the private sector; businesses owned by national or local government are in the public sector. A business may be set up for profit, public service or charitable purposes. The activities and motives of businesses have an impact on opportunities for employment.

After completing this unit you will be able to:

1 explain the purposes and types of business organisations;
2 give reasons for the location of businesses and describe the business environment, markets and products;
3 present the results of an investigation into employment.

THE PURPOSES AND TYPES OF BUSINESS ORGANISATIONS

Business organisations produce goods and services which they supply to individuals and other business organisations who require those goods and services and are prepared to pay for them.

- **goods are things you can touch and use**, such as clothes, computers and textbooks;
- **services are things that other people do for you**, such as cutting your hair, looking after your money in a bank and prescribing medicines for you when you are sick.

Business organisations supply goods and services.

INDUSTRIAL SECTORS

All business and industrial activity takes place in three broad industrial sectors.

- **The primary sector** includes business organisations involved with producing or extracting raw materials from natural resources.
- **The secondary sector** includes business organisations involved in manufacturing and construction, which use the products of the primary sector.

- **The tertiary sector** includes business organisations involved in providing services.

Fig. 1.1 shows how organisations in the three sectors form a chain of production and distribution to get goods and services to customers.

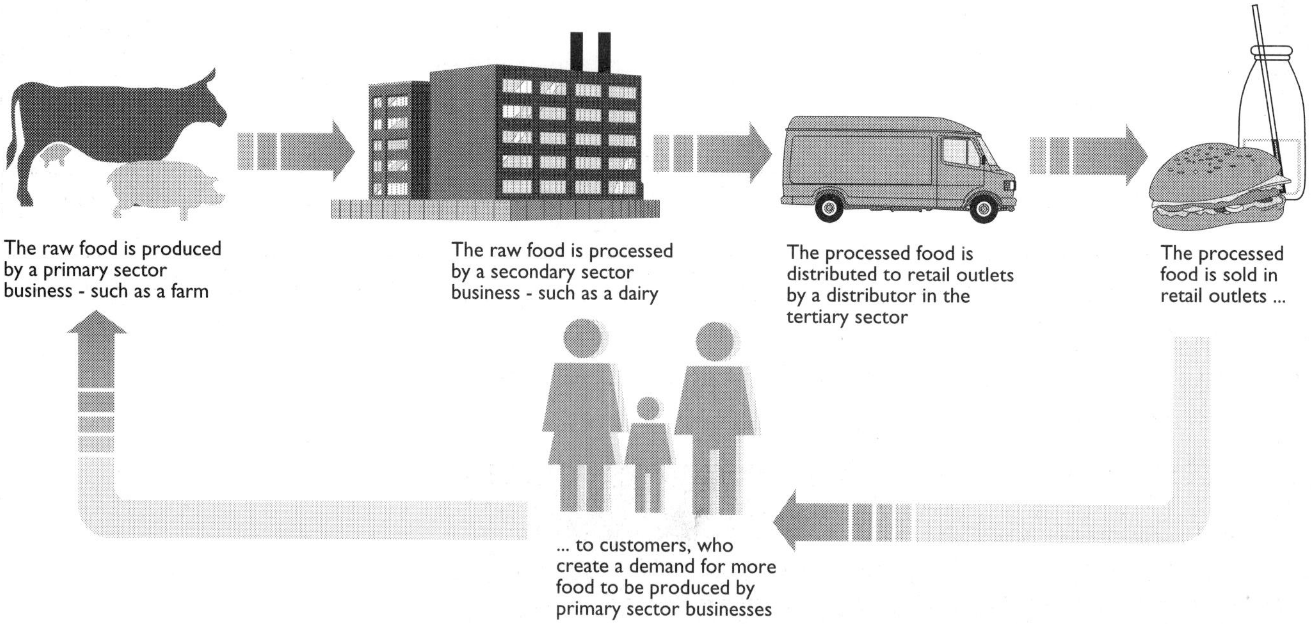

The raw food is produced by a primary sector business - such as a farm
The raw food is processed by a secondary sector business - such as a dairy
The processed food is distributed to retail outlets by a distributor in the tertiary sector
The processed food is sold in retail outlets ...
... to customers, who create a demand for more food to be produced by primary sector businesses

FIGURE 1.1 The chain of production.

PRIMARY SECTOR

Industries in the primary sector include:

- farming and agriculture;
- forestry;
- fishing;
- mining;
- oil extraction;
- quarrying.

Overall, levels of employment in the primary sector in Britain have been declining for many years as industries such as mining and agriculture have contracted. However, trends in levels of production do vary from industry to industry. For example, in the five years 1988-92, the level of British fish landings dropped from 742.0 thousand tonnes to 613.7 thousand tonnes. Production of petroleum products, on the other hand, rose from 79.1 million tonnes to 85.0 million tonnes.

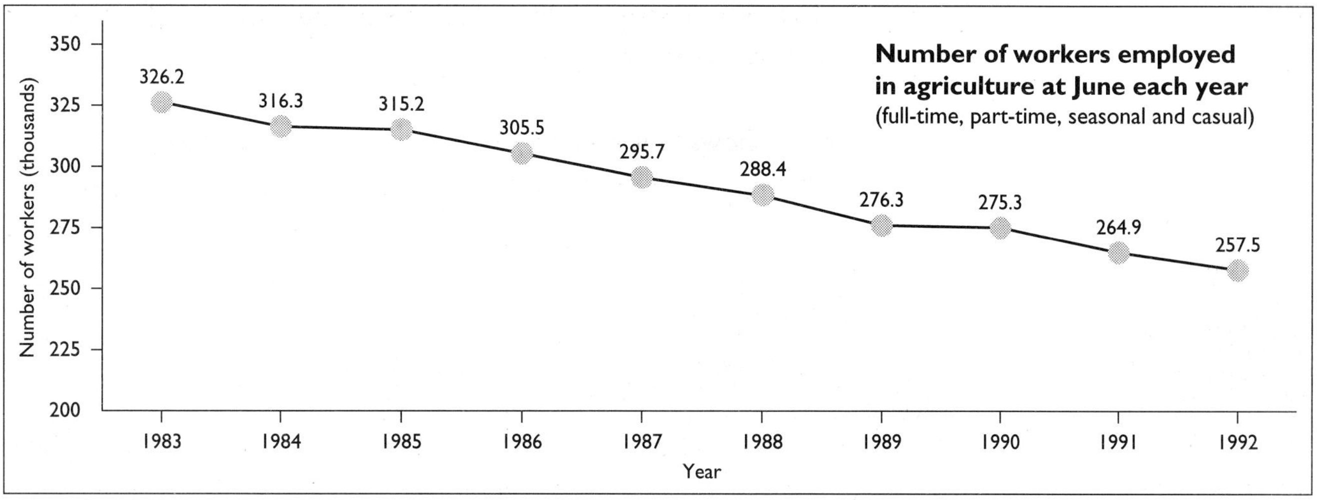

FIGURE 1.2 The decline in the number of workers in agriculture 1983–92.

One reason for the overall decline in employment is that many primary industries are becoming more efficient. New technology means that one employee can now do the same amount of work that it took several employees to do in the past.

ACTIVITY

Think of examples of work which used to be done by several people but can now be done by one person using new technology. As a group, discuss your feelings about this kind of 'progress'.

In other industries, however, the reduction in employment is due to a general decline in the industry. The present trends in the primary sector are expected to continue for the foreseeable future.

FIGURE 1.3 The decline in the production of coal between 1983/84 and 1992/93.

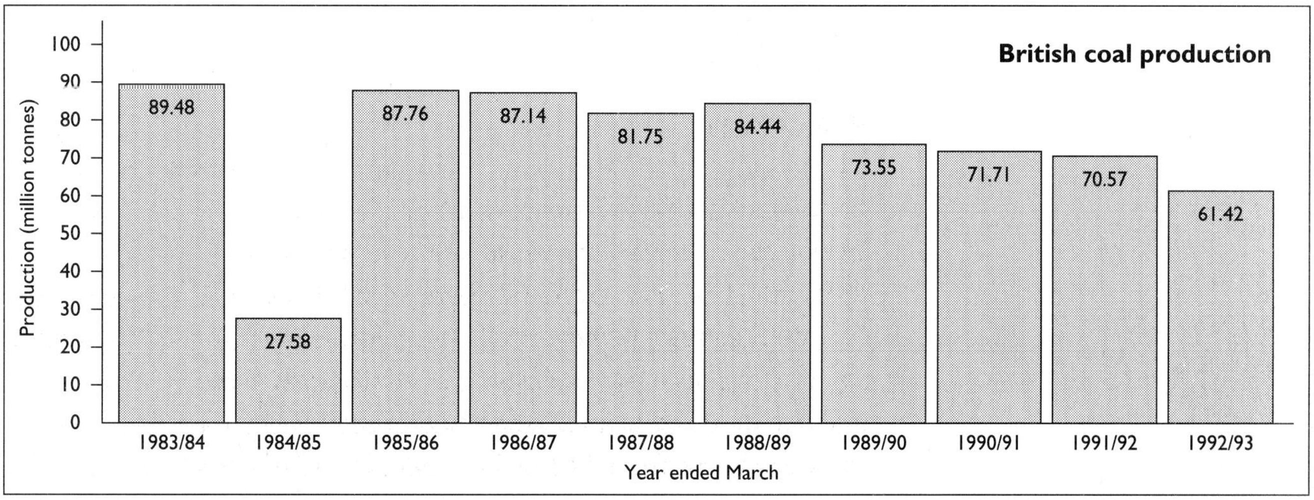

CASE STUDY

The mining industry

In the past many different metals were mined in the United Kingdom, including gold and tin. Now, however, most such mines have been closed because the supply of metals has run out or become too expensive to extract.

In the eighteenth century, for example, Cornwall was one of the most important tin-mining areas in the world. Today only one small tin mine is left in Cornwall and Britain now buys the tin it needs from as far away as Bolivia and Malaysia.

The type of mining mainly associated with Britain nowadays is coal mining. However, activity in this industry has also decreased in recent years. *Fig. 1.3* on p 5 shows the drop in production of coal between 1983/84 and 1992/93. You should note that 1984 saw a long and bitter miners' strike, resulting in a massive drop in production that year.

The decline of the coal industry is due to several factors. Most of Britain's coal reserves can only be extracted from deep mines which are expensive to operate. This, coupled with uncertainty about supply during two major strikes by British miners (in 1974 and 1984), led large coal users, such as the electricity supply industry which operates many coal-fired power stations, to look for alternative sources of coal from abroad, and also for alternative fuels, including nuclear power. Coal is now imported from countries such as Colombia where wages and other mining costs are lower than in the UK. In addition, demand for British coal has fallen because of the discovery of other, more environmentally friendly, sources of energy, such as natural gas.

The effect on employment of the decline in the British coal industry is shown in *Fig. 1.4*. No improvement is expected in the foreseeable future.

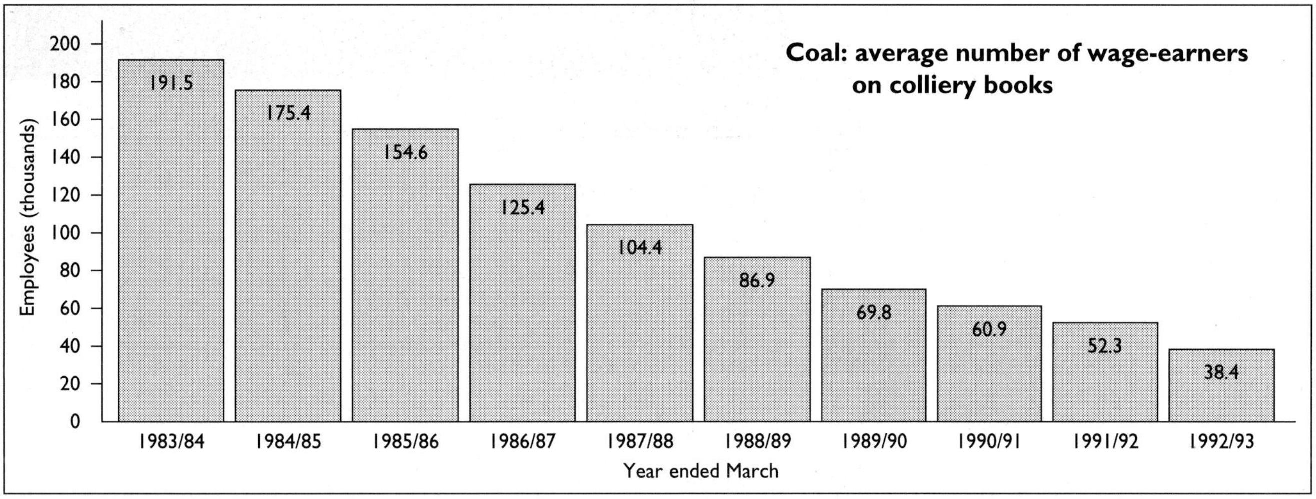

FIGURE 1.4 Employment in the coal industry between 1983 and 1993.

SECONDARY SECTOR

Industries in the secondary sector include those involved in manufacturing and construction. Secondary sector organisations use the raw materials produced by the primary sector to produce finished goods. For example, Rover Group Limited manufacture cars from the metal, plastic, glass and other raw materials that are produced by primary sector companies. Manufacturing includes:

- metals, minerals and mineral products;
- chemicals and artificial fibres;
- engineering and allied trades;
- food drink and tobacco;
- textiles, footwear, clothing and leather goods;
- other manufacturing.

Construction includes:

- building;
- civil engineering.

Some industries operate in both the primary and secondary sectors. These are called **production industries.**

QUICK response

What primary or secondary sector industries are involved in making ice-cream?

ACTIVITY

Production industries have activities in both the primary and secondary sectors. Make a list of all the production industries you can think of. What are their activities? Construct a table like this:

Production industries		
Industry	Primary activities	Secondary activities

Total UK manufacturing output rose by 17 per cent in the eight years to 1993, although this increase was not uniform across all manufacturing industries. Despite the overall increase in manufacturing output, employment in UK manufacturing is declining, especially in textiles, shipbuilding, clothing and footwear. In particular, the output of clothing and footwear fell by 6 per cent.

Manufacturing costs are high in the UK compared to other industrialised countries. Competition from abroad is fierce, particularly from within the European Union (EU), and from some newly industrialised countries such as South Korea, Malaysia, Taiwan and Singapore. New technology, which enables mass production methods to be used, thus improving efficiency and requiring fewer employees, has also contributed to the fall in employment in the secondary sector.

Manufacturing industries are expected to show significant growth in the future. A high level of foreign investment (money coming into the UK to purchase or set up businesses here), particularly from foreign companies such as Nissan, Toyota, BMW and Samsung, is creating many new jobs in this sector.

None the less, UK manufacturing industries will continue to face fierce competition from abroad, and this will limit the extent to which they can develop. In addition, new technology will continue to increase productivity, further limiting an increase in employment opportunity.

Tertiary sector

Industries in the tertiary sector include:

- retailing;
- distribution;
- hotels and catering;
- banking and other financial services;
- post and telecommunications;
- public administration;
- education;
- health services;
- other services.

New technology has led to a reduction in staffing levels.

This is the fastest growing and most diverse sector of the UK economy. Unlike the other sectors of the economy, however, employment is increasing in the tertiary sector, although, in some areas, notably banking and public administration, increased efficiency and productivity resulting from the introduction of new technology have led to reductions in employment levels.

Despite this, current trends in tertiary sector industries are expected to continue.

ACTIVITY

Carry out a survey and make a list of business organisations in your own locality. Identify their main activities and classify them according to industrial sector.

The purposes of business organisations

You have seen that business organisations can be classified according to whether their activities fall within the primary, secondary or tertiary sectors of industry. They are also classified according to whether they operate in:

- **the private sector**: that is, organisations that are owned and operated by one or more private individuals or other groups. The private sector includes organisations such as ICI, Pizza Hut, WH Smith and your local plumber;

- **the public sector**: that is. organisations owned and operated by national or local government. The public sector includes organisations such as the Post Office, the Department of Social Security, hospitals, libraries and schools.

Some types of organisations are found in both the private and the public sectors. Most schools and hospitals, for example, are owned and run by a local authority and are therefore in the public sector. However, some schools and hospitals are privately owned, taking private fee-paying students or patients, and are therefore in the public sector.

As you saw at the beginning of this unit, business organisations produce goods and services which they supply to individuals and other business organisations who want those goods and services and are prepared to pay for them. This is true whether an organisation is in the private or public sector. For example, a hospital provides a service to the public and this service is paid for by the national government out of taxes which have, in turn, been collected from the public.

A business organisation which supplies goods or services incurs costs which must be covered out of the money the business receives for the goods or services it has supplied. For example, a business organisation must pay for raw materials, wages and salaries, electricity, factory and office costs, and so on.

FIGURE 1.5 The flow of money into and out of a business.

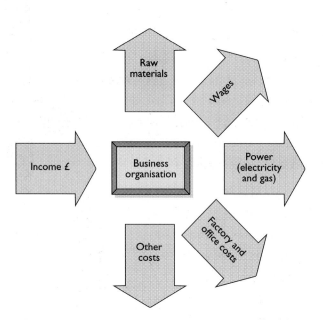

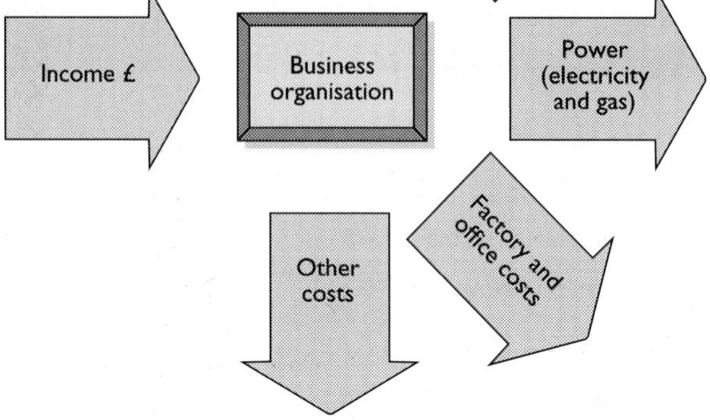

The money an organisation receives for the goods or services it sells or supplies is called its **income**. In order to pay its costs, the income the organisation receives must equal the costs it incurs. If the income of a business is less than its costs, the business will make a loss and no business can exist for long if it keeps making a loss. If the income of a business exactly equals its costs, it will break even. If the income of the business is greater than its costs, the business will make a profit.

All business organisations, whether in the public or private sector, have one or more purposes. The purposes of a business organisation may be:

- to make a profit;
- to gain a share of the market;
- to provide customer service;
- to provide a service to the public;
- charitable.

There is often a close connection between the purposes of a business organisation and the sector in which it operates.

PROFIT

The main purpose of most business organisations in the private sector is to make a profit. A business which makes a profit can do several things:

- distribute the profit among the owners of the business (this will ensure that the owners are happy with the way its managers are running the business and therefore allow them to continue);
- distribute the profit among the employees of the business as bonuses (this will ensure that the employees of the business are happy and likely to continue working hard to obtain further bonuses in the future);
- retain the profit within the business (this will ensure that there is enough money in the bank to meet any future emergencies, pay for new, up-to-date equipment, or fund expansion).

FIGURE 1.6 The distribution of profits.

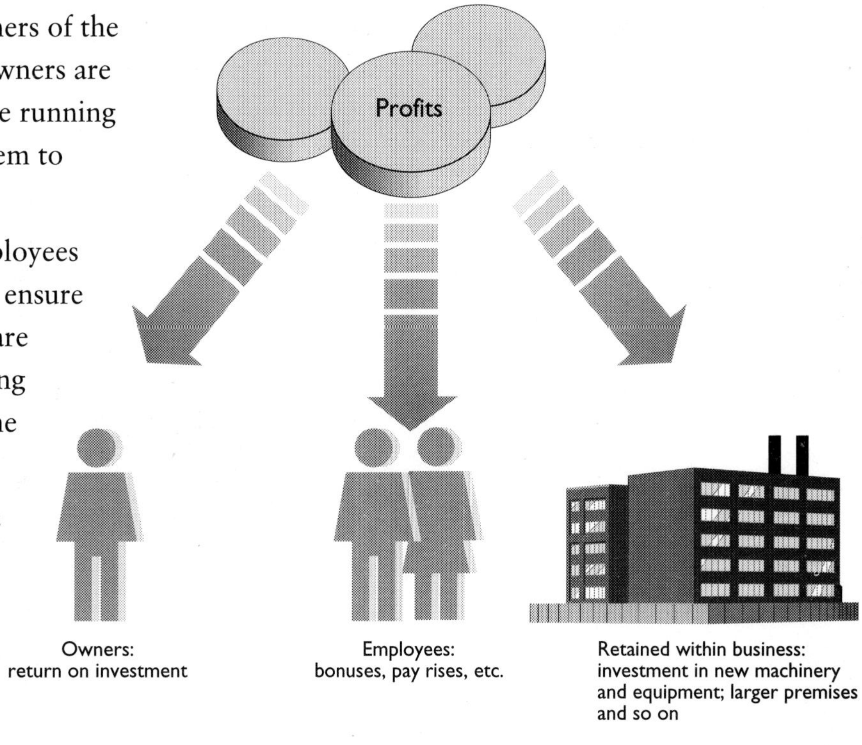
Profits
Owners: return on investment
Employees: bonuses, pay rises, etc.
Retained within business: investment in new machinery and equipment; larger premises and so on

In practice, most businesses whose purpose is to make a profit distribute their profits in more than one way, paying dividends to the owners, retaining some profit within the business and perhaps paying bonuses to employees as well.

ACTIVITY

Privatised gas, electricity and water companies are often criticised over the amount of profit they make and what they do with that profit. In groups of four or five, discuss whether you think gas, electricity and water companies should make a profit, and how their profit should be distributed: to shareholders, to employees, in the form of reduced charges to customers, or retained within the company in order to improve services and update equipment.

QUICK response

Why do most businesses retain a part of their profits?

When considering the profits made by businesses, it is important to remember that they contribute to the wealth of the nation. The higher the profits made by businesses in the United Kingdom, the greater the amount of money that will become available to buy goods and invest in British industry. This will help to make British industry more competitive in Europe and the rest of the world, so improving the UK economy.

MARKET SHARE

One of the principal aims of many organisations is to increase their market share.

The market for a product or service is the total number of customers for that product or service. The number of customers who buy a product from one organisation are that organisation's share of the total market.

Obviously, the more customers a business has, the greater its income will be and the greater its profit. It is therefore in the interests of all business organisations to supply as many customers as possible. The maximum number of customers a business organisation can supply depends on several factors, including the size and cost effectiveness of the organisation, but most business organisations try to increase their market share (i.e. the number of customers they supply).

Readers of national newspapers 1992 (millions)

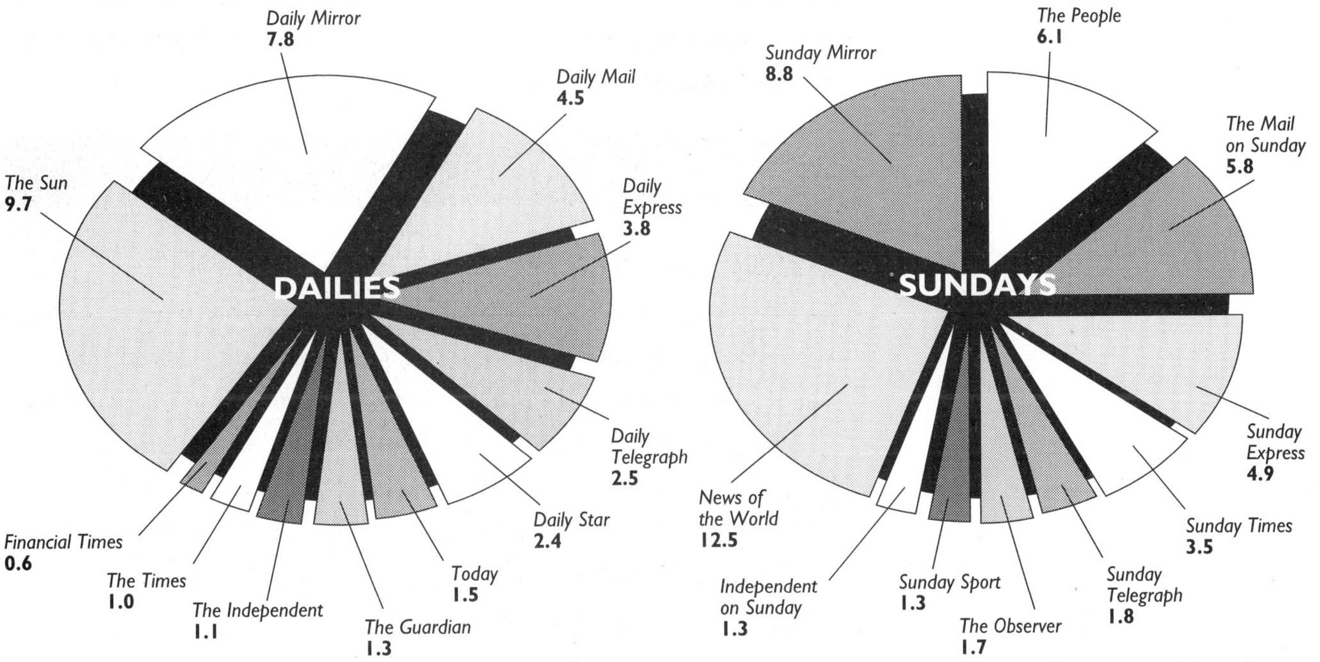

FIGURE 1.7 Readers of national newspapers.

ACTIVITY

From the pie charts showing the readership of national newspapers in *Fig. 1.7*, calculate:

- **the total market for daily newspapers;**
- **the total market for Sunday newspapers;**
- **the percentage share of the daily market for *The Sun*;**
- **the percentage share of the Sunday market for the *News of the World*;**
- **which daily or Sunday newspaper has the largest share of the total market for newspapers on all days.**

CUSTOMER SERVICE

Whether the main purpose of a business is to make a profit, to increase its market share or to serve the public, it will only achieve its aims by giving its customers what they want. This not only means providing a good-quality product or service at a price the customer is prepared to pay, but also giving good customer service.

Customer service means meeting the needs of customers by providing additional help and information to customers. (Customer service is dealt with in more detail in Element 3.3: 'Providing customer service'.) In today's competitive world all business organisations must strive to provide a high level of customer service in order to retain existing customers and attract new ones.

ACTIVITY

In groups, discuss what forms of customer service you expect to receive as a customer in a shop or restaurant.

PUBLIC SERVICE

The main purpose of some business organisations, especially those in the public sector, is to provide a service to the public rather than to make a profit.

The purpose of a school or college, for example, is to provide education facilities for the local (and sometimes wider) community. To enable it to do this, it will be allocated funds by the Government. The funds it is allocated are its income – the school or college does not have to sell its services to the public (although, in certain circumstances, it may do so in order to boost its income so that it can provide more and better services).

FIGURE 1.8 Expenditure should not exceed income.

While the purpose of an organisation may be to provide a service to the public, it still has to operate within its income. In other words, it must ensure that its costs do not exceed its total income from all sources.

Charitable

Certain other types of organisation in the private sector are set up for charitable purposes.

In the UK many large and small charities exist to obtain donations from the public and from other business organisations. The donations obtained in this way are then spent in providing goods and services to those who need them but who would be unable to obtain or afford them without the help of the charity.

Charities are normally set up to fulfil a perceived need, or to provide help to a specific section of the community. Many UK charities collect money to be spent abroad. The donations received by a charity are its income. The amount of its income remaining after the charity has paid its operating costs can be used for charitable purposes. It is essential, therefore, that the costs of any charity are kept as low as possible.

FIGURE 1.9 The income of well-known charities.

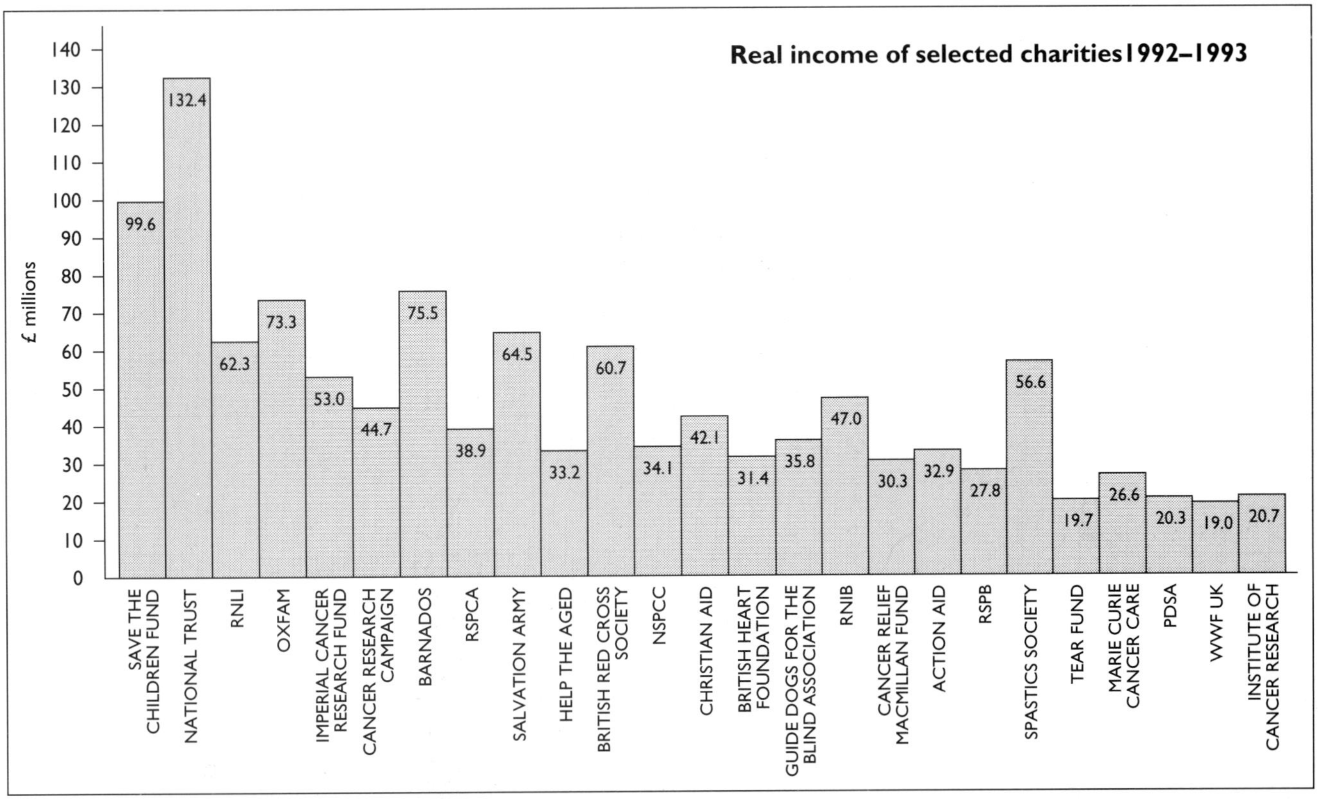

ACTIVITY

Obtain the latest annual report of one of the charities shown in *Fig. 1.9*. Identify:

- **how much income the charity received during the year;**
- **where the income came from;**
- **how much the operating costs of the charity were;**
- **how much the charity had left to spend on its charitable purposes.**

Display your answers in the form of a pie chart.

Large, medium and small businesses

The size of a business organisation can be assessed by its turnover, or total value of its sales in a year, its market share, number of employees and the scope of its operation.

A business with a turnover of £50 million, a market share of 25 per cent, 2,500 employees, and operating from depots and factories throughout the United Kingdom and Europe, would be considered large. An organisation with a turnover of £5 million, a market share of 5 per cent, 500 employees, and operating from two factories, would be considered medium. An organisation with a turnover of less than £1 million, a small market share, less than 500 employees, and operating from one site, would be considered small.

Businesses may grow in size either by increasing sales and market share, or by buying other businesses. Many businesses aim to grow in order to increase their profits. However, there are both advantages and disadvantages to becoming a large organisation. These are called **economies of scale** (advantages) and **diseconomies of scale** (disadvantages).

Economies of scale include:

- buying raw materials and other goods in bulk and so enjoying greater discounts;
- improving production methods by buying large or technically advanced machinery;
- being able to invest more in the research and development of new products;
- having greater financial resources to absorb short-term losses or to invest in expensive marketing campaigns.

Large organisations with large workforces are able to employ highly skilled and specialist staff to run the operations of the business.

Diseconomies of scale include:

- a tendency towards excessive bureaucracy, with escalating costs;
- the loss of direct contact between the senior management of the organisation, its employees and customers.

Where an organisation employs a large workforce, there is a danger that too much specialisation may lead to a reduction in the output of individual employees.

TYPES OF BUSINESS AND BUSINESS OWNERSHIP

You have seen that business organisations may be in the private or public sectors, according to whether they are owned by private individuals or the Government. Even within these categories of business ownership, however, different types of business organisations and ownership can be identified.

An important aspect of business ownership, and one which must be taken into consideration when setting up a business, is liability. Two kinds of liability are involved in owning a business:

- **unlimited liability**: where the owners of the business are personally responsible for all the debts the business incurs. This means that if the business is unable to pay its debts because it has insufficient funds available, the debts must be paid in full by the owners, even if they have to sell the business and all their own personal possessions, including their house and car, to do so;
- **limited liability**: where the owners of the business are only responsible for the debts of the business up to the amount they themselves have invested in the business. This means that if the business is unable to pay its debts, the owners will only lose the amount they originally put into the business (they may, of course, also lose the business itself if it has to be sold in order to pay off its debts).

Obviously, therefore, there are risks attached to owning a business. Businesses with limited liability for their owners are called **limited companies**. The owners of limited companies buy **shares** in the company. Shares have a nominal (face) value which is set when the shares are first issued (normally when the company is set up or first becomes a limited company). The actual cost of buying these shares, however, depends on how well the company is expected to perform, the anticipated level of profits and how many people want to buy the shares. If a company is unable to pay its debts, the owners of shares in that company lose whatever they paid for those shares.

QUICK response

List three things a business can do with its profits.

Liability is only one aspect of owning a business. Perhaps a more important aspect is profit. People and other organisations who put their money into owning businesses (that is, they invest in businesses) do so because they expect to get a return on the money they have invested. This return is paid out of the profits of the business.

- **Owners** of businesses with unlimited liability are considered to own the full profit of the business. It is for them to decide how to use the profit of the business; whether to draw it for their own personal use or retain it in the business in order to buy new equipment or fund expansion.
- **Shareholders** of limited liability companies receive a **dividend** on their shares (that is, a proportion of profits set aside by the company for distributing to shareholders according to the number of shares owned). Shareholders who own **debenture stocks** (these represent money lent to the company by the shareholder, which is therefore repayable by the company, normally on a specified date) are paid **interest** on their holding.
- **The Government** also receives a portion of the profits of a business in the form of tax – income tax on the profits of sole traders and partnerships (see p 19) and corporation tax on the profits of limited liability companies.

THE SOLE TRADER

The sole trader is the simplest form of business organisation. There is one owner of the business. The owner has complete control over all decision-making involved in the running of the business. While many sole traders are, indeed, people working on their own, a sole trader can also employ others to help to run the business.

Setting up as a sole trader is very easy. There are few legal formalities to go through, apart from the sole trader advising the Inland Revenue about the business, keeping employment records in respect of any employees (the owner of a sole trader business is not considered an employee of the business) and making sure that any business name used complies with the legislation of the Business Names Act 1985.

Setting up as a sole trader can also be the least expensive way of starting a business. Many sole traders start with the minimum of capital, often operating from small premises such as a shop, small workshop or office unit, or even from their own home.

For these reasons, starting as a sole trader is the most common way of setting up in business. In Britain today, there are more sole traders than any other type of business.

On the other hand, few sources of finance are available to sole traders, apart from the personal funds of the owner. This is partly because they are usually small businesses and partly because they have unlimited liability and will retain any profits within the business in order to finance expansion. A sole trader may take out a bank loan to help to finance the business but because the affairs of the business are legally considered to be the same as the personal affairs of the owner, any loan is, in effect, a personal loan which may need to be secured on the owner's personal property, for example in the form of a mortgage on their house. Obviously, there is a limit to the amount of money a sole trader can raise in this way. The lack of availability of other sources of finance means that sole traders usually start as small businesses and do not have real opportunities for growth.

QUICK response

List as many advantages and disadvantages of being a sole trader as you can.

There is one advantage of being a sole trader, however, which can often give a competitive edge over a larger business. In a small business, the owner and decision-maker usually maintains close and direct contact with customers and will thus be aware of any changes in customer needs and demand (see p 46). The sole trader can respond very quickly to these while, in larger organisations, it can take much longer for the decision-makers to become aware of, and respond to, these changes.

Typical sole trader businesses are local independent shops, plumbers and similar tradespeople, freelance artists and other self-employed people.

THE PARTNERSHIP

Unlike a sole trader, a partnership has two or more owners. These are the partners themselves. Generally, a partnership has between two and 20 partners but, in certain cases, such as large firms of accountants, there may be more than 20.

The partners share control of the business and profits, although there is often a 'senior' partner who has overall authority for decision-making. Legal requirements are the same as for a sole trader, although most partnerships are established with a legally drawn up **deed of partnership**. This sets out the role each partner is to play in running the business and also how any profits will be distributed among partners. Should any dispute arise at a later date, this can be settled by referring to the deed of partnership.

An advantage of a partnership is that responsibility for the business is shared between the partners. This means that no one partner has to oversee the whole business, but each partner is able to concentrate on that part of the business they are best at. For example, Jim and Mary Lloyd have a business manufacturing wooden toys. They run the business as a partnership in which Jim actually makes and packages the toys, while Mary concentrates on selling them to local shops and also does the paperwork which Jim admits he is not much good at.

The sources of finance available to partnerships are similar to those available to sole traders: principally the personal funds of the owners, profits retained within the business, or bank loans. Just like sole traders, the owners of a partnership have unlimited liability and are likely to have to use their personal property as security for a loan. As there is more than one partner, however, it is usually possible for a partnership to obtain larger amounts of capital in this way.

Typical partnerships include professional firms such as solicitors and accountants, and other small traders where two or more people have joined together to set up in business.

ACTIVITY

Identify two local sole trader businesses and two local partnerships. Find out what activities each business carries out. For each partnership, find out what role each partner plays in running the business.

LIMITED COMPANIES

Unlike sole traders and partnerships, limited companies exist as legal entities quite separately from their owners. This means that people can be employed, goods and services can be bought and sold, and finance can be raised by the limited company itself and not by the owners.

Because it is a legal entity in its own right, the owners of a limited company buy shares in the company – that is, they quite literally own a share of the company in proportion to the amount of shares they have bought. People who own shares in a limited company are called **shareholders**.

A limited company must be legally established (incorporated). In addition, it must have a written constitution (called **memoranda and articles of association**) which sets out:

- what the company has been established to do;
- the name and address of the company;
- the number of shares that have been issued and who owns them;
- the names and addresses of the directors of the company.

A limited company must also send annual accounts to the Inland Revenue as well as an annual return to the Registrar of Companies, notifying any changes in directors, shares issued or mortgage debts.

Although the shareholders are the owners of the company, they appoint a board of directors to run the company on their behalf. The directors are responsible for the running and management of the company, but the shareholders have ultimate control.

A limited company raises capital initially through the sale of shares. As a legal entity, however, a limited company is also able to take out loans from banks and other financial institutions. Being a limited company is no guarantee of profitability or success, but limited companies do tend to be larger than other forms of businesses and find it easier to raise the capital they need to operate and grow.

QUICK response

Limited liability means ...

There are two types of limited companies:

- private limited companies;
- public limited companies.

Private limited companies have the word 'limited' after their name, indicating that the company is owned by shareholders who have limited liability (see p 17). This is usually abbreviated to Ltd; for example The Lincolnshire Bus Company Ltd.

A private limited company may be owned by between two and 50 shareholders. The shareholders of a private limited company can only buy or sell their shares with the agreement of the other shareholders. Normally, because of the small numbers of shareholders and their lack of freedom to buy and sell shares as and when they like, the shareholders of a private limited company are usually closely connected with the management of the company. In fact, the

The familiar logos of some well-known private limited companies.

shareholders of a private limited company are often also the directors of the company so they are responsible for the day-to-day running of the company and also have ultimate control.

This is not always the case, however. For example, when Anita Roddick first started up The Body Shop as a private limited company, a friend helped her to raise the capital she needed by buying a substantial shareholding. As The Body Shop became a very successful company and, eventually, The Body Shop International plc, the friend, whose identity remains unknown, has seen their shareholding increase in value from a few thousand pounds to several million. This unknown shareholder has retained their shareholding but has never played any part in running the company.

The main difference between private limited companies and **public limited companies** is that with public limited companies there is no restriction on the number of shareholders or on the freedom to buy and sell shares. Shares in public limited companies can be bought and sold on the Stock Exchange at any time by private individuals, other companies or organisations.

One danger of this freedom for anybody to buy or sell shares in a public limited company is that it is possible for all the shares in one plc to be bought by another company. In this way, the company buying the shares can 'take over' the company whose shares it has bought. Although not all takeovers are unwelcome or 'hostile', they do mean that control of the company whose shares have been bought passes entirely into the hands of the company which bought them.

Shares in public limited companies are bought and sold on the Stock Exchange.

Public limited companies have 'plc' (meaning public limited company) after their name, as, for example, ICI plc.

By selling shares to the general public as well as to other companies and organisations, public limited companies can raise vast amounts of capital from sources not accessible to private limited companies. Additional shares can be issued to raise further capital if required. In this way, a public limited company can finance costly expansion, development, and research which is beyond the means of other types of businesses. For example, supermarket chains, such as Sainsbury's and Marks and Spencer, can purchase prime trading sites in order to attract more customers, while major companies like Unilever can spend huge amounts on research to keep their products ahead of those of their competitors.

Many plcs are household names.

ACTIVITY

Obtain a copy of an advertisement for the issue of shares in a public limited company. These are often carried in the financial sections of newspapers such as *The Guardian*, *The Times* and the *Financial Times*, and in magazines such as *The Economist*. What is the face value of the shares being issued? How much does the company hope to raise?

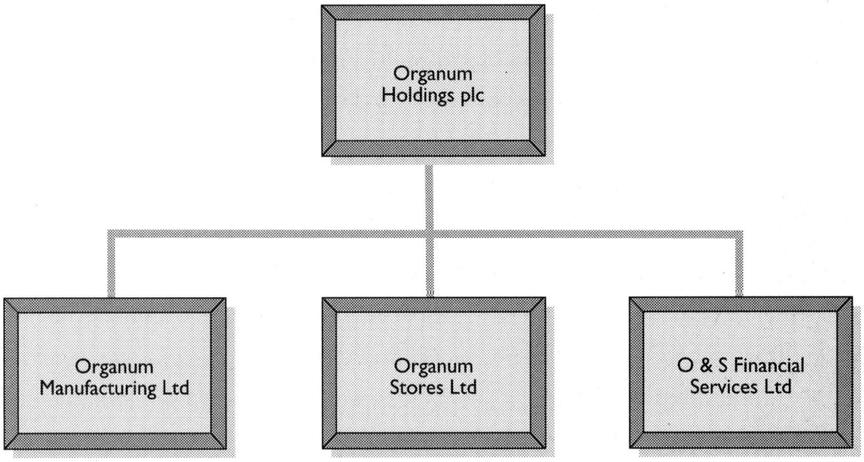

FIGURE 1.10 A public limited company may split its operations into several private limited companies.

Public limited companies are generally the largest UK companies, although some private limited companies rival even the largest public ones. Virgin, Littlewoods and JC Bamford Excavators (JCB) are all major private limited companies. As companies grow in size, however, they frequently become difficult to manage as single companies. It is not unusual, therefore, for a public limited company to split its operations into several private limited companies, each of which is wholly owned by the public company (the parent company).

FRANCHISES

Some large companies sell the right to trade under their name and to sell their products or services, usually in an exclusive area. The person buying this right, or **franchise**, is normally a sole trader who puts their money into setting up the business (perhaps with the help of a bank loan). In addition to the original purchase price of the franchise, the purchaser usually has to pay the company which has sold them the franchise an annual fee. This is often calculated as a percentage of turnover or profits.

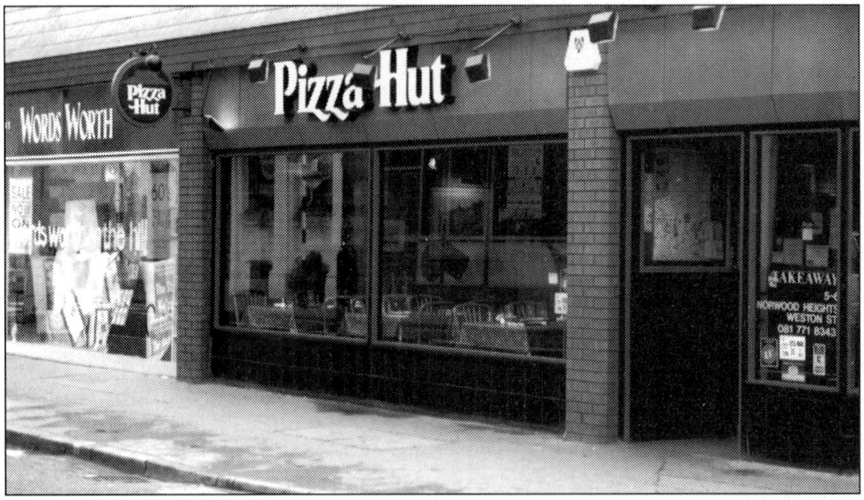

Pizza Hut operates as a franchise.

In return, the purchaser of the franchise not only obtains the right to trade under a well-known name and sell a well-known product, but may also get help with the purchase of premises and equipment. In addition, many companies which operate franchise systems offer the purchasers of their franchises training in administration, marketing and other areas. Franchises can also benefit from bulk discounts on supplies not normally available to a sole trader, and from national marketing campaigns undertaken by the main company. Owning and running a franchise is therefore often seen as a good compromise between being a small trader, with control of your own business and in touch with your customers, and a large limited company able to benefit from discounts for purchasing in bulk. The company selling the franchises can benefit from having its outlets operated by independent business people who have a strong interest is ensuring that the business is a success, while releasing the employees and capital of the main company to concentrate on other areas of the business, such as manufacturing and developing the product.

Franchises are a growing sector of business, with major companies such as Benetton, The Body Shop and Tie Rack operating in this way. By producing the goods which are sold through their franchises, they are able to protect their reputation and ensure the quality of the product.

Co-operatives

Co-operatives are business organisations which are owned by 'members', each of whom has shares in the co-operative. Co-operatives exist for the mutual benefit of the members who have complete control of the co-operative. Finance for the co-operative is raised by the members.

There are three types of co-operatives:

- co-operative retail societies, which buy goods in bulk at a discount and sell them as cheaply as possible to members;
- co-operative trading societies, which are formed to distribute and sell the products or services of their members (usually small businesses);
- worker co-operatives, which are business organisations that are owned by their employees.

The best known co-operative is, of course, the high street Co-op, which is part of the Co-operative Wholesale Society.

State-owned organisations

Many business organisations are owned and run by national or local government. These organisations are in the public sector. The purpose of these organisations is not to make a profit but to provide a service to the public. The finance for state-owned organisations is provided by national or local government out of taxes.

ACTIVITY

Identify two local state-owned organisations. Find out where the money to run them comes from. Is it all from local or national government, or is some money raised from other sources?

Libraries are not intended to make a profit.

Although their purpose is not to make a profit, state-owned organisations have to operate within tight financial budgets. They are increasingly being made responsible for managing their own affairs in the same way as businesses in the private sector. Many state-owned organisations do not make a charge for the services they provide. These include schools, government departments, such as the Department of Social Security, and libraries (unless you are late in returning your books!). Other state-owned organisations, such as leisure centres and the National Health Service which charges for prescriptions, make a nominal charge to cover the excess cost over the amount provided by the Government for providing the service.

A third type of state-owned organisation is a public corporation. These are industrial organisations, such as the Post Office, which are considered to provide such an essential product or service that they have been taken into state ownership to ensure their continued operation. Public corporations charge an economic rate for their products or services (that is, a rate at which income should cover costs – see p 10). The Government makes good any losses incurred by a public corporation and ensures that sufficient funds are available out of taxes to cover necessary expenditure. As a result of Government economic policy since 1979, many public corporations have now been sold to the private sector by creating shares in them and selling the shares to private investors. This is called **privatisation**.

ACTIVITY

Make a table of the industries which have been privatised since 1979. Were the shares sold to the general public? How much did the Government raise through the sale of each industry? Construct your table like this:

Industry	Date privatised	Shares sold to general public	Amount raised

THE OPERATION OF A BUSINESS ORGANISATION

Various factors affect the way in which a business organisation operates. These include:

- **Location**: Businesses such as potteries and timber mills, which use heavy or bulky raw materials to manufacture their products, may need to be established close to the source of these raw materials in order to keep transport costs to a minimum, while other businesses, which produce heavy or bulky products, may find it more cost effective to be sited close to their customers or outlets. Similarly, businesses such as solicitors and hairdressers, which provide services from fixed premises such as shops or offices, must operate from a location which is convenient for their customers, while the location of other businesses, such as mobile carpet cleaners and electricians, which provide their services at the premises of their customers, may not be so important.
- **Product** (goods and services): The service or product of a business affects the way it operates. A business such as Ford, for example, operates from a few large factories and uses technologically advanced machinery and equipment to build cars. The cars are then distributed to a nationwide network of garages where they are sold to customers. Other businesses, perhaps providing a service, such as a firm of accountants or solicitors, may operate from just one office in the high street with a minimum of equipment, being more dependent on the knowledge and skill of the people working in the business.
- **Links with other businesses**: All business organisations have links with other businesses which are necessary to their operation. These links may be as suppliers or customers, and contacts with them may be regular and routine or occasional. For example, a library will have regular links with publishers, book distributors, and other local authority departments, but may also have occasional links with other businesses such as decorators, electricians and so on. A business which designs and supplies computer systems will have links with computer hardware and software suppliers, and the businesses that are their own customers, as well as with other businesses from whom they may purchase vehicles, office equipment and maintenance services.

QUICK response

What factors would affect the location of a shop selling camping and outdoor wear?

ACTIVITY

Select one local business organisation and draw a network diagram of its links with other business organisations. Identify whether the other businesses are customers or suppliers.

- **Purpose**: The way a business operates will also be affected by its purpose. For example, a business which is just setting up and is trying to secure a share of the market, may pursue an aggressive marketing campaign to establish its reputation and attract customers away from competitors. An established business, which is trying to maintain sales and increase profits, may be more involved in research and development in order to improve its product and, at the same time, reduce production costs.
- **Type of ownership**: You have seen that there are several types of business ownership and that this affects the operation of a business in two ways. The number of owners can influence the structure and working arrangements of the business (see Element 2.1, p 81), while the availability of funding affects the ability of a business to grow and obtain modern technology, develop its product, adapt to consumer demand, compete with other businesses, and so on.

PORTFOLIO ASSIGNMENT

For this portfolio assignment you will need to research background information about business and a business organisation in your area. Advice on finding information about business was given on p x in the Introduction. You may wish to refer to this again before starting this assignment. Include charts and diagrams where appropriate to illustrate points you are making. You will need to carry out further research on a business organisation for Portfolio Assignment 1.2 and you may wish to look at this portfolio assignment now.

TASK 1

Write a summary describing developments in each of the primary, secondary and tertiary sectors of industry. For each sector you should give examples of typical business activities. Your summary should concentrate on the present growth or decline of the sector, rather than on the historical development of the sector.

TASK 2

Identify seven examples of business organisations with different types of ownership. Your examples should include at least one public sector organisation and also small, medium and large private sector organisations. Write notes explaining the purpose of each business organisation and the differences between the types of business organisation, especially regarding liability and other responsibilities, including the distribution of profits.

TASK 3

Select one local or national business organisation to investigate and write an informal report explaining its location, product, purpose, type of ownership, and links with other businesses. You will find advice on how to write reports in Element 1.3, p 76.

This portfolio assignment also presents an opportunity to gather evidence for the following core skills:

- Application of Number – collect and record data; interpret and present data;
- Communication – take part in discussions; produce written material; read and respond to written materials;
- Information Technology – prepare information; process information; present information.

Business Organisations – Their Location, Environment, Markets and Products

Business organisations do not operate in isolation. In this element, you will find out how various factors, such as the need for labour and raw materials, influence the location of business organisations and how the environment in which they operate affects their activities. Above all, you will see the importance of customers to an organisation and how it must respond to these in providing its product.

THE REASONS FOR THE LOCATION OF BUSINESSES

The decision where to locate a business is an important one. Several factors must be taken into consideration, the importance of each varying according to the type, purpose and nature of the business.

ACTIVITY

From the list you produced for Element 1.1 on p 8, select two primary or secondary sector industries in your locality. Identify the raw materials your chosen industries use in making their product. Where do these raw materials come from?

LABOUR SUPPLY

Apart from sole traders working on their own, all business and industrial organisations need employees. When a business is considering a location, in order to set up initially, to establish a new depot or factory, or to relocate (move) to, it must consider the availability of employees in terms of:

- numbers – will the business be able to recruit sufficient employees for its needs?
- skills – do the employees who could be recruited locally have the right skills to be able to do the work required?

ACTIVITY

Investigate the advertisements for different jobs in your local Job Centre, employment agencies and the employment section of your local newspaper. Make a list of the different types of jobs advertised in your area and the skills required. Is there a prevalence of one type of skill requirement?

High unemployment in the late 1980s and early 1990s meant that businesses had a greater supply of labour to choose from. However, the available labour often lacked the skills that were needed. The main reason for this was that, historically, certain types of industries had located in particular areas. This led to a concentration of particular skills in those areas.

For example, textiles have traditionally been produced in Leicestershire; coal was mined in certain areas of Nottinghamshire, Yorkshire and South Wales; ships were built in the north east of England and in Scotland and Northern Ireland. The decline in these industries in recent years has had a significant impact on unemployment in those areas, often leading to levels of unemployment above the national average. In order to improve this situation, local and national government has offered incentives to businesses to locate in areas of high unemployment (see p 37). On the face of it, this should make moving to areas of high unemployment attractive to businesses considering relocation. However, while a business locating in these areas would have access to a large supply of labour, the workers may not have the appropriate skills for that business.

QUICK response

What can a government do to ease high unemployment in an area after the closure of a shipyard?

Businesses therefore tend to locate in areas where the available work force has appropriate skills. This has a cumulative effect, as can be seen in the growth of hi-tech businesses along the M4 corridor in the Thames Valley.

NATURAL RESOURCES

Many businesses, particularly in the primary sector, are dependent on natural resources for their operation. An obvious example of this is mining. Coal mines, for example, must be located at the site of the coal reserves which are to be extracted.

Some land is better suited to one type of farming than to another.

In other industries, the availability of natural resources in a locality will dictate the type of activity undertaken. The type of farming carried out – dairy, sheep or arable – will depend on factors such as the type of soil available locally: its fertility, suitability for growing different crops, type of grass, and so on.

THE PROXIMITY OF OTHER BUSINESSES

No business organisation operates in isolation from other businesses, whether as suppliers, competitors or customers. Historically, the location of other businesses has had a significant effect on the location of new businesses seeking to establish themselves.

Many areas have gained a reputation for a particular type of business. Examples include:

- Sheffield for producing stainless steel – a firm manufacturing stainless steel cutlery will benefit from being able to put 'made in Sheffield' on its product;
- the City of London for banking and financial services – London has become the banking and financial capital of the world and a presence in the City is essential to the reputation of any major bank or financial institution;
- the West Midlands for the car industry – the growth of car manufacturing in the West Midlands has led to the establishment of component and material suppliers, such as Lucas Batteries and Dunlop Rubber, in the area.

In some cases, businesses can benefit from having a particular address. For example, in London, Hatton Garden is recognised as the centre of the jewellery trade, while a private medical consultant who can afford a Harley Street address immediately gains in prestige. Similarly, a firm of solicitors in Manchester will attract more clients if they have an office in Piccadilly rather than Moss Side.

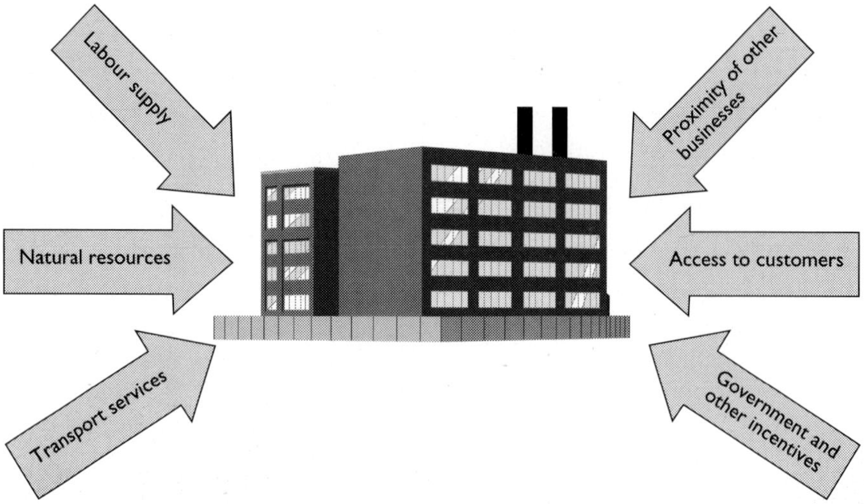

FIGURE 1.11 Influences to be considered when choosing a business location.

In the retail industry, large stores and supermarkets are often located in busy, out-of-town shopping centres and retail parks. Having ample car parking facilities, these sites suit the shopping habits of today's consumers who tend to shop less frequently and so need to buy in bulk, using a car to carry their shopping home. This has led to a decline in high street shopping, and many smaller corner shops are now facing difficulties.

ACTIVITY

Identify any areas of your locality where different business organisations have tended to congregate. Suggest reasons why this is so.

As you have seen, therefore, it is often advantageous for a business to locate near other businesses, even when they are in competition, because of the reputation to be gained from locating in a particular area or because of the proximity of suppliers dedicated to a particular industry. Some businesses, however, need to locate away from competitors in order to establish their own share of the market (see p 35).

ACCESS TO CUSTOMERS

All businesses need customers. It is important, therefore, that when deciding on a location for the business, consideration is given to where its customers are and how it will reach them.

For some businesses, particularly in the retail sector, this means locating the business where the customers are. You have already seen that large stores tend to locate in busy out-of-town shopping centres and retail parks because that is where their customers want to go to shop. Smaller retail outlets, however, are also located near their customers. A small corner shop or newsagent's customers are usually local residents, although the business may also attract passing trade if it is located on a busy road or near a bus stop.

Business in the retail sector are sited in places that are most convenient for their customers.

Similarly, businesses such as solicitors and local banks are sited close to their customers or clients. They are often in prominent high street positions so that their location is well known and easily accessible to their customers.

As you have seen, some businesses choose a particular location because other businesses are already there. If there is a large concentration of businesses in one industry in a locality, such as car manufacturing in the West Midlands or potteries around Stoke on Trent, other businesses which supply that industry will tend to locate near them so that they are close to their customers.

For other businesses, locating close to their customers is not so important. This may be the case with service industries where the service is carried out on the customers' premises, or with larger manufacturing companies whose customers are spread over a wide area, perhaps throughout the UK.

TRANSPORT SERVICES

Before the development of modern transport networks, manufacturing industries were generally located close to their sources of raw materials, while service industries needed to be close to their customers. The development of fast and efficient rail links and motorway networks has tended to give businesses more freedom of choice over location.

In practice, the availability of transport services influences the location of businesses in several ways.

- A manufacturing organisation which produces easily transportable goods from heavy or bulky raw materials will be likely to locate close to its source of raw materials.
- A manufacturing organisation which produces heavy or bulky goods from easily transportable raw materials will tend to locate close to its customers.
- A manufacturing organisation seeking to distribute its goods nationally or internationally will take the availability of appropriate transport facilities into account, perhaps locating close to a motorway junction or port.
- A service industry which carries out its service on customer premises will consider the location of its customers, the ease of access to them, and how far it is prepared to travel to provide its service.

The Japanese car giant Nissan chose to open a plant in the north east of England, partly because of incentives from the Government (see p 37), but also because the site was close to motorway and rail links

The Nissan car plant in the north east of England.

for distributing cars throughout the UK, while the Tyne and Wear port facilities were easily accessible for exporting to Europe.

Manufacturing in south east England is moving away from expensive town and industrial park locations to cheaper locations closer to motorway networks. The newly refurbished London Docklands only started to develop as a commercial centre once businesses were convinced that the area would be properly served by the transport network. In the Midlands, new towns such as Telford and Milton Keynes have also attracted businesses due to their easy access to the rest of the country via the motorway system.

Some businesses choose particular locations in order to be easily accessible to their employees or customers. One of the reasons why London developed as a major centre for business and commerce was the existence of a vast and complex commuter network enabling employees to work in the City or the centre of London while living in the fast growing suburbs. Likewise, when the Disney Corporation decided to establish a theme park in Europe, they chose a location with easily accessible road, rail, air and ferry links with the rest of Europe.

Incentives

The decline, and even closure, of many manufacturing industries in different areas of the UK has led to an unequal distribution of unemployment between the regions, as shown in *Fig. 1.12*. There is a similar pattern across Europe.

In order to rectify this situation, a variety of incentives have been developed by the European Union, the British Government and local government, designed to encourage new business into areas of high unemployment.

The EU provides aid through the European Regional Development Fund which gives grants to projects concerned with developing areas of industrial decline, in some cases supporting businesses and improving transport links.

The UK Government has introduced financial incentives aimed at creating new jobs in areas of high unemployment. These incentives include free or subsidised rent on premises, subsidies per employee and grants for additional employees taken on. The overall level of aid to such regions fell from £900m in 1982 to £110m in 1991, but many large businesses have located in depressed areas as a result of Government action.

QUICK response

Where is the headquarters of the European Parliament?

5.4 Employment structure of the civilian workforce[1]: by gender

Thousands

	1976	1981	1986	1991	1992	1993	1994
United Kingdom							
Civilian workforce	25,895	26,685	27,644	28,264	28,155	27,986	27,736
Males	16,040	16,212	16,198	16,042	15,928	15,754	15,549
Females	9,856	10,473	11,446	12,221	12,227	12,232	12,187
Employees in employment	22,557	21,892	21,387	22,262	21,937	21,626	21,562
Males	13,401	12,562	11,744	11,530	11,239	10,978	10,911
Females	9,156	9,331	9,644	10,731	10,698	10,648	10,651
Self-employed (with or without employees)	2,073	2,272	2,802	3,408	3,215	3,184	3,290
Claimant unemployed (males and females)	1,266	2,521	3,229	2,241	2,678	2,865	2,586
WRGTP[2]	.	.	226	353	325	311	298
North							
Civilian workforce	1,450	1,407	1,424	1,383	1,407	1,401	1,393
Males	918	865	844	785	801	799	791
Females	533	541	580	598	606	602	602
Employees in employment	1,255	1,122	1,061	1,089	1,106	1,081	1,084
Males	769	654	585	567	574	553	553
Females	486	468	476	522	531	527	531
Self-employed (with or without employees)	96	92	111	118	119	124	126
Claimant unemployed (males and females)	100	192	232	141	151	167	156
WRGTP[2]	.	.	20	35	31	29	27
Yorkshire & Humberside							
Civilian workforce	2,244	2,258	2,320	2,365	2,361	2,363	2,326
Males	1,407	1,389	1,368	1,336	1,325	1,326	1,296
Females	837	868	951	1,029	1,036	1,037	1,030
Employees in employment	1,967	1,852	1,762	1,866	1,859	1,850	1,843
Males	1,190	1,083	970	962	945	938	928
Females	777	768	792	904	914	912	915
Self-employed (with or without employees)	167	169	223	258	240	240	230
Claimant unemployed (males and females)	109	237	312	203	227	240	221
WRGTP[2]	.	.	22	38	35	34	31
East Midlands							
Civilian workforce	1,696	1,774	1,888	1,940	1,916	1,899	1,919
Males	1,054	1,083	1,112	1,096	1,091	1,059	1,074
Females	642	691	776	844	825	841	845
Employees in employment	1,497	1,467	1,490	1,535	1,514	1,493	1,514
Males	900	855	831	796	786	755	766
Females	597	613	659	739	729	739	748
Self-employed (with or without employees)	128	152	181	245	214	207	222
Claimant unemployed (males and females)	71	155	199	139	169	180	166
WRGTP[2]	.	.	17	22	20	20	17
East Anglia							
Civilian workforce	780	833	915	999	1,008	1,021	1,016
Males	493	521	543	572	579	578	567
Females	286	312	371	427	429	442	450
Employees in employment	669	681	717	795	784	788	793
Males	404	400	402	417	412	405	403
Females	265	281	314	377	372	383	390
Self-employed (with or without employees)	78	91	109	139	143	142	142
Claimant unemployed (males and females)	32	61	81	57	74	82	72
WRGTP[2]	.	.	7	8	8	9	8
South East							
Civilian workforce	8,224	8,573	9,049	9,172	9,118	9,016	8,949
Males	5,027	5,158	5,232	5,195	5,134	5,085	5,025
Females	3,196	3,414	3,817	3,977	3,984	3,930	3,925
Employees in employment	7,246	7,263	7,255	7,316	7,119	6,929	6,892
Males	4,243	4,135	3,968	3,791	3,649	3,540	3,504
Females	3,003	3,128	3,287	3,525	3,470	3,389	3,389
Self-employed (with or without employees)	687	762	986	1,173	1,115	1,105	1,175
Claimant unemployed (males and females)	290	548	772	628	826	919	818
WRGTP[2]	.	.	36	56	58	63	64
South West							
Civilian workforce	1,812	1,972	2,098	2,305	2,243	2,264	2,261
Males	1,133	1,209	1,228	1,302	1,261	1,270	1,256
Females	679	763	870	1,004	982	994	1,004
Employees in employment	1,513	1,541	1,579	1,731	1,694	1,687	1,693
Males	894	883	862	881	849	842	840
Females	619	658	717	850	845	845	853
Self-employed (with or without employees)	204	275	307	399	330	346	362
Claimant unemployed (males and females)	94	156	196	153	197	210	185
WRGTP[2]	.	.	17	23	21	21	21

FIGURE 1.12 A section from a table showing the employment of the civilian workforce across regions. (WRGTP = Work-related Government Training Programme.) Source: *Regional Trends 30*, Crown copyright 1995.

ACTIVITY

Find out what incentives to businesses are available in your local area, either from the Government or the EU. Suggest reasons for these incentives. If no incentives are available in your area, where is the nearest area where incentives are available?

To qualify for regional aid from the Government, a business must either locate in a designated development area, where a grant for the creation of new jobs will be available, or in intermediate areas, where financial aid may be available.

The Government has also provided some money for the regeneration of inner-city areas. An example of this is London Docklands where the decline of the docks had created a run-down, almost derelict area. Government funding was used to reclaim the land and create an infrastructure (roads, communications and so on) to make it an attractive area for commercial organisations. Further examples may be found in many provincial cities.

Local authorities have also sought to attract firms to their areas, particularly if they have high levels of unemployment. Ways of doing this often include the easing of planning restrictions to allow new building development, the creation of business parks to attract new businesses and of retail parks to attract supermarkets and large stores, normally with the added incentive of a subsidised or rent-free period.

ACTIVITY

Obtain publicity material from a region in the UK which is trying to attract businesses to locate there. What incentives are they offering? Are they offering any incentives in addition to those available from the Government or the EU?

THE INFLUENCE OF THE BUSINESS ENVIRONMENT

Business organisations are affected by a number of external factors which influence their activities and performance. These factors form the business environment in which organisations operate. They are largely outside the control of individual business organisations.

Because the business environment influences the activities and performance of organisations, it is important for the management of a business organisation to be aware of the factors involved and how they can affect the organisation. In this way, account can be taken of the business environment when planning future courses of action, and the organisation can respond to any changes in the business environment which might adversely affect performance.

While some factors in the business environment, such as legislation, place constraints on an organisation, other factors should be seen positively, as opportunities for the organisation to develop.

COMPETITION

All business organisations, whether in the private or public sector, profit-making, non-profit-making or charitable, are faced with competition.

Today the world market for goods and services is vast, and there are millions of large and small business organisations supplying that market. Yet as vast as the world market is, it contains only a finite number of consumers and customers (see Unit 3, p 163). Each consumer has only a limited amount of money available to spend on goods and services. This means that business organisations must persuade customers to buy their goods or services rather than the goods and services of other businesses.

Foreign competition for British goods and services has been increasing for many years. All restrictions on trade within the EU were removed in the early 1990s. This means that goods and services produced in any EU member state can flow freely into Britain, thus competing with goods and services produced within the UK. The converse is also true: British goods can now be sold anywhere within the EU on equal terms with other EU goods and services. In addition, products from the developing economies of Asia and Eastern Europe are also providing competition for British manufacturers.

On the face of it, the competitors of a particular business are other businesses providing the same goods or services. Vauxhall, for example, is a competitor of Ford as both companies make cars and both companies must persuade the same customers (in this case people who wish to buy cars) to buy the cars that they produce.

In the public sector, schools financed by the local authority or directly by the Government (grant-maintained schools) have found themselves in competition with other schools in the same locality as the Government has given parents more freedom to choose which school they wish their child to attend. Schools are allocated funding according to the number of pupils they have on roll. Schools with too few children will not be viable and therefore have to close.

Additionally, schools in the public sector are in competition with other schools in the private sector. These schools (often confusingly called 'public schools') charge the parents of their pupils a fee. They depend on pupils for their income and, obviously, the more pupils they can attract, the higher their income. Public schools compete with local authority and grant-maintained schools, and with other public schools.

QUICK response

How does increased competition for a product benefit the customers who purchase that product?

All sorts of items can be bought as gifts.

There are many occasions when the competition that a business faces comes not from other businesses providing the same goods or services, but from those providing goods or services which could be considered a substitute. For example, the competition for an expensive Parker fountain pen is obviously a similar pen made by Waterman or Sheaffer. However, expensive fountain pens are often bought as gifts. The true competition is therefore other items which may also be considered suitable as gifts.

Charities, such as Age Concern, the Save The Children Fund, the RSPCA and Oxfam, all collect money for, and support, very different causes. Yet each of these charities must compete with the others for a share of the money that people are willing to give. Some would argue that the total amount of money given to charities as a whole is also being adversely affected by the National Lottery. Only 25 per cent of the money spent on National Lottery tickets goes to 'good causes', but the publicity surrounding it has persuaded many people to give to charity through the National Lottery.

ACTIVITY

Select three local business organisations. Identify the competition for the product of each business.

ACTIVITY

As a group, discuss whether you think there should be competition in areas such as gas, electricity and water supply, education and the health service. What are the benefits or disadvantages of competition in these areas?

Legal constraints

Many laws control the activities of business organisations. Some of these laws, such as the Health and Safety at Work Act 1974 which places an obligation on employers to ensure that their employees have a safe and healthy environment in which to work, are designed to protect the interests of employees. Others protect the interests of customers and the general public.

Legislation passed by Acts of Parliament to protect the interests of customers places constraints and restrictions on the production, sale and supply of goods and services. These laws are dealt with in detail in Unit 3 (p 221), but the main Acts are:

- **the Trades Descriptions Act 1968**, which makes it illegal to describe a product as something other than it is;
- **the Unfair Contract Terms Act 1977**, which makes it illegal for businesses to attempt to take away the statutory rights of customers by including clauses to that effect in contracts of sale, whether or not these are in writing;

- **the Sale of Goods Act 1979**, which makes it the responsibility of the supplier to ensure that goods supplied are as described, of an appropriate quality and fit for the purpose the supplier has indicated;
- **the Supply of Goods and Services Act 1982**, which places an obligation on businesses to supply goods or services ordered in a satisfactory manner, within a reasonable period of time and at a reasonable price;
- **the Consumer Protection Act 1987**, which places responsibility for any damage or injury caused by a faulty product on the supplier of the product, and not just on the manufacturer;
- **the Sale and Supply of Goods Act 1994**, which extends the Sale of Goods Act 1979 to state that goods and services supplied must not only be suitable for their stated purpose, but they must also be suitable for the purpose for which the purchaser has bought them.

QUICK response

If you bought an oak table which turned out to be stained to look like oak, under which Act could you claim compensation?

Other legislation which puts constraints on the activities and behaviour of business organisations covers areas such as the construction and use of premises and vehicles, the hours during which certain types of business can operate (particularly affecting shops, pubs, racecourses and so on).

Laws passed by the European Parliament, which must be implemented by the parliaments of EU member states, have had a significant impact on the business environment in Britain. For example, the Common Agricultural Policy (CAP) has restricted the activities of farmers throughout the EU. Quotas are now imposed on how much farms can produce. A similar situation exists within the fishing industry.

ENVIRONMENTAL CONSTRAINTS

In recent years considerable concern has been voiced about what is happening to the natural environment. Organisations and pressure groups such as Friends of the Earth and Greenpeace have been set up to bring pressure on governments and businesses to show more care for the environment in what they do.

Consumers, and the general public, want more consideration to be shown in preserving the environment we live in. This trend in public opinion has meant that many businesses have had to take action to ensure that their operations do not harm the environment. New terms, such as 'environmentally friendly' and 'green' have come into common usage to show that products have been developed, and processes used, which will help to maintain the environment.

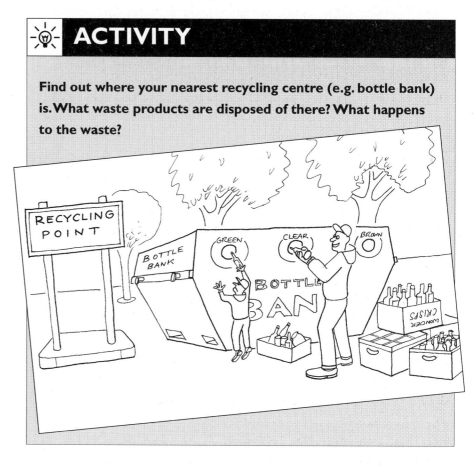

ACTIVITY

Find out where your nearest recycling centre (e.g. bottle bank) is. What waste products are disposed of there? What happens to the waste?

In response to public opinion and pressure from environmental groups, the Government has introduced laws constraining the activities of businesses by, for example, reducing the permitted levels of pollution of the land, sea, rivers and atmosphere. The 1990 Environmental Protection Act has forced manufacturers to reduce the environmental damage they cause by introducing methods of production and waste disposal that eliminate harmful emissions. This has resulted in the development of an entire new business sector concerned with waste disposal, pollution control and the recycling of used materials.

Aerosols no longer contain CFCs.

Pressure from the general public, environmentalists and environmental groups, combined with new legal restrictions, including EU regulations, has brought about significant changes in production and consumption. For example, since 1976 there has been a considerable reduction in the use of chlorofluorocarbons (CFCs) in manufacturing, for example in refrigerators and aerosol sprays, as these are believed to damage the protective ozone layer in the Earth's atmosphere. There has also been a reduction in the use of fossil fuels, such as coal, which produce gases which contribute to global warming.

Indeed, many businesses now publicise the fact that their products and processes are 'green' and 'environmentally friendly'. In this way, they try to enhance their reputation and develop relations with an increasingly environmentally aware and concerned public. Any business which fails to respond to public opinion in this way is likely to lose customers to competitors who do.

PUBLIC PRESSURE

Many organisations exist to protect the interests of consumers by bringing pressure on business organisations. Some of these are sponsored by the Government, while others are fully independent. In some cases they may even be sponsored by the industry involved.

A pressure or consumer group may represent a particular area of concern affecting a few individuals, such as worry over noise levels in a locality created by an individual factory working at night, or a more general area of interest, such as concern for the environment. We have already discussed the effect on business of environmental pressure groups such as Friends of the Earth and Greenpeace. *Fig. 1.13* shows some of the major consumer organisation pressure groups representing the interests of consumers.

FIGURE 1.13 Some of the major consumer pressure groups.

Organisation	Sponsored by	Purpose
Office of Fair Trading	Government	Established by the Fair Trading Act 1973 to protect consumers against unfair business practices. Works with businesses and consumers. Will prosecute businesses where necessary.
Consumers Association	independent	Tests goods and services and campaigns on various issues on behalf of consumers. Publishes the consumer magazine *Which?*.
National Consumer Council	Government	Investigates and publishes reports on various matters of interest to consumers.
British Standards Institute	Government	Sets standards of manufacture and service provision for a wide range of goods and services. Goods conforming to a BSI standard are entitled to display a 'kitemark'.
Nationalised Industry Consumer Councils	Government	Sometimes called 'watchdogs', these exist to regulate the activities of nationalised industries
Advertising Standards Authority	independent	Maintains a watching brief over the content of advertisements, which should be 'legal, decent, honest and truthful'. Publishes the results of its investigations and asks for adverts to be withdrawn if appropriate.

ACTIVITY

In groups, choose either one of the organisations listed in *Fig. 1.13* or another pressure group to investigate. Find out about its purpose, the consumers it represents, how it operates and how it can be contacted. Each group should make a presentation of its findings to the class as a whole.

DEMAND, CUSTOMERS AND MARKETS

DEMAND AND SUPPLY

Businesses exist by producing and supplying goods and services for which there is an effective demand. If there is an effective demand for something, that demand is likely to be met by one or more business organisations. Demand for a particular product is created when:

- people or other organisations *want* that product;
- the people or organisations who want the product are *able and willing* to pay for it;
- the amount they are willing to pay is *sufficient* to cover the costs of producing and supplying the product.

If enough people or organisations want a product and are able and willing to pay enough to cover the costs of producing and supplying it, then there is an effective demand for the product.

For example, there is a demand today for food that is produced without the use of artificial or forced means, such as 'organic' vegetables which are grown without the use of chemical fertilisers, and 'free range' eggs, which are produced by chickens kept in as natural an environment as possible. This is part of an overall trend towards healthy eating habits.

However, if you compare the prices of organically grown vegetables and free range eggs with the prices of other vegetables and eggs in a supermarket, you will find that the organic and free range varieties are more expensive. They is because they are comparatively more expensive to produce. Therefore, although there is a demand

QUICK response

We all use the services of the police, although we do not pay for these ourselves. How are the police paid for? Does this cover their costs?

Free range eggs are expensive to produce and buy.

for these products, because people want them, they will only be produced and offered for sale *if sufficient people are prepared and able to pay the higher price for them.*

If there are not enough people willing and able to pay the higher price, perhaps because they prefer to pay a lower price for ordinary vegetables and eggs or because the weekly family budget for food simply won't stretch to the higher price, then supermarkets and shops will not offer them for sale and farmers will not produce these more expensive items.

ACTIVITY

The modern trend towards healthy lifestyles covers much more than organically grown foodstuffs. For example, many people now include an exercise regime as part of their daily lives. Make a list of all the other products you can think of that have been made available because they help people to follow a more healthy lifestyle.

CUSTOMERS AND CONSUMERS

Demand is created by customers and consumers.

- **Customers** are the people or organisations who actually buy and pay for particular goods and services supplied by business organisations.
- **Consumers** are the people or organisations who use goods and services supplied by business organisations. Consumers may or may not buy the goods and services they use.

We are all consumers of goods and services as we all use some goods and services. For example, we all:

- use electricity, for lighting, to watch television, to play a CD, and so on;
- wear clothes which have been made by manufacturers and sold in shops;
- go to the doctor when we are unwell.

However, we do not necessarily buy these goods and services ourselves and therefore may not be a customer of the organisations that supply them.

- The electricity may be paid for by our parents or guardians, or another organisation, such as our school or college.
- A sweater you like to wear may have been bought for you as a present.
- You may not pay NHS contributions which are collected by the Government out of wages and salaries and which pay for the National Health Service.

ACTIVITY

Identify the customer and the consumer in the following cases:

- **a young mother in a supermarket buying the weekly family shopping;**
- **a doctor buying drugs from a drugs company to prescribe to a patient;**
- **you, buying Christmas presents;**
- **somebody in a camera shop buying a camera to take photographs on holiday.**

In most cases, the demand for a product is created by the consumer of the product who is also the customer, as with anything you buy for your own use, from a can of Coke to drink at lunchtime to the latest CD of your favourite group. However, demand can also be created by consumers who are not customers (as with the demand for education, which is created by parents although it is paid for by the Government out of taxes), or by customers who are not consumers (for example, the demand for a particular perfume may be created by people who buy it to give as a gift rather than to wear themselves). The

Government is a customer of many organisations providing goods and services, including the police and armed services, the National Health and Education Services, although the entire population of the UK may at some time be consumers of these goods and services.

We have said above (p 46) that demand is created when people or other organisations want a product and are *able and willing to pay* for it. However, what people need and what they want are often two different things.

Everybody has basic needs which they have to satisfy in order to sustain life. However, people can often choose what they will use to satisfy those needs. For example, you *need* to eat in order to live, but you may go into a hamburger bar at lunchtime because you *want* to eat a burger.

In addition to the basic needs for things like food and drink, warmth, clothing and so on, there are many other things that people want in order to make life more enjoyable, such as:

- computers to play games on or to help them with their work;
- CDs and CD players so that they can hear their favourite music;
- the services of hairdressers to help them look and feel good.

Food is a need but a burger is a want.

ACTIVITY

Make a list of all the things you have bought during the last week. Which were needs and which were wants? Compare your list with your fellow students. Have any of them listed as needs some of the things you identified as wants?

Often, demand for a particular product can be created by persuading customers and consumers that the product is exactly what they want – even if they had not thought of it before. In this way, by careful use of marketing techniques (see Unit 3, p 189), an organisation can create a demand for its own products. Demand may be created, or stimulated, for:

- an existing product – as when SmithKline Benson began to advertise Lucozade as a healthy drink for today's lifestyle, rather than as a drink for invalids;

- a new development in an existing field – as when CDs were introduced as improvements on traditional vinyl records;
- a new idea – as when Sir Clive Sinclair brought out his first home computer.

However, when a business tries to stimulate demand for one of its products, it is important to remember that, ultimately, it is the consumer or customer who will decide what they want.

MARKETS

A market is a place where customers and suppliers come together to buy and sell goods or services. The term 'market' is also used to describe the total actual and potential customers and demand for a particular product or organisation. Markets may be described in terms of numbers of customers or value of sales.

There are all sorts of markets – some sell futures in the money market; others sell food.

A business may sell its goods and services in the **domestic market**, that is, within its own national boundaries, or in the **international market**, that is, anywhere in the world. A small computer consultancy based in Bristol may, for example, only sell its services to business organisations within the UK – the domestic market – or even within the county of Avon. A large organisation like Coca-Cola, on the other hand, sells its product to customers all over the world.

The success of an individual business organisation depends on:

- the value of the total market for the type of goods or services it supplies (including similar goods and services supplied by other businesses);

- the share of the market supplied by the individual business organisation.

For example, in 1992, food sales in the UK (the domestic market) totalled more than £45 billion. Of this, about 60 per cent was sold by the major supermarket chains, such as Tesco, Safeway and Sainsbury. The value of the share of the market supplied by the large chains was therefore in excess of £27 billion. As this was shared by several supermarket chains, it is easy to see why individual chains try to increase their own share of the total market.

One of the aims of many business organisations is to increase their share of the market (see p 12). There are, however, some businesses which supply the whole, or at least a major part, of the market for their goods or services. These businesses are called **monopolies.**

QUICK response

What would an increase in the market share of food sales by major supermarket chains mean for independent retailers?

THE PRODUCTS OF BUSINESS

As you have seen, business organisations exist by providing products to customers and consumers. By products we mean:

- **goods** – that is, things you can touch and use, such as clothes, computers and textbooks;
- **services** – that is, things that other people do for you, such as styling your hair, looking after your money in a bank and prescribing medicines for you when you are sick.

Goods can be classified as:

- **consumable;**
- **durable.**

Consumable goods are those goods that are produced to satisfy short-term wants. Consumable goods are used up, or *consumed*, in the satisfaction of those wants, and the life of consumable goods is therefore also short. Examples of consumable goods are food and drink, newspapers and clothes.

Durable goods are those goods that are produced in order to satisfy long-term or recurring wants. Durable goods are *not* used up in the satisfaction of those wants, although they may wear out in time.

Examples of durable goods are computers, personal stereos and cars.

Business organisations may provide their products to:

- individual customers;
- governments;
- other businesses.

A company like Reebok, which produces trainers, provides those trainers to individual customers; manufacturers of weapons systems provide their products to governments; companies such as British Steel provide raw materials and components to other businesses. Many other companies provide their products to all three types of customers. For example, Rover Cars supply cars to private individuals, to governments and to other businesses.

Rover cars are sold to many sectors of the market.

ACTIVITIES UNDERTAKEN BY BUSINESSES TO IMPROVE THEIR MARKET POSITION

Whatever product they provide, and whoever the customers or consumers of their products are, most business organisations seek to improve their market position – in other words, to increase their share of the market for their product.

A business organisation may improve its market position by:

- **advertising** – to attract new customers;
- **improving existing products** – to ensure they meet the changing needs of customers and take advantage of new, improved materials;
- **creating new products** – to meet the needs of customers.

ACTIVITY

Identify at least two improved products and at least two new products. What needs do these products meet that were not being adequately met before?

A business can undertake several types of activity which may help it to improve its market position.

MARKETING RESEARCH

The first thing a business must do is to find out exactly what the customers in its chosen market want, and what they think of the products already being supplied by both the business trying to improve its market position and by its competitors. By finding out what customers want, a business can supply a product which fulfils that want, whether that want is for an existing product, an improvement to an existing product, or a new product which more closely meets customers' requirements. Businesses find out what their customers want from a product, and also monitor what they think of and how satisfied they are with existing products, by undertaking **marketing research**.

A business organisation can carry out various methods of marketing research which will show:

- existing and potential sales of a product;
- the attitudes of customers to a product;
- the strengths and weakness of competitors;
- expected trends in the market and demand for a product.

DESIGN

When a business knows what its market wants from a product, it can design the product so that it closely matches market requirements. This may involve developing an existing product or designing a new one.

In designing products, a business must take account of new technology and future trends. This is particularly important in areas of hi-tech manufacture, where new developments in, for example, computers mean that higher specification products are becoming available almost daily.

Businesses must also be aware of technological developments in methods of manufacture and materials. For example, technological developments may mean that a product can be produced to a higher specification or more cheaply by using the new technology. In this case the design of the product must take the new technology into account as customers will expect to buy the product with the higher specification or lower price.

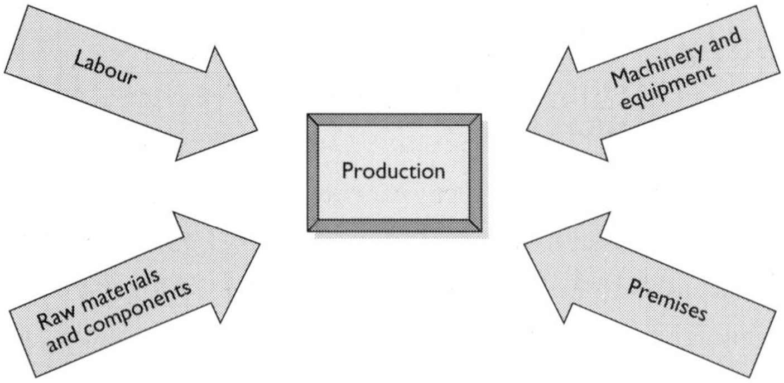

FIGURE 1.14 The factors influencing production.

PRODUCTION

When trying to improve its market position, a business organisation must take account of the additional production requirements needed to meet the increased level of sales. It is no good a business gaining more customers and improving its market position if it is then unable to supply those customers with the goods they want when they want them. Factors involved in ensuring that an increased level of orders can be met include:

- **Labour** – is the current workforce large enough, or will more employees with the right skills need to be recruited or trained?
- **Machinery and equipment** – is the current capacity of manufacturing machinery and equipment sufficient, or will more, and perhaps more advanced, machines need to be bought?
- **Raw materials and components** – increased production will mean an increased need for raw materials and components used in making the finished product. Can these be obtained from existing suppliers, or will additional sources of supply be needed to meet the increased demand?
- **Premises** – increasing the market share of a business may lead to a larger workforce, more machinery, a larger customer base, increased production and storage to meet orders, and a growing business organisation. The present premises may not be large enough for the new production and other requirements of the business.

Marketing communications

Finding out the requirements of the market, designing a suitable product and ensuring that the production capacity of a business organisation is sufficient to supply the market will not, in itself, increase the market share of the business. The business must take steps to let the market know about the business and its product. There are several ways of doing this.

- **Advertising** – in the media, such as newspapers, magazines, radio and television. The medium used should be appropriate to both the product being advertised and the customer. For example, a manufacturer of diesel engines for commercial vehicles would choose to advertise in a trade journal such as *Commercial Motor* which is read by people likely to be interested in purchasing the product. Advertising a diesel engine on national television would be very expensive, and only a very small proportion of viewers would be interested in the product. A large supermarket chain, such as Safeway, on the other hand, whose potential customer base is vast, will choose a national medium seen by the maximum number of people, such as television.

ACTIVITY

Suggest appropriate media in which a producer of computer games could advertise.

- **Promotion** – usually at the point of sale. Promotion of a product can take many forms, including special display stands, cut-price offers, money-off coupons, and so on. Promotion is used to persuade people to buy a new product or one they might not normally use, or else to buy more of a product than usual.

ACTIVITY

Visit a local supermarket. How many different types of promotion can you find? As a group, discuss which form of promotion you think is most effective. Is it different for different types of product?

- **Sponsorship** – of events and personalities. Sponsorship can bring the name of a business organisation to the attention of potential customers by linking that name with an event or person. For example, many sporting events are linked with business organisations, such as the NatWest Trophy in cricket.
- **Sales literature** – giving information about a business and the goods or services it provides.

(Marketing communications are described in more detail in Unit 3, p 189.)

SALES

QUICK response

List five goods or services and say where they are sold.

The purpose of a business in trying to increase its share of the market is to increase its level of sales. Until a business actually sells more of its product to more customers, its efforts in marketing research, in designing a product to meet the needs of the market, in ensuring production capacity is sufficient to fulfil the increased level of orders that is anticipated, and in marketing communications will not have achieved their objective. It is essential, therefore, that these activities are followed up by further action to convert any increased customer interest in a product into actual sales.

Selling a product may take place in a shop or other retail outlet, or in the office of a buyer in another company, depending on the product being sold and whether the customer is a private individual or another business organisation. There are five stages in the selling process:

1. **Introduction** – where the relationship between buyer and seller is established.
2. **Finding out the needs of the customer** – in order to show how the product meets those needs.
3. **Presentation of the product** – in such a way as to convince the buyer it is what they need.
4. **Answering questions** – about the product or the business organisation.
5. **Closing the sale** – getting the buyer to decide to purchase the product

AFTER-SALES SERVICE

An important factor in attracting new customers can be the level of after-sales service offered by a business. Customers who purchase a product want to know that if the product is faulty when they buy it, or else does not suit their needs, they can get it replaced or have their money refunded. If a product develops a fault in use, then customers need to know that the product can be repaired – free of charge under guarantee, if appropriate.

After-sales service is an important part of sales.

PROPOSE PRODUCTS WHICH WOULD MEET MARKET DEMAND

The results of its marketing research will tell a business organisation what its customers want and expect from a product. However, the needs and wants of customers change over time and this gives rise to changes in demand for products. Some of the factors affecting demand are:

- changing fashions, for example, in clothes and leisure pursuits;
- changing tastes and customer preferences, for example, in food and drink;
- changing social trends, for example, more women going out to work;
- customer concerns, such as for the environment;
- developments in technology, for example, the introduction of multi-media computers and the so-called 'information superhighway';
- changes in the law, for example, health and safety requirements;
- the availability of new developments, such as liquid detergents for low-temperature automatic washing machines.

Business organisations must be aware of, and take account of, these factors when proposing and designing products to meet market demand. In order to respond to and meet changes in market demand, a business may need to develop an existing product or propose an entirely new product.

For example, a recent development in safety measures in cars has meant that many new cars are being built with airbags as a standard safety feature. The trend towards healthy lifestyles and more people taking part in fitness programmes has led to the development of many new products, such as step exercise machines.

A business failing to respond to the changing requirements of the market will lose customers and sales to other businesses which do.

PORTFOLIO ASSIGNMENT

For this portfolio assignment you will need to research a business organisation in your area. This may be one of the businesses you investigated for Portfolio Assignment 1.1. Advice on finding information about business was given on p x in the Introduction. You may wish to refer to this again before starting this assignment. Include charts and diagrams where appropriate to illustrate points you are making.

TASK 1

Select a local business organisation to investigate. This could be one of the organisations investigated for Portfolio Assignment 1.1 on p 29. On a map, identify the location of the business and any relevant natural resources or sources of raw materials and components. You should also indicate on the map the proximity of other businesses, customers and transport services.

TASK 2

Write notes explaining the reason for the location of the business in Task 1.

TASK 3

Explain the effects of the business environment and legal, environmental and public influences on business activities, with particular reference to the business organisation chosen for Task 1.

TASK 4

Write an informal report on the business organisation chosen for Task 1, describing the market for its goods or services, the demand for goods and services, and explaining how any marketing communications used by the business have improved its market position.

TASK 5

Identify a need or demand for a product or service which is not at present being adequately met by products or services currently available. This may be due to any of the factors on p 57. Design and propose a new or improved product or service which you believe will meet that need or demand. Write notes supporting your proposal, with sketches of the product or service where appropriate, describing the product or service, justifying your belief that there is a need or demand for it, and explaining how it will meet that need or demand.

This portfolio assignment also presents an opportunity to gather evidence for the following core skills:

- Communication – take part in discussions; produce written material; read and respond to written materials;
- Information Technology – prepare information; process information; present information.

INVESTIGATING EMPLOYMENT

When you have finished this course, and obtained your Intermediate GNVQ in Business, you may either go on to further education or out to work. In either event, when you have finished your full-time studies you will probably need to find employment. Indeed, you may already have some form of employment now, to help you to afford some of the things you want while you are still studying.

In most industrialised countries, like Britain, the majority of people go out to work in a business organisation of one or other of the types you have looked at in this unit: a sole trader, partnership, private or public limited company, franchise, co-operative or state-owned organisation. The organisation these people work for may be in the primary, secondary or tertiary sectors, and its main purpose may be for profit, not for profit or charitable. Refer back to Unit 1 for an explanation of types of business (pp 17–26), industrial sectors (pp 3–9) and purposes of business organisations (pp 9–15).

Just as there are many different types of business organisation, there are many different types of employment to choose from. In this element you will find out about the different types of employment, and employment in different regions of the UK, locally and nationally, and in different regions of the EU. You will also compare working conditions for employees in different organisations.

TYPES OF EMPLOYMENT

As you carry out your investigation into employment, you will find that not only do people do an almost endless variety of jobs, but that, within the variety of jobs they do, there are also different types of employment.

- **Full-time employment** consists of employment for 30 hours or more per week *for one employer*. In practice, most full-time jobs require the job holder to work for between 35 and 40 hours per week. A full-time employee receives a contract of employment (see Unit 2, p 113) which states the number of hours per week they are expected to work. A set weekly wage (calculated on an hourly basis) or monthly salary (calculated on an annual basis) is normally paid for this. An employee may work more than the number of hours stated in their contract, but such hours are considered **overtime**. The employee may receive further payment for overtime, in addition to the normal wage or salary.

QUICK response

Give three reasons why part-time employment in Britain is increasing.

- **Part-time employment** consists of employment for less than 30 hours per week for one employer. In Britain part-time employment is increasing, partly at the expense of full-time employment. This is largely due to the increase in service industries (see p 68) and the decline in manufacturing (see p 67). Jobs in service organisations, such as shops, banks, hotels and the Health Service, are often part-time, while many manufacturers are now cutting down on full-time jobs and creating part-time jobs. Part-time employees in Britain do not have the same employment rights (to pensions, redundancy payments, holidays, etc.) as full-time employees, although legislation introduced by the EU is closing the gap. In other member states of the EU, part-time employees generally do enjoy the same rights as full-time employees.
- **Job sharing** is an arrangement in some organisations, particularly local authorities, whereby one job which would normally be full-time is shared by two employees, each working part-time but, between them, covering full-time hours.
- **Permanent employment** occurs when an employee is hired for an unspecified length of time and the employment is likely to continue for the foreseeable future. This does not mean that the employment cannot be terminated by either the employee or the employer in certain circumstances, such as the employee retiring, leaving to take up other employment, or losing their job through redundancy. Traditionally, permanent employment has been seen as having advantages to both employers and employees. Employers have been able to build a stable and appropriately skilled and trained workforce; employees have had job security which has allowed them to plan for the future, both in their careers and in their private lives.
- **Temporary employment** is employment which is for a limited

period of time, and usually for a specific purpose. For example, many shops take on additional, temporary employees at Christmas or sale time, to help them to cope with the rush of customers at those times. Business organisations also take on temporary employees to cover for permanent employees who are absent, perhaps on long-term sick or maternity leave. Many businesses employ additional temporary staff during the summer months to cover for permanent staff who are away on holiday.

- **Skilled and unskilled employment**: Many jobs require workers to have specific knowledge and skills in order to be able to do the job properly. People who do these jobs are in skilled employment. Skilled employment ranges from operating certain types of machines, including computer-controlled equipment, to crafts requiring specific skills, and highly skilled jobs such as the work of a brain surgeon or airline pilot. Skilled employment normally calls for special training in order that the employee has the appropriate skills. This training may have been done prior to starting employment, so that the employee already has the necessary skills, or during employment so that the employee gains the skills while in employment.

Airline pilots do highly skilled jobs.

Unskilled employment, on the other hand, requires no special skills. Unskilled jobs can be performed by anyone, without training, although they will probably need some 'on the job' training in the workplace to be shown how to do the job and to ensure they are doing it correctly.

ACTIVITY

- **Collect as much information as you can on jobs which are advertised in your local newspaper, Job Centre and other employment agencies. Identify which jobs are full-time and which part-time, which skilled and which unskilled. Construct a table like this:**

Job title	Full- or part-time	Skilled or unskilled	Skills/knowledge required

- **Start a noticeboard in your class on which to put details of job advertisements in newspapers, the Job Centre, etc. Have separate sections for jobs which will be suitable for employment when you have finished your GNVQ Intermediate course and jobs which will be suitable for later progression.**

- **Self-employment**: The owner of a sole trader business, or a partner who is joint-owner of a partnership (see pp 19–20) works for themself rather than for an employer or organisation. This is because a sole trader or a partnership business has no legal identity separate from the owner or owners of the business (unlike a limited company). Other people, who are employed to help the owner or owners to run the business, are considered to be employed by the owner or owners. The owner or owners themselves, however, are said to be self-employed. Some people enjoy the freedom of being self-employed, they like the feeling that they are their own boss and will reap the rewards of their own hard work. Many people, however, prefer the security of being employed by a larger company or business organisation where they are assured of a regular weekly wage or monthly salary.

ACTIVITY

As a group, discuss the advantages and disadvantages of being self-employed rather than employed. What special skills or abilities do you think you would need to become self-employed?

CASE STUDY

Karen Harper

Karen Harper is the Personnel Manager of Western Distribution Services Limited in Bristol. This is a skilled job, calling for specific qualifications and experience, and the position is full-time and permanent. Karen went into personnel work when she left college because she enjoys working with people. She started with a large national company as a personnel assistant, gaining experience in personnel work and also studying for further professional qualifications. She likes the security of being employed and of knowing that her salary will be paid into her bank account regularly each month. She feels that she can develop her career and get to the top in personnel.

CASE STUDY

Michael Adobe

Michael Adobe is a college lecturer in business studies. He is a single parent, however, and needs to be able to be around for his young daughter, Katy, taking her to school and collecting her again at the end of the day. For this reason, Michael is unable to work full-time and has part-time positions at three nearby colleges of further education. This means that he has to do a considerable amount of lesson preparation and marking of students' work at home, but at least he is there to look after Katy. The positions are only temporary, and Michael has to renew his contract with each college at the beginning of the academic year. So far, the colleges he works for have wanted him back each year but he knows that if the number of students taking his courses drops significantly, he could lose his position with one or more of the colleges. While he would like more job security, Michael needs the flexibility of the part-time positions. He is glad that he has the skills to be able to do the work he enjoys and still have the necessary time to devote to his daughter.

CASE STUDY

Jane Sharman

Jane Sharman is an accountant. She is self-employed and works for herself. Hers is only a small business but she has a number of regular clients. Jane went to university to study accountancy, after which she worked for a large firm of accountants for ten years before deciding to set up on her own. It was hard at first when the regular monthly salary stopped coming in. She also found that going out and finding clients wasn't as easy as she had expected. When she worked for the big firm, the clients were always there – somebody else had gone out and got the business, she only had to do the work. Now, however, she is glad she became self-employed. She likes being her own boss and not having anybody else telling her what to do, but it does call for strict self-discipline. Wth regular clients, the money is coming in more regularly now, and she is able to draw money out of the business on a regular basis.

REGIONAL EMPLOYMENT

Although unemployment is often considered to be a national problem, there are considerable variations between regions, both within the UK and in the EU as a whole. These can be seen in the numbers of people employed and unemployed. There are also variations in employment in different industrial sectors, locally and nationally within the UK, and within the EU.

ACTIVITY

From the map in *Fig. 1.15*, select two regions to investigate. One region should be within the UK and the other in an EU member state. Find out what you can about those regions: major towns, communications, tourist attractions, population, and so on. You will investigate employment in those regions in later activities.

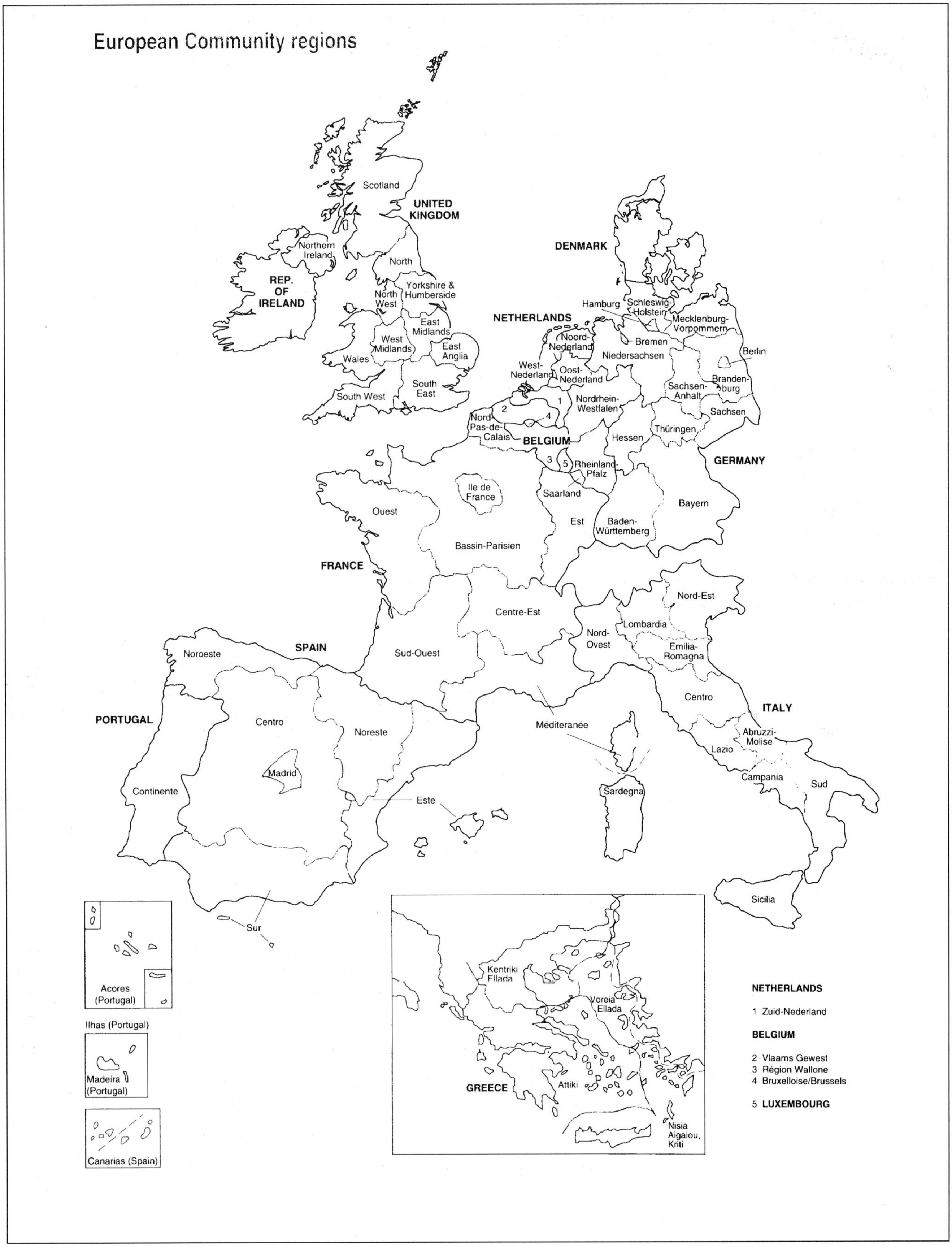

FIGURE 1.15 European Union member states and regions. Source: *Regional Trends 30*, Crown copyright 1995

NUMBERS OF PEOPLE EMPLOYED

When considering numbers of people employed and unemployed in a region, it is useful to analyse these in terms of percentages of the available workforce. The available workforce is the number of people available and suitable for work. This may be analysed in terms of:

- **gender** – that is, male or female;
- **age** – for example, under 25, 26–40, 40–60, over 60;
- **industrial sector** – for example, manufacturing, service.

Many factors contribute to employment in a region, although not all factors will necessarily apply in all situations. These factors may be:

- **historical** – for example, historically, car manufacturing has been based in the West Midlands;
- **geographical** – for example, shipbuilding is carried out close to the estuaries of large rivers;
- **cultural** – where a local community is predominantly of one culture, industries and businesses serving that community and

FIGURE 1.16 The labour force in spring 1994. Source: *Regional Trends 30*, Crown copyright 1995

5.1 The labour force[1], Spring 1994

Percentages and thousands

	Manufacturing employees	Construction employees	Service employees	Other employees	Self employed	On GETP[2]	ILO unemployed	Total labour force[3] (=100%) (thousands)
United Kingdom	*16.0*	*3.6*	*55.4*	*2.0*	*11.7*	*1.2*	*9.5*	28,239
North	*16.4*	*4.6*	*53.7*	*2.2*	*8.9*	*2.1*	*11.7*	1,417
Yorkshire & Humberside	*18.6*	*4.3*	*53.8*	*2.0*	*9.6*	*1.3*	*9.8*	2,394
East Midlands	*22.0*	*3.6*	*50.4*	*3.1*	*11.0*	*0.9*	*8.3*	2,020
East Anglia	*18.2*	*3.3*	*53.6*	*3.4*	*13.0*	..	*7.4*	1,098
South East	*11.6*	*2.9*	*59.8*	*1.3*	*13.1*	*0.9*	*9.6*	8,943
Greater London	*7.9*	*2.7*	*61.3*	*0.7*	*12.9*	*1.0*	*13.0*	3,370
Rest of South East	*13.9*	*3.1*	*58.9*	*1.7*	*13.3*	*0.8*	*7.6*	5,573
South West	*14.3*	*2.8*	*55.8*	*2.4*	*15.3*	*1.2*	*7.5*	2,360
West Midlands	*23.6*	*3.3*	*49.2*	*1.8*	*10.2*	*1.4*	*9.9*	2,585
North West	*19.0*	*3.7*	*54.8*	*1.3*	*9.6*	*1.0*	*10.2*	2,971
England	*16.3*	*3.4*	*55.6*	*1.8*	*11.8*	*1.1*	*9.5*	23,789
Wales	*16.2*	*3.9*	*51.9*	*2.2*	*13.9*	*1.5*	*9.4*	1,297
Scotland	*14.3*	*5.7*	*55.6*	*3.3*	*9.0*	*1.5*	*9.9*	2,471
Northern Ireland	*12.3*	*3.5*	*53.9*	*2.3*	*12.4*	*3.0*	*11.5*	683

1 Based on SIC 92. See Appendix notes.
2 Government employment and training programmes.
3 Includes unpaid family workers.

Source: Labour Force Survey, Employment Department; Department of Economic Development, Northern Ireland culture tend to develop; this can be seen, for example, in areas of Leicester which have large Asian communities. Likewise, in Oxford the presence of the university has largely influenced the type of business which is carried on in the town;

- **industrial** – the existence of an industry in a region attracts other organisations operating in the same industry to that region because of the availability of a skilled workforce, raw materials, transport systems, etc. (see p 31), and also other businesses which supply that industry;
- **political** – political factors which influence the numbers of people employed in a region include job creation schemes and other incentives to business organisations to set up in that region;
- **economic** – economic factors affecting employment include the effects of changes in supply and demand. (Where demand for the output of an industry is falling, output will contract to a level at which it equals the reduced demand, possibly resulting in a reduction in employment – where demand is increasing, as with many service industries, the converse is true.) Changes in the general economic climate also have an effect. (In times of depression, business organisations generally tend to postpone investment and plans for expansion, often having to reduce expenditure as much as possible, which sometimes means reducing the workforce);
- **technology** – automated manufacturing techniques often mean that one employee can do the same work that two or more did previously – and often to a higher standard – resulting in a reduction in numbers employed.

QUICK response

Describe two effects that the development of computers has had on employment.

NUMBERS EMPLOYED IN DIFFERENT INDUSTRIAL SECTORS

Employment in the different sectors of industry was discussed in Element 1.1 (pp 3–9).

Overall, levels of employment in the manufacturing sectors in Britain have been declining for many years, partly due to the contraction of these industries and partly due to methods of manufacturing becoming more efficient. In addition, manufacturing costs are high in the UK compared to other industrialised countries. Competition from abroad is fierce, particularly from within the EU and also from some newly industrialised countries such as South Korea, Malaysia, Taiwan and Singapore. In some areas, however, a high level of foreign investment (money coming into the UK to purchase or set up businesses here), particularly from foreign companies such as Nissan, Toyota, BMW and Samsung, is creating many new jobs in this sector.

Employment in the service sector, on the other hand, is increasing as this sector of the UK economy continues to develop. In some areas, however, notably in banking and public administration, increased efficiency and productivity resulting from the introduction of new technology has led to reductions in employment levels.

ACTIVITY

Information about employment can be obtained from sources such as libraries, business information centres, local authorities, Economic Development Units, Training and Enterprise Councils (TECs), Chambers of Trade and Commerce, and government departments. From these and other appropriate sources, investigate employment in the two regions you have selected. Your investigation should include the numbers of people in employment, with percentages, broken down by gender, age and sector. Suggest reasons for the figures and breakdown, with reference to the factors described above. The information you gather for this activity will be used in your portfolio assignment for this element.

CASE STUDY

Employment in the North of England

In January 1994, unemployment in the north of England stood at 12.3 per cent. This was the second highest level of unemployment of any region in the UK. Between 1983 and 1994, the unemployment rate in the north was always at least 2 per cent above the national average. The region had also suffered from a high level of redundancies. In the spring of 1993, one in 60 employees in the region had been made redundant.

This was accompanied by a fall in the average level of income. In 1983, average weekly earnings in the north were at a level 95 per cent of the national average. By 1993, however, the level had fallen to 90 per cent of the national average.

Historically, manufacturing industries have been an important part of the economy of northern England. In 1983, for example, manufacturing accounted for 35 per cent of business activity in the north, compared with 28 per cent in the UK as a whole. In 1993 the levels had dropped to 29 per cent and 21 per cent, respectively. This suggests that the decline in manufacturing industries has had a greater effect on employment in the north than it has on employment nationally.

Among the industries prominent in the region were iron and steel making, shipbuilding and coal mining, all of which have suffered a decline in recent years. As these industries, which were dominated by full-time male employees, declined in importance, and service industries, such as tourism and financial services, began to develop, there was a shift in employment towards a growth in the employment of women – much of this work being part-time. *Fig. 1.17* (p 70) shows the make up of employment in the north, analysed by occupation and gender. By examining these figures, it is possible to draw the following conclusions:

- The percentage employed in manufacturing has declined significantly since 1981.
- The decline has been especially significant in energy and water supply.
- The decline in these industries has particularly affected male employment.
- The percentage employed in the service sector has increased significantly since 1981.
- Between 1981 and 1994, male employment fell by over 100,000, whereas female employment increased by over 60,000.

In the nineteenth century, the north of England was the home of many of Britain's traditional manufacturing industries. The Tyne and the Wear were major shipbuilding areas; Cleveland

5.5 Employees in employment: by Standard Industrial Classi[illegible]n and gender, 1981 and 1994[1]

Percentages and thousands

	Agriculture, forestry, fishing (0)	Energy and water supply (1)	Metals, minerals and chemicals (2)	Metal goods, engineering and vehicles industries (3)	Other manufacturing (4)	Total manufacturing (2)-(4)
1981 Males						
United Kingdom	2.2	4.9	5.9	18.4	10.9	35.2
North	1.8	9.6	10.8	19.0	8.7	38.6
Yorkshire & Humberside	2.0	9.9	9.9	15.4	12.6	38.0
East Midlands	2.8	10.0	5.6	20.6	14.8	41.0
East Anglia	6.7	2.5	3.7	15.7	13.3	32.7
South East	1.2	2.4	3.2	16.2	9.5	28.9
South West	4.1	2.7	3.8	18.6	11.2	33.6
West Midlands	1.7	3.9	8.3	32.4	9.1	49.8
North West	0.9	3.9	7.5	19.8	14.1	41.4
England	1.9	4.6	5.8	19.2	11.0	36.0
Wales	3.3	10.1	11.3	13.6	7.2	32.1
Scotland	3.4	5.7	5.0	15.5	11.1	31.6
Northern Ireland	5.6	3.1	3.9	11.3	13.6	28.9
1981 Females						
United Kingdom	1.0	1.0	2.1	6.5	10.6	19.2
North	0.4	1.3	2.4	6.0	10.1	18.6
Yorkshire & Humberside	0.9	1.2	2.7	4.8	14.8	22.3
East Midlands	1.5	1.1	2.6	5.9	21.1	29.6
East Anglia	3.9	0.6	1.2	5.6	12.7	19.5
South East	0.8	0.9	1.8	6.6	7.2	15.6
South West	1.5	0.9	1.3	5.5	8.5	15.3
West Midlands	1.0	1.0	4.0	13.3	8.5	25.7
North West	0.4	1.0	2.6	6.2	13.0	21.8
England	1.0	1.0	2.3	6.9	10.5	19.6
Wales	1.1	1.4	2.2	6.1	8.0	16.3
Scotland	0.7	1.0	1.2	4.6	11.9	17.7
Northern Ireland	1.5	0.6	0.6	3.4	14.4	18.4
1994 Males						
United Kingdom	1.8	2.2	4.0	13.4	10.3	27.7
North	1.6	3.3	7.1	14.2	10.8	32.1
Yorkshire & Humberside	1.8	2.3	6.7	12.7	13.4	32.8
East Midlands	2.2	2.1	4.6	17.0	16.4	38.1
East Anglia	4.1	2.5	2.7	12.7	12.9	28.2
South East	0.9	1.8	2.1	10.0	7.6	19.7
Greater London	-	1.5	1.0	5.2	7.3	13.6
Rest of South East	1.7	2.0	3.0	14.1	7.8	24.9
South West	3.2	1.8	3.0	13.9	9.8	26.7
West Midlands	1.6	1.6	6.0	23.6	9.7	39.2
North West	0.9	2.0	4.8	15.2	12.4	32.4
England	1.6	2.0	4.0	13.7	10.4	28.1
Wales	2.9	2.7	8.2	13.0	10.9	32.0
Scotland	2.2	4.1	2.4	12.0	9.2	23.7
Northern Ireland	5.9	1.9	3.1	8.5	12.6	24.2
1994 Females						
United Kingdom	0.6	0.7	1.4	3.6	7.2	12.2
North	0.3	0.9	1.5	3.4	8.5	13.4
Yorkshire & Humberside	0.5	0.6	1.7	2.8	9.3	13.7
East Midlands	0.8	0.5	1.8	3.7	14.7	20.2
East Anglia	1.9	0.7	0.7	3.6	8.0	12.3
South East	0.5	0.7	1.2	3.1	4.8	9.2
Greater London	-	0.7	0.6	1.7	5.0	7.3
Rest of South East	0.9	0.6	1.6	4.2	4.7	10.6
South West	1.0	0.7	0.7	3.3	5.1	9.0
West Midlands	0.7	0.6	2.2	7.1	6.7	16.0
North West	0.4	0.7	1.8	3.4	7.8	13.0
England	0.6	0.7	1.4	3.7	7.1	12.2
Wales	0.7	0.8	1.4	4.9	7.4	13.7
Scotland	0.4	0.8	1.1	3.4	7.5	12.0
Northern Ireland	0.8	0.3	0.6	2.1	9.8	12.5

FIGURE 1.17 Employment between 1981 and 1994. Source: *Regional Trends 30*, Crown copyright 1995

5.5 *(continued)*

Percentages and thousands

	Construction (5)	Distribution, hotels and catering, repairs (6)	Transport and communication (7)	Banking, finance, insurance, business services & leasing (8)	Public administration and other services (9)	All industries and services (= 100%) (thousands)
1981 Males						
United Kingdom	8.1	15.2	9.1	7.2	18.1	12,562
North	9.8	11.7	7.8	4.4	16.3	654
Yorkshire & Humberside	8.2	13.9	8.0	4.8	15.2	1,083
East Midlands	6.8	13.9	6.7	4.5	14.3	855
East Anglia	8.7	16.8	9.1	5.8	17.8	400
South East	7.3	17.3	11.6	10.9	20.5	4,135
South West	8.2	17.7	8.0	6.4	19.3	883
West Midlands	6.8	13.0	5.8	5.1	13.9	1,199
North West	8.0	14.1	9.2	6.0	16.5	1,391
England	7.6	15.4	9.2	7.5	17.7	10,600
Wales	9.1	12.6	8.2	4.8	19.9	551
Scotland	11.4	13.9	9.4	5.7	18.8	1,128
Northern Ireland	9.3	14.3	5.9	4.8	28.0	283
1981 Females						
United Kingdom	1.2	24.3	3.0	9.0	41.3	9,331
North	1.1	28.4	2.2	6.3	41.7	468
Yorkshire & Humberside	1.2	25.6	2.3	6.9	39.6	768
East Midlands	1.0	22.2	2.7	6.2	35.8	613
East Anglia	1.2	24.7	2.7	7.9	39.5	281
South East	1.4	23.1	4.1	12.5	41.6	3,128
South West	1.2	28.8	2.4	8.6	41.3	658
West Midlands	1.2	22.9	2.3	7.4	38.5	852
North West	1.1	24.5	2.5	7.8	40.9	1,075
England	1.2	24.3	3.1	9.4	40.4	7,845
Wales	1.1	24.8	2.2	6.0	47.3	389
Scotland	1.4	26.1	2.6	7.4	43.1	874
Northern Ireland	0.9	17.3	1.7	5.8	53.9	224
1994 Males						
United Kingdom	6.8	19.4	8.5	12.3	21.1	10,911
North	8.6	16.5	7.6	8.6	21.7	553
Yorkshire & Humberside	8.1	19.0	8.0	9.1	18.8	928
East Midlands	6.8	18.9	6.7	7.6	17.6	766
East Anglia	6.6	19.5	9.2	10.4	19.5	403
South East	5.5	20.7	10.5	18.5	22.5	3,504
Greater London	4.7	19.9	12.7	23.4	24.1	1,622
Rest of South East	6.1	21.3	8.7	14.2	21.2	1,882
South West	5.1	22.2	6.8	12.2	22.0	840
West Midlands	6.7	18.6	6.7	9.1	16.5	1,017
North West	6.8	19.1	8.7	10.1	20.1	1,139
England	6.4	19.8	8.7	13.0	20.5	9,151
Wales	7.1	17.1	7.1	8.3	22.6	487
Scotland	11.1	17.9	8.3	9.5	23.1	996
Northern Ireland	6.9	17.6	5.9	7.1	30.5	276
1994 Females						
United Kingdom	1.3	23.9	2.8	12.8	45.7	10,651
North	1.2	25.3	2.0	8.2	48.6	531
Yorkshire & Humberside	1.5	25.4	2.3	10.4	45.6	915
East Midlands	1.3	23.9	2.2	9.0	42.2	748
East Anglia	1.2	26.0	2.2	11.6	44.1	390
South East	1.4	22.1	3.8	17.8	44.5	3,389
Greater London	1.4	20.2	4.8	22.3	43.2	1,469
Rest of South East	1.4	23.6	3.1	14.4	45.4	1,919
South West	1.2	27.4	2.1	13.4	45.2	853
West Midlands	1.4	23.5	2.5	10.7	44.5	943
North West	1.2	25.0	2.8	10.6	46.3	1,140
England	1.3	24.0	2.9	13.4	44.9	8,909
Wales	1.1	24.3	1.9	8.4	49.2	478
Scotland	1.4	24.0	2.4	11.1	48.0	990
Northern Ireland	0.8	20.9	1.6	7.7	55.3	274

1 At June. Figures are based on SIC 80. See Appendix notes.

Source: Employment Department

and Cumbria were both centres of the iron and steel industries; Northumberland and Durham had large coalfields. Each of these industries was a major employer.

As these industries have declined and closed down, so jobs in them have disappeared. The last coal mine in Durham closed in the early 1990s, leaving few coal mines still working in the region. Traditionally, these industries have employed a predominantly male workforce, and this has led to a loss in male employment opportunities.

Service industries, on the other hand, have traditionally offered a greater range of employment opportunities to women. Many service industries are particularly suited to flexible, part-time employment, again traditionally a preserve of women. This largely explains the increase of female employment in the face of a decline in male employment.

Sometimes action by the Government has affected levels of employment in the region. When unemployment was particularly bad in the 1980s, the Government played a major role in creating jobs in both the manufacturing and the service sectors. Nissan, the Japanese car giant, was given subsidies and encouraged to establish a large factory in the region. As an employer, the Government also created jobs in the service sector by relocating some departmental offices from London to the north.

Despite action to help the employment situation, in 1994 well over 50 per cent of unemployed males in the north of England had been unemployed for more than six months, with over 22 per cent having been unemployed for more than two years. When people are unemployed for as long as this, it becomes difficult for them to re-enter the employment market as they lose their skills and relevant experience, especially in the face of new technology.

Fig. 1.18 shows projected employment figures for the north of England in the year 2001.

5.2 Civilian labour force[1]: by age, 1994 and 2001

Percentages and thousands

	1994[2]					2001[2]				
	Percentages aged					Percentages aged				
	16-24	25-44	Females 45-59 Males 45-64	Females 60+ Males 65+	All ages (= 100%) (thousands)	16-24	25-44	Females 45-59 Males 45-64	Females 60+ Males 65+	All ages (= 100%) (thousands)
United Kingdom	17.8	49.5	30.1	2.6	28,851	16.4	49.7	31.4	2.6	29,577
North	17.0	51.8	29.3	1.9	1,445	15.7	51.7	30.7	1.9	1,444
Yorkshire & Humberside	17.9	49.9	30.2	2.0	2,446	16.3	49.8	32.0	1.9	2,495
East Midlands	16.7	50.3	30.7	2.3	2,098	15.0	50.5	32.2	2.3	2,182
East Anglia	17.3	48.4	31.2	3.1	1,066	15.9	48.8	32.4	2.9	1,138
South East	17.6	48.9	30.2	3.3	9,117	16.3	49.3	31.3	3.1	9,398
Greater London	17.6	50.7	29.0	2.8	3,444	16.2	51.5	29.8	2.6	3,499
Rest of South East	17.7	47.8	31.0	3.5	5,673	16.4	48.1	32.1	3.4	5,899
South West	17.6	48.4	30.9	3.1	2,394	16.1	48.7	32.2	3.0	2,534
West Midlands	18.0	48.6	31.1	2.4	2,646	16.6	48.6	32.5	2.3	2,671
North West	17.9	50.2	29.6	2.2	3,121	16.6	49.8	31.3	2.2	3,139
England	17.6	49.3	30.3	2.7	24,332	16.2	49.5	31.7	2.6	25,001
Wales	18.6	50.3	28.9	2.1	1,351	17.1	51.0	29.8	2.1	1,393
Scotland	18.7	50.0	28.9	2.4	2,468	16.8	50.0	30.7	2.4	2,454
Northern Ireland	20.2	50.5	27.1	2.1	699	18.7	51.5	27.9	2.0	730

1 See Appendix notes.
2 Projections from 1991 estimates.

Source: Labour Force Survey, Employment Department; Department of Economic Development, Northern Ireland

FIGURE 1.18 The civilian labour force in 1994 and as a projected figure for 2001. Source: *Regional Trends 30*, Crown copyright 1995

WORKING CONDITIONS

Just as employment conditions vary from region to region, so working conditions vary from organisation to organisation. In selecting an organisation to work for, these conditions must be taken into consideration as they can affect your contribution to the organisation, and also the satisfaction you get from your work. Some of the most significant working conditions are:

- **Travel to work** – most people have to travel some distance to get from home to their place of work. Travelling takes time and costs money. Both of these factors must be borne in mind when considering employment.
- **Physical conditions** – often connected with the nature of the job. Some conditions are clean and comfortable, while others are less so. For example, the physical conditions in which a paint sprayer in a garage works

differ greatly from the physical conditions in which the receptionist at the same garage works. Of course, not everybody wants to work in the artificial environment of a sterile office, perhaps preferring to work on an oil rig, and enjoying the physical as well as the mental aspect of the work.

- **Hours of work** – these can vary between jobs. A typical office job, for example, may be from 9.00 am to 5.00 pm, although more senior managerial employees will often find themselves working considerably longer than this – perhaps even working at home in the evenings and at weekends. Other workers may have to work hours to suit their customers – shops, for example, have to open on at least one late night during the week, on Saturdays, and, in many cases these days, on Sundays as well, as these are the times when most people have leisure to do their shopping.
- **Pay** – employees are normally paid weekly, in the form of wages calculated by multiplying the hourly rate for the job by the number of hours worked, or monthly in the form of a salary which is calculated as one-twelfth of the annual salary for the job. Other forms of extra payments, such as overtime, bonuses or commission, which are based on hours worked in excess of the basic contractual hours, performance of the employee or the success of the employer, are also made. Rates of pay vary enormously between different jobs in the same organisation, and between different organisations. While not everybody chooses to work in a particular industry or for a particular employer because they pay the highest wages, pay is an important factor in choosing employment.
- **Safety** – is of prime importance in many jobs. This is especially true where potentially dangerous machinery is operated, or potentially dangerous substances, such as chemicals and cleaning fluids, are used. The Health and Safety at Work Act 1974 and the Control of Substances Hazardous to Health Act 1988 have laid responsibilities on both employers and employees for taking action to ensure safety in the workplace. This topic is dealt with in more detail in Unit 2, p 120.

QUICK response

Why is job insecurity a feature of a recession?

- **Job security** – is especially important in times of economic uncertainty. As you have seen, the decline in the manufacturing sector has led to a reduction in employment. Similarly, employment in some service industries has been affected by the introduction of new technology (see below). There is therefore less job security for employees in these industries. A low level of job security creates stress among employees, who find it difficult to plan for the future or commit themselves financially by, for example, taking out new mortgages to buy houses if they are not sure how long their employment will last.

- **Career opportunities** – can make employment within one particular organisation or industry as attractive as the lack of job security makes it unattractive in another. Many people choose employment with the aim of improving their position as they progress in their job. An organisation which provides clear opportunities for career development will attract employees with a higher degree of loyalty and commitment than an organisation which is not interested in the career development of its employees.
- **Training opportunities** – are closely linked with career opportunities, enabling employees to acquire the skills necessary to do their current jobs to the best of their abilities and also to progress to other types of employment in accordance with their career plans.
- **Use of new technology** – can affect employment and the effectiveness of an organisation in three major ways. First, as you have seen, the use of new technology can sometimes mean that one person can do the same work that was done by several people before. This can cause a reduction in employment opportunities in an organisation or industry. Second, the use of new technology can make the production of goods or services more efficient and cost effective, contributing to the success and profits of the organisation. Third, new technology can give rise to the production of new goods and services, using new materials and components or processes. This, in turn, can lead to the development of new employment opportunities and, in some cases, entirely new industries.

You will study working conditions and the rights and responsibilities of employees and employers in Unit 2.

ACTIVITY

As a group, discuss how important each of the working conditions described above is in deciding on employment. What other factors might influence your choice?

PRESENTING THE RESULTS OF YOUR INVESTIGATION INTO EMPLOYMENT OR A COMPARISON OF WORKING CONDITIONS

The portfolio assignment for Element 1.3 requires you to write a report comparing working conditions, and to make a presentation of the results of an investigation that you have conducted into employment. The final part of this unit, therefore, gives some general guidance and advice on report writing and making presentations.

WRITING A REPORT

You will be asked to write two types of report during your course: informal reports (sometimes called memo reports) and formal reports. An **informal report** normally contains:

1 a title or subject;

2 a brief introduction, setting out the purpose of the report;

3 a main section, giving relevant facts and the findings of any research you have carried out;

4 a conclusion explaining the significance of your findings and containing any recommendations you have been asked for.

A **formal report** is generally longer and more structured. It should contain:

1 a title, often on a separate title page;

2 the terms of reference (the purpose of the report, what it covers and any limitations or constraints on its coverage);

3 the research methods used;

4 the findings of your research;

5 your conclusions or explanations of your findings;

6 a summary;

7 appendices containing any material not included in the body of the report, such as other published material, copies of questionnaires used in your research, and so on.

Any statistics or other numerical data contained in a report should, where possible, be shown in the form of a table or chart.

MAKING PRESENTATIONS

There are six basic stages to making a successful and effective presentation.

1 **Identify the purpose of the presentation** – Is it to inform, persuade or teach? What is it about? Who is your audience, and how much do they already know about the topic?

2 **Define your objectives** – What do you want your audience to know, understand or be able to do at the end of your presentation. Make sure your objectives are attainable.

3 **Prepare your presentation** – Carry out the necessary research, decide what you are going to say and prepare any visual aids you are going to use. (Visual aids include such things as flip charts, transparencies for use on an overhead projector, diagrams or figures you are going to draw on a marker board.)
Give your presentation an attention-getting opening – perhaps an unexpected statistic or surprising fact. Beware of humour, however – unless this is done well it will fall flat. The opening should lead smoothly into the middle section of your presentation, containing the core material – information, statistics, facts and so on. Try to make this sound interesting. The conclusion of your presentation should be logical and based on the facts and information already given. Finally, add a summary to remind your audience of the information and conclusions you have given.

4 **Practise the presentation** – Does it sound right? Is it the right length? Does it convey the right message? Can you deliver it confidently?

5 **Make the presentation** – Be prepared with notes and visual aids. Speak confidently and enthusiastically. Under no circumstances talk down to your audience. Try varying the tone of your voice and expression to hold their attention.

6 After you have given your presentation, **evaluate your performance** – Did you achieve what you set out to do? How did the audience react? What went well? What could you improve?

Few people find making presentations easy, even when they do it regularly. Being systematic in making the presentation and reviewing your performance will help you to develop your skills and confidence as a presenter.

PORTFOLIO ASSIGNMENT

For this portfolio assignment you will research employment. Advice on finding information is given on p x in the Introduction. You may wish to refer to this again before starting this assignment.

Task 1

Identify seven examples of different types of employment. Your examples should include at least one example of full-time, part-time, permanent, temporary, skilled, unskilled and self-employment.

Construct a table like this:

Job title	Type of employment	Description of job

Task 2

In previous activities for this element you have investigated employment in two regions of the European Union, one of which was in the UK. Write a summary of your findings for each region. Your summary should include a graph or chart showing percentages of people in employment, with a breakdown by gender, age and industrial sector. Explain the differences in the number of people employed and describe the growth or decline of at least one manufacturing or service sector industry in each region.

Task 3

Arrange to interview two people who work for different organisations to find out about their working conditions. These may be people you know, such as friends or family, one an employee at your school or college, or they may be people in businesses given in the Introduction. You may interview each person individually or as a group. Individually, write a short report describing and comparing the working conditions of the people you have interviewed.

Task 4

Make a presentation to the rest of your class and your tutor of either the summary of employment information produced for Task 2, or the report produced for Task 3. Your presentation should be supported by appropriate visual aids. A record of your presentation should be made by your tutor. This can be in the form of a video or audio tape recording, or a record of observation prepared by your tutor.

This portfolio assignment also presents an opportunity to gather evidence for the following core skills:

- Application of Number – collect and record data; interpret and present data;
- Communication – take part in discussions; produce written materials; use images; read and respond to written materials;
- Information Technology – prepare information; process information; present information.

2

UNIT

People in business organisations

Contents

Outline

In this unit you will look at the different kinds of organisational structures in business and see how these can affect the way employees work. You will investigate how people work, look at the benefits and responsibilities of employment and gain an understanding of employment law, in particular equal opportunities and health and safety at work. You will also begin to assess the skills you need for employment or self-employment, and to develop organisational, planning and presentation skills.

After completing this unit you will be able to:

1 examine and compare structures and working arrangements within organisations;
2 investigate employee and employer responsibilities and rights;
3 present the results of an investigation into job roles;
4 prepare for employment or self-employment.

Structures and Working Arrangements in Organisations

Organisational structures

Most business organisations consist of people working together to achieve the overall goals of the business. In order to achieve those goals, and to ensure that employees are working together effectively, the goals must be communicated to the employees, jobs must be allocated to individuals and the individual activities of employees must be co-ordinated. If employees are unsure of what goals they are working towards, jobs are not allocated, or their individual activities are not co-ordinated, the employees will not know what they are supposed to do or what is expected of them. This can result in:

- some jobs being done twice by different people, resulting in duplication of effort and waste of effort because they did not know someone else was also doing the job;
- some jobs not being done at all because everybody thought someone else was doing them;
- some jobs not being done to an appropriate standard, or at the right time, because no one told the people doing them what standard was required or when the task should be completed.

It is obvious, therefore, that unless employees are told what their goals are, jobs are correctly allocated, and the individual activities of employees are effectively co-ordinated, the result will be chaos – and a far from efficient business!

In other words, a business must plan and organise the work and activities of its workforce. Even a sole trader, working on their own, must plan and organise their work, just as you have to plan and organise your work when doing an assignment for GNVQ Intermediate Business.

When more than one person works in a business, the business must develop a structure which establishes:

- **job roles**, so that every employee knows what they are supposed to do and what is expected of them;
- **levels of authority**, so that employees know who they are responsible to (and for), and who makes the plans and takes the decisions which affect the way the business is run and the jobs the employees do;
- **channels of communication**, so that every employee knows what the business is trying to achieve (and therefore what they are working towards) and is aware of decisions that have been taken which affect their own work. Good channels of communication also allow employees to feed back information to their superiors about any problems which may occur, and to make suggestions about how performance could be improved.

HIERARCHICAL STRUCTURES

Traditionally, business organisations in the UK have been given hierarchical structures. A hierarchical structure is based on levels of authority and responsibility, with each person in the organisation having a clearly defined position which sets limits on the amount of authority and responsibility they have. Hierarchical structures are usually shown in the form of a pyramid, as in *Fig. 2.1*.

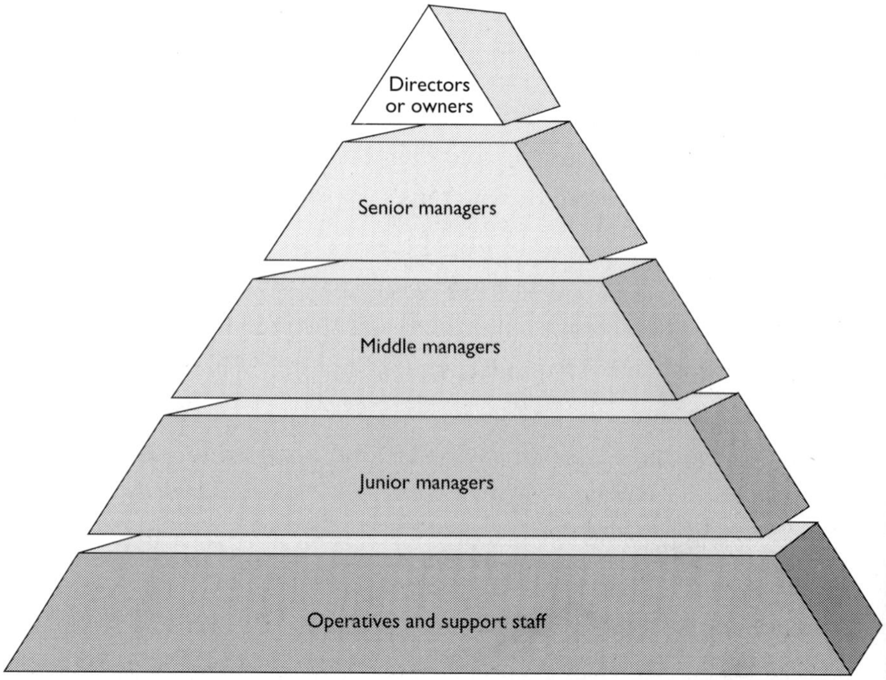

FIGURE 2.1 A hierarchical structure.

ACTIVITY

Consider the hierarchical structure in *Fig. 2.1* and suggest why this is shown as a pyramid.

At the top of the structure is the most senior manager of the business, usually the owner or the managing director. Below this are levels of less senior managers, middle managers, junior managers, supervisors, operatives, and support staff.

Except at the top and the bottom, employees at each level are responsible to a supervisor or manager at the level above and have authority over a number of employees at the levels below. For example, a middle manager reports to a senior manager and may have authority over three junior managers. The number of employees a manager or supervisor has authority over is called their **span of control**. The span of control of the middle manager in the example is therefore three.

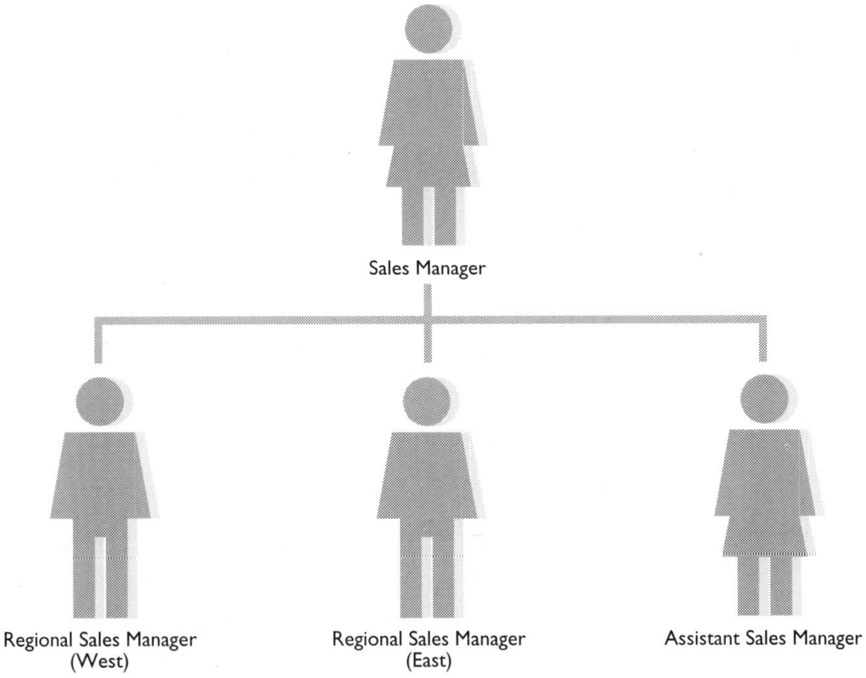

FIGURE 2.2 The span of control.

The advantages of this type of hierarchical structure are:

- Control of the organisation is kept in the hands of the person at the top of the organisation.
- It is easy to maintain a particular identity or standard of service and quality in a large organisation. This is especially important in

QUICK response

How can a hierarchical structure help an organisation like a large hotel chain to maintain a particular identity? Why do you think this is important?

large service organisations with several branches, such as major banks, building societies, hotel chains, supermarkets, and so on.

- There is a clearly defined chain of command, with instructions flowing downward through all levels of employees, and information about performance, problems, and so on, flowing upwards.
- All people in the organisation know their role within the organisation, who they are responsible to and who they have authority over.

The main disadvantages of hierarchical structures are:

- There is no limit to the number of levels of management between the top decision-maker and the shop-floor operatives or other support staff.
- Decision-making can be slow or delayed as it takes a long time for information to flow upwards and for decisions to be taken at the top and then communicated downwards again to be implemented by production operatives or support staff.
- At each level, information and instructions may be interpreted differently so that information passed on, or action taken, may be biased by the attitudes of individual managers.

ACTIVITY

In groups, discuss how the attitudes of individual managers may affect the way in which information and instructions are interpreted. Give examples of such attitudes and the effects they may have.

Flat structures

In order to overcome the disadvantages of hierarchical structures, while still retaining their advantages, many large organisations have reduced their number of levels of management, thus bringing the most senior managers closer to operatives and support staff. As you can see from *Fig. 2.3*, the removal of several levels of management gives an organisation a 'flatter' structure.

The advantages of a flat organisational structure are:

- The flow of information between upper and lower levels is much

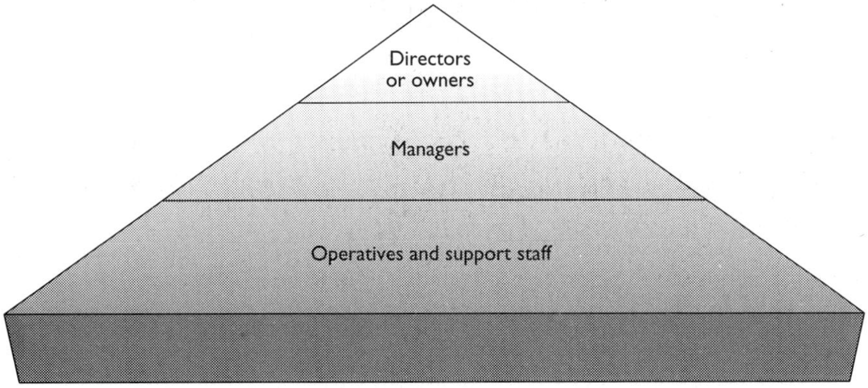

FIGURE 2.3 A flat organisational structure.

faster, enabling quicker decision-making and faster response to problems.

- With fewer levels of management to answer to, many managers and operatives feel they have more responsibility for their own work, which increases motivation and job satisfaction.

In recent years, more and more business organisations, in both the public and private sectors, have developed flatter structures by cutting out layers of middle management. This has enabled them to save money and has been encouraged by the increasing use of information technology.

In some organisations, the move towards a flatter structure has been combined with **decentralisation**. In a **centralised** organisation, decision-making is kept in the hands of a few people at the top of the organisation. In a **decentralised** organisation, on the other hand,

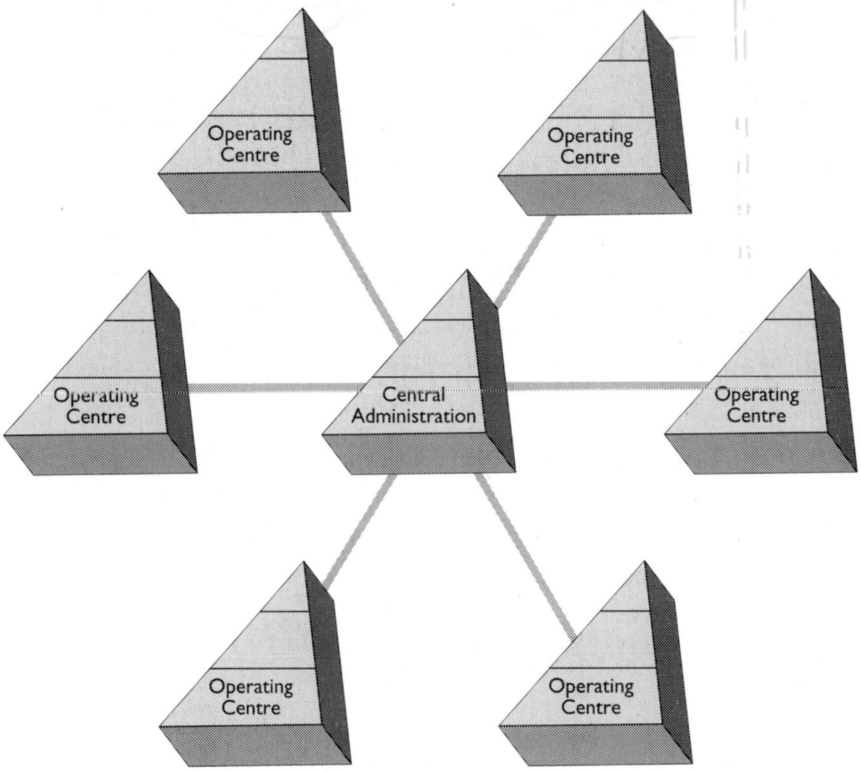

FIGURE 2.4 A decentralised organisational structure.

responsibility is given (or **delegated**) to senior managers in different departments or divisions. Thus each department or division develops its own structure. This can be seen in *Fig. 2.4*.

MATRIX STRUCTURES

A third type of organisational structure, which is more flexible than the hierarchical structures described above, is known as a matrix structure. This type of structure is often used for running specific projects, such as developing a new product.

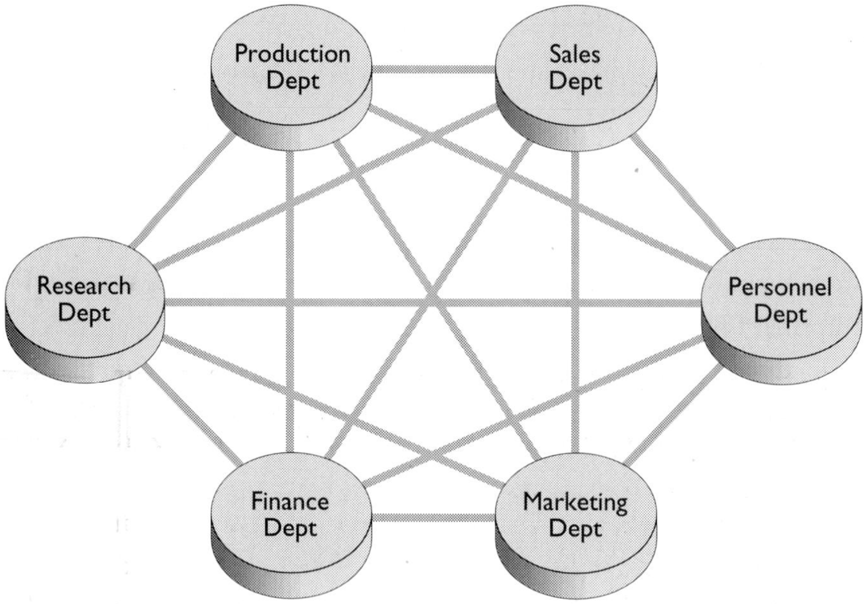

FIGURE 2.5 A matrix structure.

In a matrix structure, specialists are brought together from different functions or departments within the organisation, to share their knowledge and give advice about various aspects of the project. Matrix structures therefore tend to be based on functions or key processes which may cross the more traditional departmental boundaries of hierarchical organisations. For example, when Firenze Holdings plc wanted to develop a new type of aircraft engine, they formed a project group consisting of people from the research and development, production, marketing, and finance departments. In this way, all aspects of the development and production of the new engine were considered, including costs, production needs and what was required by the customers.

A group organised on a matrix structure is usually disbanded once the project for which it has been formed is finished.

ORGANISATIONAL CHARTS

The structure of an organisation is usually shown on an organisational chart. Organisational charts are normally constructed in the form of a tree diagram (see *Fig. 2.6*), although this is not suitable for matrix structures (see *Fig. 2.5*). An organisational chart for a small organisation may show the names and job titles of employees. An organisational chart for a large organisation, however, perhaps with hundreds or even thousands of employees, will normally show the departments in the organisation.

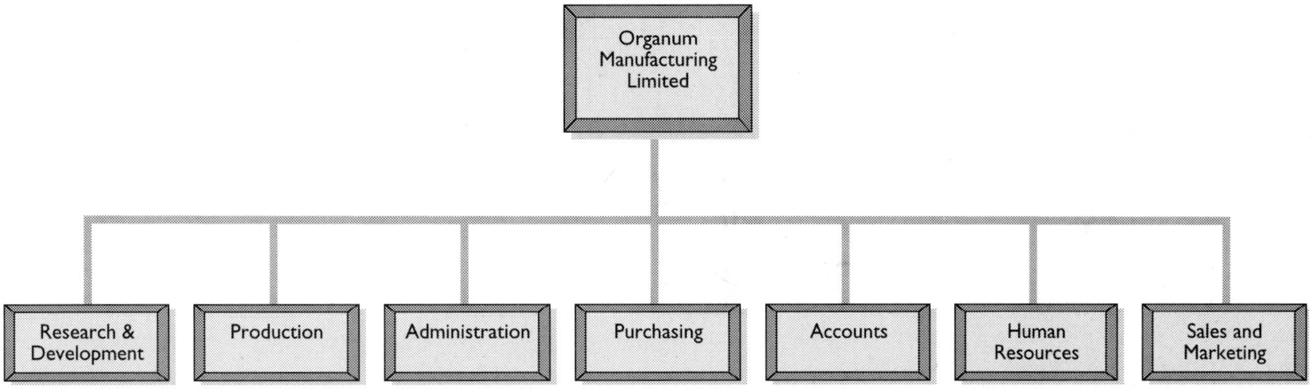

FIGURE 2.6 An organisational chart.

Organisational charts are useful because they show the relationships between people and departments within the organisation, and also lines of formal communication. *Fig. 2.6* shows the departments in a typical large business organisation. You should note, however, that different types of organisations have different departments which reflect their functions and activities. For example, in addition to the departments in a typical business organisation, an organisation which publishes newspapers or magazines will have an editorial department, a features department and an advertising department (for handling advertisements placed in the newspaper or magazine).

ACTIVITY

Construct an organisational chart for your school or college, or for another business organisation you can investigate. Identify the different departments in the organisation. Which departments do you think would be found in other organisations, and which are specific to the type of organisation you have investigated?

THE WORK AND INTERDEPENDENCE OF DEPARTMENTS IN BUSINESS ORGANISATIONS

All business organisations have to carry out various activities. Some activities, or functions, are directly concerned with developing, producing and distributing the goods or services which the business provides. These include research and development, production, and distribution. Other functions are concerned with the actual running of the business. These include purchasing, accounting, human resources, marketing, and administration.

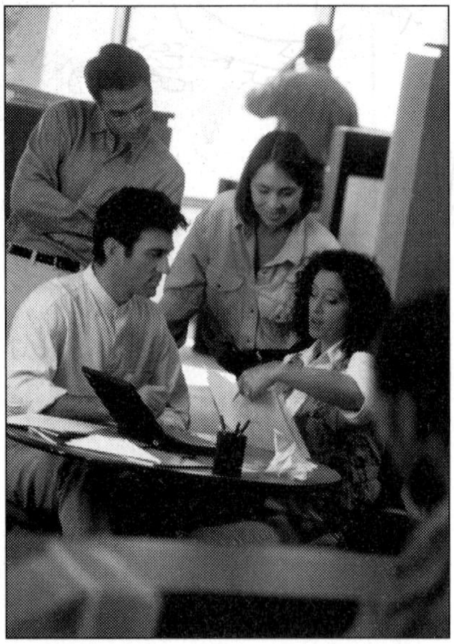

Hillgrove Associates is a small business which markets computer software.

In a small business organisation, such as a sole trader, partnership or very small private limited company, several of these functions will be performed by one person. Jim Thomson and Davina Hillgrove, for example, are the partners in Hillgrove Associates, a small business which develops and markets computer software. Besides Jim and Davina, there is Jessica Meadows, the secretary, and Bob Simpson who designs much of the software. Because it is a small organisation, Jim and Davina share the operation of the business between them. Jim looks after the administration, accounting and purchasing; Davina sees to the marketing, production and distribution of the software.

In larger organisations, however, the amount of work involved in each function is much greater. As organisations grow, they tend first to employ specialists to perform each function and then, as the work involved becomes too much for one person, other employees are taken on to help them. In this way, larger organisations tend to be structured on the basis of departments, each with a specific function.

As we have seen, the actual departments found in a given organisation depend on the type and purpose of the organisation. It is impossible, therefore, to describe every department to be found in any organisation but it is important to understand the work of departments typically found in larger organisations.

RESEARCH AND DEVELOPMENT

The work of the Research and Development Department involves:

- developing new products;
- improving existing products.

New products and improvements to existing products are needed to meet the requirements of customers, taking into consideration changes in consumer demand and the availability of new materials and technology. Information about changes in consumer demand and the requirements of customers is collected by the Marketing Department. The Research and Development Department must also keep abreast of information about new materials, technology and products which affect customer requirements. For example, the development of multimedia computer technology has led to the availability of interactive encyclopaedias and other materials on CD-ROM.

New technology can also enable an organisation to manufacture a product which meets a consumer need more fully than was possible without the technology. For example, research into methods of improving safety in cars, coupled with technological advances, has enabled many cars to be fitted with airbags as standard.

Many large companies spend millions of pounds every year on research and development, to try to stay ahead of their competitors in providing the latest product for their customers.

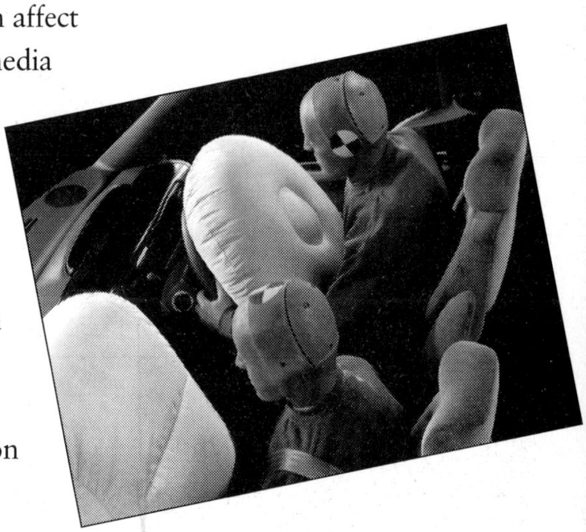

Many cars are now fitted with airbags as a standard safety feature.

ACTIVITY

Choose a well-known, large manufacturing company (a drugs or other pharmaceuticals, household electrical goods, computer manufacturer or similar is ideal). Try to find out how much the company spent on research and development in their last financial year. This information may be found in their latest company report. Compare this with the findings of other students in your class.

PRODUCTION

It is the job of the Production Department to make the products designed by the Research and Development Department. This involves:

- planning production – to ensure that there are enough raw materials, components, personnel with the right skills, and machines or other equipment available to make the product in sufficient quantities and at the right time to meet the needs of customers;
- controlling production – to ensure that there are no delays or problems in the production process, so that customers' orders are fulfilled on time and as planned.

In order to carry out these functions, the Production Department must work closely with the Research and Development, Purchasing, and Marketing and Sales Departments.

PURCHASING

QUICK response

Why is it better to have a separate Purchasing Department rather than letting the Production Department buy raw materials and components as they need them?

The function of the Purchasing Department is to buy (purchase) the raw material and components needed by the Production Department in order to complete planned production. If the Purchasing Department has not ensured that the Production Department has enough of the raw materials it needs, the raw materials will run out, production will stop and the organisation will lose sales. It is essential, therefore, that the Purchasing Department works closely with the Production and Sales Departments so that there are enough materials available to meet production and sales targets. Too many materials, on the other hand, will mean that the organisation carries a stock of unused materials which is an unnecessary expense. It is also the responsibility of the Purchasing Department to negotiate prices for the goods it purchases. These are negotiated with the suppliers. Prices should be kept as low as possible, without compromising on quality, in order to yield the maximum profit for the organisation while maintaining a competitive price to the customer.

In service industries which do not use raw materials, the Purchasing Department may buy other goods. For example, the Purchasing Department of a large retailer will buy goods from wholesalers and manufacturers to sell to customers.

ACCOUNTING

The work of the Accounting Department, sometimes called the Finance Department, involves:

- setting financial targets;
- preparing accounts;
- monitoring financial performance and advising when action is needed;
- compiling and sending out invoices for sales;
- receiving and paying invoices for expenditure;
- paying wages and salaries;
- chasing overdue bills;
- checking that there is sufficient money coming into the organisation to cover expenses it has to pay (cash flow).

The financial targets of an organisation are set out, normally on a monthly basis, in a document called a **budget**. Actual financial performance, as shown in the accounts of the organisation, are then compared with these targets, normally also on a monthly basis. Any significant variation can then be analysed and senior management informed so that decisions on appropriate action can be taken.

In order to complete the budgets and accounts, the Accounting Department must work closely with all other departments within the organisation. The work of the Accounting Department is covered in more detail in Unit 4, 'Financial and Administrative Support'.

HUMAN RESOURCES

The Human Resources Department is often called the Personnel Department. The work of the Human Resources Department involves:

- planning the personnel requirements of the organisation and departments within the organisation in terms of numbers of employees needed to carry out its functions;
- recruiting the employees needed by each department, including advertising job vacancies, interviewing and advising on selection;
- keeping employment records of all employees;
- arranging training of employees to ensure that they possess appropriate skills for the job;
- ensuring that the organisation complies with relevant employment legislation, including equal opportunities, racial discrimination, and employee contracts;
- advising and negotiating on pay and conditions of service with management, employees and trade unions.

The work of the Human Resources Department is closely involved with other departments who rely on the Human Resources Department to ensure that they have sufficient employees with the appropriate skills to carry out their tasks. Aspects of the work of the Human Resources Department will be looked at in detail in Element 2.2, 'The Rights and Responsibilities of Employers and Employees'.

MARKETING

The work of the Marketing Department involves:

- establishing the needs of the organisation's customers;
- ensuring that the organisation's products meet those needs (this may be achieved through the Research and Development Department);
- ensuring that customers and potential customers are aware of, and interested in, the organisation and its product.

Much useful information can be found in Government publications.

The Marketing Department establishes the needs of customers by carrying out market research. This may be done by analysing information on consumer spending patterns and demand which has already been published – for example, in the Government publication *Social Trends* – or by actually asking the customers and consumers themselves, perhaps using a questionnaire by post, telephone or face to face. Customers are made aware of the organisation and its products through advertising and other forms of promotion. Such advertising and promotion are designed to stimulate an interest in the organisation and its products. Some aspects of the work of the Marketing Department are described in Unit 3.

SALES

The Sales Department is responsible for converting the customer interest in the organisation and its products that has been generated by the Marketing Department into actual sales. Without sales, the organisation will receive no income and will go out of business. The Sales Department of an organisation is therefore one of the most important departments, although it cannot function without the help of the Marketing Department to find out what customers want and to make them aware of the organisation and its products, the Production Department, to produce products to sell, or the other departments within the organisation which provide essential back-up services.

ADMINISTRATION

No organisation can operate effectively without an efficient administration system. In larger organisations this will comprise an Administration Department whose job is to provide back up for all the other functions and departments of the organisation.

Sometimes called the Office Services Department, the Administration Department provides services such as:

- typing and secretarial services;
- desk-top publishing;
- photocopying;
- design and production of forms;
- reception and telephone;
- post room.

The actual services provided will depend on the type and size of an organisation. Every other department in the organisation relies heavily on the Administration Department to help it to carry out its work.

In addition to providing services such as those listed, the Administration Department may also be responsible for the legal and insurance aspects of the organisation.

QUICK response

In a large organisation, why is it better to have a central Administration Department rather than to let every other department do its own administration?

COMPUTER SERVICES

In smaller organisations, the Computer Services, or Information Technology, Section may be a part of the Administration or Office Services Department. Nowadays, however, the importance of computers and information technology is so vital to the success and efficiency of an organisation, and the work involved is so complex, that it requires a separate department.

The Computer Services Department works closely with other departments, obtaining data and inputting them on to the computer. The data are then processed and information produced in a form that is useful and easily understood by senior management. The speed with which this can be done, enabling decisions on future courses of action to be taken quickly and based on timely and accurate information, has meant that computers are now accepted tools in most business organisations.

The Computer Services Department may also be involved in areas such as:

- raising sales invoices;
- processing purchase invoices for payment;
- compiling budgets and accounts;
- planning production;

- checking and maintaining stock levels;
- keeping records (including employee records);
- developing specialised software to suit the needs of the organisation.

Customer services

In today's increasingly competitive world, business organisations must ensure that they provide what their customers want in order that the customers do not go elsewhere. This involves not only providing a product which does what it is supposed to do, but also providing a standard of service in dealing with the customer which the customer finds satisfactory.

A customer is just as likely to take their custom elsewhere if they have received poor, perhaps even rude or unhelpful, service as if the product is unsatisfactory. This aspect of customer relations is so important that many larger organisations have established Customer Service Departments specifically to deal with customers' enquiries, complaints and requests and, where appropriate, to pass these on to the appropriate department. A Customer Service Department can be a valuable source of market research information The subject of providing customer service is dealt with in Unit 3, p 210.

Distribution (logistics)

For many organisations, a sale is not completed until the product has been delivered to the customer. For example, if a farmer wants to sell eggs to a supermarket, the eggs must be delivered to the supermarket before the supermarket will buy them.

When this is the case, arrangements must be made to distribute the product to customers, and this is the function of the Distribution Department. Distribution may be by post, the organisation's own vehicles, an outside haulier's vehicles, rail, sea or air, depending on the product, its destination and whether the organisation has its own vehicles.

Obviously, if an organisation has to distribute its goods to its customers, by whatever method, the customer must receive these on time and in good condition. The method of distribution chosen must also be cost effective, as distribution can be a major expense to an organisation.

ACTIVITY

In groups of four or five, discuss why departments in organisations need to work together. Identify problems which could arise when departments do not work together. Write out your conclusions individually and keep them in your portfolio.

WORKING ARRANGEMENTS IN BUSINESS

Many factors affect the working arrangements of people in business organisations. Some people work in formal teams for organisations with a centralised structure; others in less formal teams in organisations with decentralised structures. For an increasing number of employees working arrangements are now flexible, and many now have fixed-term rather than permanent contracts. The workbase, too, is changing as more and more people move away from working in traditional factory or office environments.

TEAM WORKING

A team can be defined as a group of people working together towards a common goal. While it is true that some people work entirely on their own, most employees in organisations work as part of a team.

Most employees in organisations work as part of a team.

This is because a team can:

- carry out jobs and procedures which could not be carried out successfully by one person;
- call on the skills and experience of all members of the team;
- help the management and control of the organisation's activities, as it is easier to manage a team working together than several individuals doing their own thing;
- help communications within the organisation;
- increase the commitment and motivation of employees because members of a team are likely to feel a commitment to the team and want to work towards the success of the team.

The effectiveness of a team is influenced by five main factors:

1 **The structure of the group**: A team in a hierarchical organisation is likely to have a fairly rigid structure with set procedures and roles for team members. This can inhibit the creativity of team members and restrict their opportunities to contribute fully to the work of the team. In a flatter or matrix organisation, teams are more likely to be able to develop their own structure and procedures, and team members may adopt the roles they are most suited for. This may increase motivation as the team feels it has greater ownership of its task.

Another aspect of the structure of teams which influences effectiveness is size. A large team may contain members with a greater range of skills and experience, while a small group can offer more opportunities for individual members to participate fully in the activities of the team.

ACTIVITY

In groups of four or five, discuss why some people find it easier to participate fully in a small team than they do in a large team. Which do you find it easier to participate in?

2 **The members of the team**: To a large extent, the effectiveness of a team depends on how its members work together. Obviously, they must have the skills and abilities necessary to carry out the tasks of the team, but they must also support and work with each other.

Attitudes play an important part. When members share similar attitudes, the team will be more stable; when members display a range of attitudes there is likely to be some internal conflict. In some circumstances, however, conflict within the team can lead to greater productivity.

It must be remembered that team members are individuals with their own needs and objectives (known as 'personal' or 'hidden' agendas). In any team, individual members will try to pursue their own objectives as well as those of the team. The leader of a team must ensure that, as far as possible, the objectives of team members are compatible with the objectives of the team, and that individual members have opportunities to fulfil their own objectives.

> **QUICK response**
> **How can conflict within a team lead to greater productivity?**

3 **The team's task or objectives**: Four aspects of the task or objectives of a team affect the team's effectiveness. A team which believes in the **importance** of its task is also likely to believe in its own importance. This leads to greater commitment and positive behaviour among members. If the **time scale** for completion of the task is tight, pressure may be exerted to finish in the allotted time. This can lead to frustration and negative behaviour if members resent the pressure. **Criteria** for success that are set too high also inhibit the behaviour and performance of the team as members are under pressure to meet the criteria. The **clarity** of the task is important in that uncertainty caused by unclear or ambiguous requirements, criteria or instructions causes confusion and ineffectiveness. There may also be conflict within the team as members interpret the team objectives and procedures differently.

4 **The style of leadership**: Ultimately, the effectiveness of the team is the responsibility of the leader. It is the team leader who must co-ordinate the activities of all the team members and ensure that they contribute fully towards the team's objectives. A leader may be:

- **autocratic:** that is, is planning and controlling the activities of the team without reference to other team members;
- **democratic:** that is, sharing the planning and decision-making about team activities and procedures with other team members;
- **laissez-faire:** that is, allowing team members to plan and carry out their functions and tasks without interfering. A leader who adopts a laissez-faire approach remains in the background, co-ordinating and supporting the work of other team members.

5 **The expected life-span of the team**: A team that has been formed to undertake a specific project may have a life-span which is limited to the completion of the project. This is often the case with matrix teams. A life-span linked to the progress of the task can affect the motivation and effectiveness of a team. Individual team members may find it difficult to commit themselves to a team that is soon to be disbanded.

ACTIVITY

Think of a group or team to which you belong. Analyse it in terms of the factors described above. How do these influence the effectiveness of the group or team? Could any of these factors be altered in any way to improve its effectiveness?

CENTRALISED AND DECENTRALISED ORGANISATIONS

A centralised organisation is characterised by the traditional hierarchical structure (see p 82). It has set channels of communication and levels of authority. Control of the organisation is kept in the hands of a few senior managers or directors at the top of the pyramid. Some advantages of a centralised structure are:

- a greater control of the organisation;
- uniform standards can be more easily maintained;
- planning and decision-making are in the interests of the organisation as a whole, rather than individual centres;
- managers at the top of the pyramid tend to have more experience on which to base their decisions.

In a decentralised organisation, authority and control are delegated to the managers of individual 'centres' of activity or operation – such as divisions, factories or branches. This brings the decision-making in large and complex organisations closer to customers and the workforce, helping the organisation to respond quickly to their needs and so foster good customer and employee relations. A decentralised organisation may develop a 'satellite' organisational structure, as in *Fig. 2.7*. Some advantages of a decentralised structure are:

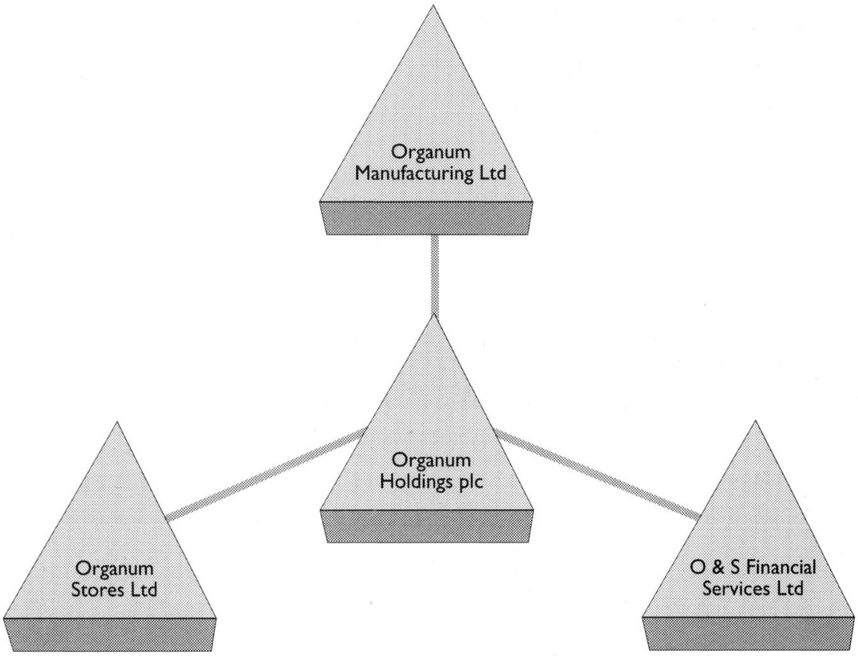

FIGURE 2.7 A satellite organisational structure.

- faster response to the needs of customers and employees;
- greater flexibility and faster decision-making based on the needs of the 'centre' of activity or operation;
- the involvement of junior managers and their teams in the decision-making process (leading to greater ownership of their work and increased motivation);
- increased responsibility and opportunities for junior staff to develop their careers;
- a reduction in the involvement of top managers and directors in the day-to-day running of the organisation, resulting in less stress and increased effectiveness in other areas of their responsibility.

ACTIVITY

Look at the organisational chart you constructed for the activity on p 87. Does this show a centralised or decentralised organisation? Do you think the organisation would benefit from changing from a centralised to decentralised, or decentralised to centralised, structure? Identify any benefits or disadvantages and give your reasons.

QUICK response

List three reasons why a leisure centre may want its staff to work flexible hours.

FLEXIBLE WORKING HOURS

In many jobs these days, employees no longer work a traditional nine to five, Monday to Friday working week. This may be due to the needs of the job or the requirements of the employee.

For example, hospitals must operate for 24 hours a day, seven days a week; many shops and supermarkets stay open late on at least one night a week – and also open on Sundays. Some manufacturing organisations which operate expensive equipment find it cheaper and more effective to keep the equipment running for 24 hours a day, rather than starting it up and shutting it down every day. Additionally, in periods of high demand an organisation may need to operate for more hours than normal in order to meet the demand.

In these cases, many organisations operate a **shift system** in order to cover the long hours. Under a shift system, individual employees only work for the normal number of hours, but they are formed into teams or 'shifts', where all the employees on one shift may work, for example, for eight hours from six in the morning until two in the afternoon, at which time the second shift takes over and works until ten at night. As you can see, in this way, by running three shifts, an organisation can operate for 24 hours a day, although each employee works for only eight hours.

Working shifts, however, can place a strain on employees, especially when the shift changes and sometimes the employee has to start work at six in the morning, while at other times they don't finish until ten at night. For this reason, shifts are normally worked for set periods of at least a week, and usually three or four weeks, to give employees time to adjust to the different hours of waking and sleeping. In some cases, shifts are permanent and an individual employee's hours do not change. Employees who do shift work normally receive additional payments for the shift work, which may vary according to whether they are working an early or late shift.

In times of heavy demand, requiring extra hours to be worked in order to meet the demand, employees cover this by working **overtime**, without changing their normal basic hours. Additional hours worked as overtime are normally paid at a premium rate. However, many employees in senior and managerial positions often have to work long hours in order to complete their tasks and no additional payments are normally made for this.

Where Saturday or Sunday working is required, for example in shops and stores, employees often do this on a rota basis. With

Sunday opening, however, many stores are employing part-time staff to work on this day only.

An alternative approach to fixed working hours is flexi-hours. Under this system, employees choose their hours of work – often varying these from day to day – provided a set total is worked over all (such as 37 hours per week, or 160 per month). Working flexi-hours, for example, can enable a single parent to collect their child from school each day. Sometimes it may be possible to accrue hours worked above the fixed number, to be taken as time off later. An employee who works, say, 168 hours one month rather than 160, may be able to take a day off during the following month.

ACTIVITY

Obviously, not all jobs are suitable for working flexi-hours. What do you think would be the effect if the teaching and other staff at your school or college started working flexi-hours. Make a list of advantages and disadvantages.

CONTRACTS

You have seen that employees may have either fixed-term or permanent contracts of employment (see p 59). In recent years there has been a steady decline in the number of permanent jobs that are available, and a trend towards business organisations employing people on fixed-term contracts.

- **A permanent contract** is a contract of employment which does not give a finishing date. A permanent contract gives certain rights and places responsibilities on both employees and employers (see p 60). Such a contract can only be terminated after a stated period of notice.

- **A fixed-term contract** does give a date on which the employment will come to an end. An employee on a fixed-term contract does not enjoy the same rights as an employee on a permanent contract, and the employer does not have the same obligations to the employee. The rights and responsibilities of the employee and employer depend on the length of time the employee is employed.

Many organisations prefer to employ people on fixed-term contracts to cover periods of known high demand or temporary increases in the workload. In some organisations, particularly in the public sector, there may be uncertainty over whether the organisation will be able to maintain its number of employees in the future, and fixed-term contracts may help by creating flexibility in levels of personnel.

When an increasing number of employees are on fixed-term contracts, it is harder for a hierarchical organisation to maintain its long chains of command due to employees leaving when their contracts expire. Organisations may therefore become flatter. It is also harder for employees on fixed-term contracts to become fully effective members of teams in which other members are on permanent contracts.

ACTIVITY

Some organisations find it convenient to employ people on fixed-term contracts while they can afford to do so, so that they can easily reduce the number of employees when times are tight. As a group, discuss whether you think the use of fixed-term contracts in this way is fair. Give your reasons.

THE WORKBASE

The place where a person works is called their workbase. This may be:

- an office;
- a factory;
- a shop;

- outdoors;
- the person's home;
- mobile – such as a mobile shop or library.

Some workbases offer more freedom; others offer more comfort.

Obviously, the type of workbase will influence working arrangements. Different workbases affect:

- the need for rigid time-keeping;
- the need to follow set working routines and procedures;
- the cohesiveness of teams and dependency of employees on each other;
- the type and variety of work.

Employees who work in factories and offices are likely to have set times of work as their work and the work of others frequently depend on them all being available in the workplace at one time. Shops, restaurants and other service and leisure industries, where customers come to the organisation, normally require employees to be present at set times (such as shop opening times), often to suit the customer. In these cases, good time-keeping is important, and the presence of many employees encourages the development of team working.

On the other hand, people who work from home, on behalf of their employer or as self-employed, may be able to set their own daily routine and hours of work. This, again, depends on the needs of customers and any other people with whom the homeworker must liaise. People whose workbase is mobile, such as mobile hairdressers, electricians and sales representatives, can also often work independently to their own daily routine as they are relatively free from the constrictions imposed by any hierarchical structure or their employer.

People who work out of doors, such as farmers, window cleaners and so on, often work alone. They may be largely responsible for their own working arrangements. Other outdoor workers are part of a team and have to conform to the requirements of the team in respect of times of work, routines and procedures. Such workers include the crew of a fishing boat, teams on building sites and professional footballers.

REASONS FOR CHANGE IN WORKING ARRANGEMENTS

There are several reasons why an organisation should want to change its working arrangements. These include:

- **Productivity**: Businesses which are competing in the market place, perhaps trying to increase sales and gain a larger share of the market, must strive to achieve the maximum output while keeping the cost of production to a minimum. One way of doing this is by increasing productivity – the amount produced per employee or machine. It may be possible to increase productivity, for example, by operating a shift system, so that machines can be operated for a longer period, producing more goods per machine. Some businesses have developed methods of team working to increase the contribution made by each team member who can concentrate on one aspect of the work.

QUICK response

What might be the effect of a business increasing productivity at the expense of quality?

- **Quality assurance**: While increasing productivity is an aim of many business organisations, the quality of the product or service must always remain a prime consideration. Sometimes the quality of a product can be improved by changing working arrangements. For example, workers on assembly lines are often bored and poorly motivated by the monotony and repetition of their jobs. This leads to lack of interest and care, resulting in a poor quality product. For this reason, in many manufacturing industries, such as the car industry, there has been a move away from assembly-line working arrangements towards team working.
- **Competition**: Business organisations in the private and public sectors face increasing competition from other organisations. To survive, they must continually strive to improve their competitive advantage. This includes responding to changes in demand and economic uncertainty by keeping personnel costs to a minimum in all areas, including administration and other 'non-production' functions. Many organisations have responded to uncertainty about the future by changing working arrangements and introducing fixed-term contracts.
- **Technology**: The availability and introduction of new technology have played a significant part in shaping the working arrangements which exist in business organisations. The use of computers and computer-controlled equipment has meant that in many areas one person can now do the work previously done by several. This has

Computer-controlled equipment has taken the place of people on car-assembly lines.

altered the structure of teams – and may even have taken away the need for a team at all. The increased use of fax machines and modems linking computers through the telephone line has meant that employees can work in different locations – in some cases even from home – while remaining in close contact with their base and having instant access to the information they need via e-mail.

PORTFOLIO ASSIGNMENT

For this portfolio assignment you will need to research two business organisations in your area. Advice on finding information about business is given on p x in the Introduction. You may wish to refer to this again before starting this assignment. The work you do for this portfolio assignment can build on work carried out for Unit 1. This portfolio assignment also combines well with the portfolio assignment for Element 2.3 and you may wish to look at that before starting the present assignment.

TASK 1

Identify and investigate the organisational structures of two businesses with different structures. They may be large, medium or small businesses which you have already investigated for previous activities or assignments. Construct an organisational chart of each business (two charts in all). One chart could be the one you constructed for the activity on p 87.

TASK 2

Identify the departments in each organisation and write notes describing the work of each department. Show how the work of each department is interrelated.

TASK 3

Write a short, informal report describing and comparing the working arrangements in each organisation. Show the extent to which team-working operates in each organisation, how it is encouraged, and the benefits gained.

TASK 4

Choose one of the organisations you have investigated in the above tasks and write a summary describing changes which have occurred in the organisation as a result of:

- the need to improve productivity;
- the need to introduce quality assurance procedures;
- the impact of competition;
- the impact of technology.

This portfolio assignment also presents an opportunity to gather evidence for the following core skills:

- Communication – take part in discussions; produce written material;
- Information Technology – prepare information; process information.

THE RIGHTS AND RESPONSIBILITIES OF EMPLOYERS AND EMPLOYEES

The relationships between employers and employees are important. Good relationships can help a business to achieve its goals, while poor relationships can lead to the failure of the business. The impact of relationships on employees is therefore considerable.

If a business achieves its goals, the employees of the business will gain in terms of satisfaction, benefits (including pay), and job security. If a business fails, on the other hand, the employees of the business will find themselves having to work harder for little reward and may even become out of work if the business has to close down.

Relationships largely depend on employers and employees recognising and fulfilling their rights and responsibilities towards each other. Increasingly, these rights and responsibilities are being defined in law, so that any dispute may be settled by legal procedures, including going through the courts if necessary.

Before considering how disputes are settled, or looking at the specific rights and responsibilities of employers and employees, we shall consider the benefits of co-operation without recourse to legal procedures.

A good relationship between employer and employees is a key factor in the success of a business!

THE BENEFITS OF EMPLOYER AND EMPLOYEE CO-OPERATION

Co-operation between employers and employees has benefits in three interrelated areas:

- the survival of the business;
- improved employee commitment to the business;
- improved efficiency.

QUICK response

Give three reasons why co-operation between employer and employees is important.

All employers rely on the efforts of their employees to achieve their business goals. Without the efforts of employees, the business would not be able to supply its customers with a product or service of the quality they require and at the price they are willing to pay. The business would become uncompetitive and customers would go elsewhere. Without sales, the business would not survive. It is therefore in the interests of an employer to co-operate with their employees in order to encourage them to produce their best efforts for the business.

Equally, it is in the interests of employees to co-operate with their employers. If they do not co-operate, the business will suffer and may be unable to provide the benefits they look for. If the business fails to survive, then the employees will lose their jobs.

Good co-operation between employers and employees develops a climate of positive employer/employee relations. This leads to a greater commitment to the business from employees, who are likely to work harder and with more care. Their contribution will be greater and this, in turn, will lead to improved efficiency and enhanced performance by the organisation.

ACTIVITY

You work in the Administration Department of Office Paper Supplies Limited. For some months now, there has been a growing problem with office staff being slow to return to their desks after the permitted ten-minute tea breaks in the morning and afternoon. Management have stated that this is affecting productivity. It has also been pointed out that the breaks are a concession and unless staff keep within the permitted ten minutes the breaks will be withdrawn and a drinks vending machine placed in the corridor so that staff can get a cup of tea or coffee to drink while they continue working at their desks.
Jim Spiers, the trade union representative, has accused the company of being mean-minded and says that as the tea breaks are obviously not long enough, they should be extended rather than withdrawn.
This has given rise to a situation which could result in either co-operation or non-cooperation between management and workforce. As a group, discuss what the effects would be of each side adopting a position of (a) co-operation, and (b) non-cooperation. Which position would bring the greatest benefits to each side?

RESOLVING DISAGREEMENTS

Disagreements can arise even when there is a good level of co-operation between an employer and employees. For example, an employer may want to retain profits within the business to fund future expansion which could bring benefits to both employer and employees. The employees, on the other hand, being unconvinced of the benefits that expansion would bring, and conscious of the fact that the profits of the business were made because of their co-operation and hard work, may feel that the profits should be distributed in the form of a pay rise or bonus.

Sometimes both employer and employee feel that profits should be distributed more evenly!

Where co-operation between an employer and employees is poor, and relationships are at a low ebb, disagreements and conflicts are even more likely to arise. In order that such disagreements do as little harm to the business or the interests of employees as possible, they should be resolved quickly, preferably through negotiation.

If the disagreement is between a single employee or a small group of employees and their employer, perhaps because they feel they have been treated unfairly, the first step is to try to resolve the disagreement by direct negotiation between the employee or employees and the employer. In the case of a single employee, this may be done by following a laid-down grievance procedure which sets out the way in which such disagreements may be resolved. A small group of employees may ask for a meeting with the employer's senior management who have the authority to resolve the disagreement.

ACTIVITY

As a group, write a grievance procedure which members of your class could follow in cases where there is a disagreement with your tutor or another member of school or college staff. Discuss the procedure you have written with your tutor.

When a disagreement cannot be resolved in this way, however, or when it involves a number of employees – or employers if the disagreement involves a number of business organisations – the matter can be taken up by the relevant trade union who will negotiate with employers on the employees' behalf.

Trade union strength protects the individual members.

A trade union is an organisation which is set up to represent the interests of employees in a particular trade or industry and to promote good relations and co-operation between employers and employees. Activities of trade unions in representing their members (that is employees who have joined the union) include negotiating with employers or employers' representatives over pay and conditions, acting on behalf of members and providing legal advice and support in disputes. Negotiations with employers can take place on two levels:

- **nationally**, where the trade union is trying to reach an agreement with all employers in an industry, for all its members, or for all its members in a business which operates nationally;
- **locally**, where the trade union negotiates on behalf of its members with employers in a specific part of the country, or with one employer on behalf of members at a particular factory or base.

Most disputes and disagreements are resolved by trade unions negotiating with employers, but where agreement cannot be reached in this way, other courses of action are open to both parties to the disagreement.

An important organisation in the field of industrial relations is the Advisory, Conciliation and Arbitration Service (ACAS). ACAS was set up by the Government in 1974 to provide a wide range of services to employers and employees. In an industrial dispute either side can ask ACAS to arbitrate and help to reach an agreement. ACAS will look objectively at each side of the disagreement and suggest solutions which might be acceptable to both.

There are ACAS offices throughout the UK.

Where no solution is acceptable to both sides of the dispute, various courses of legal action can be taken. The most common way for an employee to try to settle a dispute with an employer is through an Industrial Tribunal. Industrial Tribunals were established in 1964 and were intended to be an informal type of court which would decide on cases where employees felt they had been treated unfairly by their employers. The intention was that these tribunals, which consist of a chairperson who is an expert in employment law, an employee's representative and an employer's representative, should be very informal and accessible to employees. There has been a tendency, however, for both sides to employ highly qualified barristers to put forward their case.

The decision of an Industrial Tribunal is enforceable in law. Both sides have the right to appeal to an Employment Appeal Tribunal if they do not agree with the decision of the Industrial Tribunal.

If none of these methods gives a satisfactory resolution, disputes between employers and employees can be taken to a County Court, High Court or even the House of Lords. In 1995, for example, the Law Lords (the House of Lords sitting as an Appeal Court) ruled that the British Armed Forces could dismiss people because they are gay. As a final resort, disputes involving employment matters such as health and safety, maternity rights, discrimination and so on can be taken to the European Court of Justice which consists of judges from each member state of the EU. Decisions of the European Court of Justice are binding and take precedence over decisions of national courts.

The European Court of Justice in Luxembourg.

ACTIVITY

Find examples of employment disputes that have been resolved by the European Court. These are fully reported in national newspapers such as *The Times*, *The Daily Telegraph*, *The Independent* and *The Guardian*, and also in magazines such as *The Economist*. Your school, college or local library may hold back copies or have extracts from these publications on CD-ROM, and may be able to help you locate appropriate articles and reports.

Do you think the ruling of the European Court was fair? Did it differ from the ruling of the British courts? Do you think that decisions of the European Court should take precedence over decisions of national courts? Explain your answers.

EMPLOYER AND EMPLOYEE RIGHTS AND RESPONSIBILITIES

People at work have a right to expect certain things of their employers. For example, an employee has a right to expect:

- to be paid at an agreed rate;
- to be treated fairly;
- to be provided with a workplace that is healthy and safe to work in;
- to be provided with equipment that is safe to use;
- to receive appropriate training;
- not to be asked to do anything that is dangerous, unethical or illegal.

Employers have a responsibility to their employees to fulfil these expectations, and the degree of co-operation between employers and employees depends on their fulfilment. In addition, employees have a right to be told, and employers have a responsibility to tell their employees, the objectives of the business.

In return, employers have a right to expect their employees:

- to work conscientiously in accordance with the agreed terms of the employment;

- to maintain standards of quality;
- to co-operate in trying to achieve the objectives of the business;
- to follow laid-down procedures;
- to comply with health and safety regulations.

The rights and responsibilities of employers and employees are largely covered by two areas of legislation:

- employment legislation;
- health and safety legislation.

The Employment Protection (Consolidation) Act 1978 provided, among other things, for employees to be given a written statement of the terms and conditions of their employment. This states the basic rights and responsibilities of the employee and the employer and is the foundation of the relationship and co-operation between them.

THE CONTRACT OF EMPLOYMENT

A contract of employment is an agreement, which can be enforced in law, between an employer and an employee, by which the employer offers the employee employment to do a particular job, and the employee agrees to work for the employer in return for some kind of remuneration (usually a wage or salary).

Under the terms of the Employment Protection (Consolidation) Act 1978, any employee who works for a minimum of 16 hours per week must be given a contract of employment *within* 8 weeks of starting their employment. In practice, many employees who work for less than 16 hours per week are also given a contract, and this hours rule is currently under review by the Government in the light of legislation in the EU.

The contract must state at least the following basic facts about the employment:

- the name of the employer;
- the name of the employee;
- the job title;
- the date the employment covered by the contract began;
- the date on which the current period of continuous service with the employer began;

- the basic hours the employee is expected to work;
- the remuneration to be paid by the employer;
- any entitlement of the employee to participate in a pension scheme;
- how absence through sickness should be reported to the employer, and details of any sick pay entitlement;
- the amount of holiday the employee is entitled to each year;
- the amount of notice an employee must give of their intention to leave the employer, and the amount of notice the employer must give of any intention to terminate the employee's employment;
- details – or where these may be found – of procedures to be followed in the event of (a) a grievance by the employee, or (b) the need for the employer to take disciplinary action against the employee.

QUICK response

When an employee signs a contract of employment, what are they agreeing to?

The date on which an employee's continuous service with an employer begins may be different to the date of the contract if, for example, the employee moves to a different organisation which is considered to be a part of the same employer. This may happen when an employee of a government department moves to work for a different government department, or an employee of one company within a group of companies moves to work for another company within the same group.

ACTIVITY

You are starting employment with a company next Monday as a Personnel Assistant. Your salary will be £7,500 per year and your hours of work will be 9 am to 5 pm, Mondays to Fridays. You will get four weeks' holiday each year. Write down the main details you would wish to see in your own contract of employment using a computer word processing package.

REMUNERATION

The remuneration for which an employee works is normally their wage or salary.

- Production workers and operatives normally receive wages.
- Managerial and administrative staff normally receive salaries.

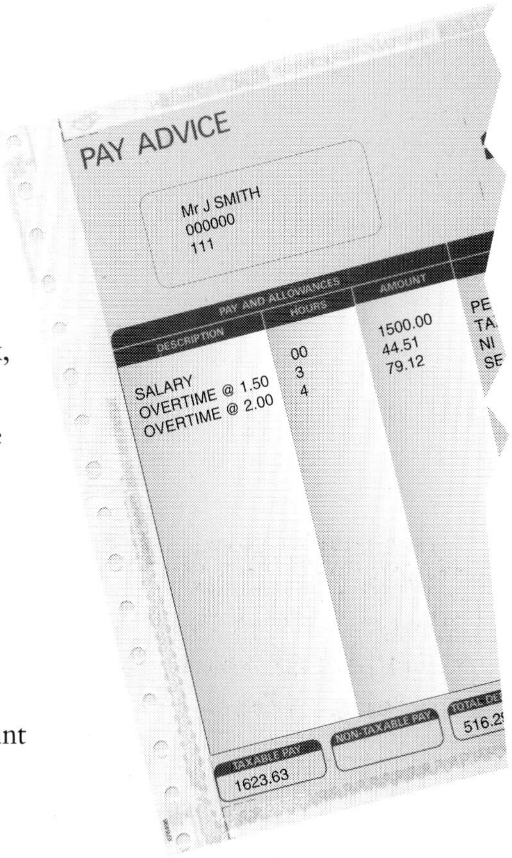

A pay slip.

A wage is a payment which is calculated on an hourly rate. Wages are usually paid weekly. The hourly rate is shown on the contract of employment, and this is multiplied by the number of hours the employee actually works each week in order to arrive at the wage to be paid for that week. For example, an employee who is paid at a rate of £8.56 per hour, and works 40 hours in one week, will receive wages of £8.56 × 40 = £342.40 for that week.

A salary is a payment based on an annual, or yearly, rate (the rate per annum). The annual rate is shown on the contract of employment. Salaries are usually paid monthly.

The amount of salary paid each month is found by dividing the annual salary by 12 monthly payments. For example, an employee whose annual salary is £12,000 will be paid £12,000 ÷ 12 = £1,000 per month. Salaries are frequently set within a range or scale for the job. This means that the salary of an employee will rise by a set amount (or **increment**) each year, as the employee gains more experience and becomes more proficient at the job, up to a maximum salary.

If the position of sales clerk has a salary scale of £12,000 to £15,000 per year, with annual increments of £500 per year, for example, an employee would start at £12,000 per year and expect to be earning £15,000 per year after six years. However both starting point and increments may be flexible according to circumstances. An employee who has already gained experience with one company may start employment with a new company one or two increments above the bottom. If they gained an appropriate qualification after a year, they might then rise by more than one increment for that year.

Although an employee's contract of employment states that they will be paid a wage or salary at a certain rate, this is not the actual amount the employee receives to spend as they like. Before an employer makes a wage or salary payment to an employee, the following must be deducted from the total amount:

- income tax – which is paid to the Government through the Inland Revenue;
- National Insurance – which is paid to the Government to pay for the National Health Service and state pensions;
- pension deductions – if the employee is in a private pension scheme and this is stated in the contract of employment.

ACTIVITY

Your salary is £9,000 per annum (your gross pay). Of this the first £3,445 is tax free (your basic allowance), the next £3,000 is taxed at 20 per cent and the remainder is taxed at 25 per cent (the basic rate). National Insurance contributions of £55.24 per month will be deducted from your salary. Calculate the amount you will actually receive each month.

GRIEVANCE PROCEDURES AND DISCIPLINARY ACTION

Employers and employees should co-operate to find ways of resolving disagreements!

The need for employers and employees to co-operate, and ways to resolve disagreements, have already been discussed on pp 107–11. A contract of employment should explain, or state where the employee can find out, what action should be taken:

- by the employee, if they feel that they have been treated unfairly by the employer or by a superior working for the employer;
- by the employer, if the employer feels that the behaviour of the employee is unreasonable or breaks the terms of the contract.

The procedure to be taken if an employee feels they have been treated unfairly is called a **grievance procedure**. Most organisations have set grievance procedures which are based on discussion and consultation in order to resolve the grievance. Grievance procedures normally follow three steps:

1 The employee formally states their grievance to their immediate superior or manager, who must investigate the grievance fully and try to resolve it.

2 If the employee's superior cannot resolve the grievance then the employee can take the matter to a higher level within the organisation. This may involve the Personnel Department and other senior managers of the organisation, and possibly trade union representatives.

3 If the grievance still cannot be satisfactorily resolved, the employee has recourse to legal representation, such as taking the grievance to an industrial tribunal, ACAS or even a court of law (see p 111).

The procedure to be taken by an employer if the employer feels that the behaviour of the employee is unreasonable or breaks the terms of the contract, is known as a **disciplinary procedure**, or **disciplinary action.**

Disciplinary action must follow two stages:

1 informal discussion;

2 formal procedures.

At the informal stage, the employer will again try to resolve the matter by discussion with the employee, to find out why the employee has acted in such a way that the employer feels disciplinary action is necessary. If the matter can be resolved at this stage, no further action is necessary.

If a disciplinary matter cannot be resolved informally, however, the employer must follow a set disciplinary procedure involving:

- **A verbal warning** by which the employee is warned that certain behaviour of the employee will not be tolerated and, unless the behaviour changes within a certain period, further disciplinary action against the employee will be taken.
- **A written warning** which will detail the offence for which the employee is being disciplined, explain what is expected of the employee in the future and state what action will be taken if the employee continues to offend. Reference will be made to any previous formal or informal verbal or written warnings about the present offence, and the employee must sign a copy of the written warning to show that they have received and understand it. An employee may be given a first or a final written warning.
- **Disciplinary action**: If an employee continues to commit an offence, despite receiving verbal and final written warnings, the employer may take disciplinary action consisting of **dismissal, suspension**, or, in some cases, **transfer** or **demotion** according to the severity of the offence.

QUICK response

Before you read the rest of this section, make a list of types of behaviour which you think would result in an employee being disciplined.

Some types of employee behaviour can be termed as **gross misconduct** which normally results in **instant dismissal** of the employee (that is, without the need to go through the full procedure of verbal and written warnings). Gross misconduct includes:

- dishonesty and theft, for example, of the company's products;
- physical violence, for example, fighting;

Sometimes instant dismissal seems the most obvious solution!

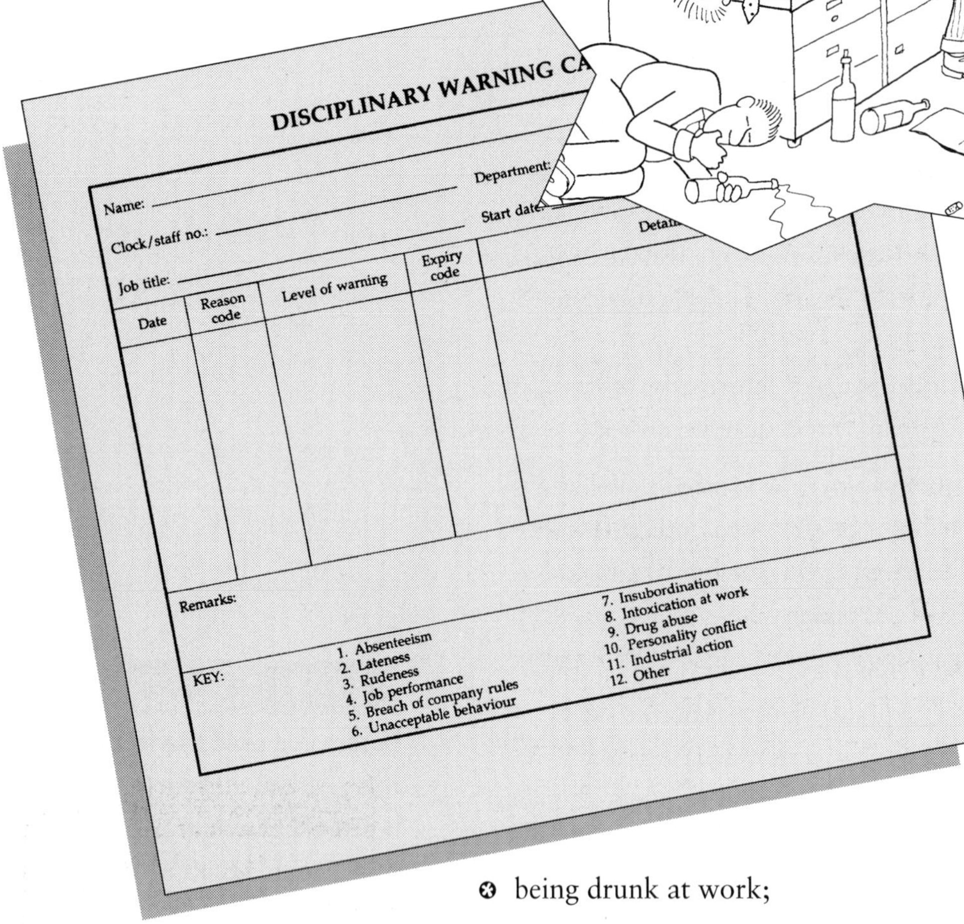

DISCIPLINARY WARNING CA

Name:
Department:
Clock/staff no.:
Start date:
Job title:

Date	Reason code	Level of warning	Expiry code	Details

Remarks:

KEY:
1. Absenteeism
2. Lateness
3. Rudeness
4. Job performance
5. Breach of company rules
6. Unacceptable behaviour
7. Insubordination
8. Intoxication at work
9. Drug abuse
10. Personality conflict
11. Industrial action
12. Other

A disciplinary warning card.

- being drunk at work;
- refusing to comply with a reasonable request;
- swearing;
- some other gross violation of an established works rule.

Other forms of misconduct which are not serious enough to warrant instant dismissal, but may warrant disciplinary procedures, include:

- persistent absenteeism or lateness;
- carelessness or negligence, including failure to follow health and safety procedures;
- sexual or other harassment.

ACTIVITY

- **As a group, discuss the reasons for instant dismissal given above. Do you think they are, in fact, sufficient reason for an employer to dismiss an employee without further warning?**
- **In pairs, choose one of the reasons warranting disciplinary action given above. Make notes for an interview between an employee being disciplined and their manager. Act out the interview as a role play exercise, one student playing the employee and the other playing the manager. Afterwards, discuss what you think your feelings would be as an employee being disciplined and as a manager having to discipline an employee.**

In most cases, where an offence by an employee has been fully investigated by the employer and the disciplinary procedures carried out correctly, the disciplinary action will be considered fair and justified. If, however, an employee feels they have not been treated fairly, the employee can take action against the employer for **unfair dismissal**. In this case the employee can take the employer to an Industrial Tribunal, and even seek other forms of legal representation, right up to the European Court of Justice (see pp 109–11). An Industrial Tribunal will consider whether the employer has acted in accordance with *natural* justice. The principles of natural justice which govern the way in which an employer should handle a disciplinary case are:

QUICK response

What does 'natural justice' mean?

- The employee should know the standards they are expected to achieve and the procedures they are expected to follow.
- It should be clearly explained to the employee where they are failing to achieve the standards of performance or to follow procedures.
- The employee should be given a chance to improve prior to disciplinary action being taken (except in cases of gross misconduct).
- The employee should be advised of the nature of the offence.
- The employee should be given the opportunity of stating their case.

- Anyone involved in disciplinary proceedings should act in good faith.
- The employee should be given the opportunity of appeal.

A dismissal may be shown to be unfair if:

- The employer does not have an admissible reason to dismiss the employee.
- The employer can be shown not to have acted reasonably in dismissing the employee, or not to have followed a normal dismissal procedure, including formal warnings if appropriate.
- It can be shown that **constructive dismissal** has taken place.

A constructive dismissal is where the attitude and behaviour of the employer is such that the employee can reasonably consider their contract terminated by the employer.

HEALTH AND SAFETY

Health and safety are important factors in every area of employment. Two principal items of legislation set out the rights and responsibilities of employers and employees regarding health and safety.

1 **The Health and Safety at Work Act 1974 (HASAW)** This places responsibilities on employers to:
- provide a workplace that is safe and healthy to work in;
- carry out safety procedures such as fire drills, displaying safety notices, indicating fire exits and so on;
- provide machinery and equipment that is safe to operate and properly guarded;
- provide trained safety staff;
- have a written statement of health and safety policy which is available to all employees.

HASAW also places responsibilities on employees to:
- follow health and safety procedures;
- use machinery and equipment in a safe manner, including using any safety devices and guards;
- always act in ways that will not endanger themselves or others;
- not misuse any safety equipment provided or deface safety notices.

2 **The Control of Substances Hazardous to Health Regulations 1988 (COSHH)** These cover the storage, handling and use of substances which are hazardous to health, such as chemicals and cleaning materials.

QUICK response

Why does health and safety legislation place respons-ibilities on employees as well as on employers?

The combined effect of these regulations is to make employers, their managers and employees responsible for health and safety in the workplace. Employers are responsible for providing, and employees have a right to expect, a safe and healthy workplace with proper safety procedures and safe machinery and equipment. Managers and employees are responsible for following safety procedures and acting in a responsible way with regard to the health and safety of themselves and others. Employers have a right to expect that their employees will do this.

ACTIVITY

Much health and safety legislation has been introduced to protect employees in the workplace. Do you think it is right that health and safety should be a matter for legislation, or should it be a matter for employers and employees to agree between themselves, in a spirit of co-operation?

EQUAL OPPORTUNITIES

All employees – and prospective employees – have a right to be treated fairly and without prejudice on the behalf of the employer with regard to sex or race. There is no legal requirement for an employer to have a formal equal opportunities policy, but all employers must conform with the relevant legislation.

All employees have the right to be treated fairly and without prejudice on the grounds of their gender or ethnic origin.

- **The Equal Pay Act 1970** states that women performing comparable tasks to men should be treated equally, including receiving the same rates of pay.
- **The Sex Discrimination Acts 1975** and 1986 rule against discrimination in any form on the basis of sex or marital status.
- **The Race Relations Act 1976** makes it illegal to discriminate against employees or potential employees on the grounds of race or ethnic origin.

Complaints of discrimination on the grounds of sex or marital status are investigated by the Equal Opportunities Commission. Complaints of discrimination on the grounds of race or ethnic origin are investigated by the Commission for Racial Equality.

ACTIVITY

It can be argued that equal opportunities legislation places unnecessary restrictions on employers in deciding who they can employ, and may, in turn, restrict employment opportunities. As a group, discuss whether equal opportunities should be a matter for legislation or whether employees should be able to offer employment to whom they like at whatever salary or wage the employee is willing accept.

PORTFOLIO ASSIGNMENT

For this portfolio assignment you will research employer and employee co-operation in a business organisation. The organisation you select to investigate may be one you have investigated for previous activities or assignments. Your task is to find out about the benefits the organisation has gained from employer and employee co-operation, and how health and safety and equal opportunities legislation places rights and responsibilities on both employers and employees.

Analyse your findings in a formal report. Your report should include examples of disagreements or potential disagreements, explaining how these were or might be resolved. Discuss how trade unions or courts may be involved when disagreements cannot be resolved. You should include at least two examples of the rights and responsibilities of employers and employees imposed by health and safety and equal opportunities legislation.

This portfolio assignment also presents an opportunity to gather evidence for the following core skills:

- Communication – take part in discussions; produce written material; read and respond to written materials;
- Information Technology – prepare information; process information; present information.

LEVELS AND JOB ROLES IN ORGANISATIONS

You have seen (p 82) that, traditionally, organisations were given hierarchical structures. These are based on levels of authority and responsibility, with each person in the organisation having a clearly defined position in the hierarchy.

LEVELS WITHIN BUSINESS ORGANISATIONS

The levels within an organisational hierarchy are usually referred to as:

- senior;
- middle;
- junior.

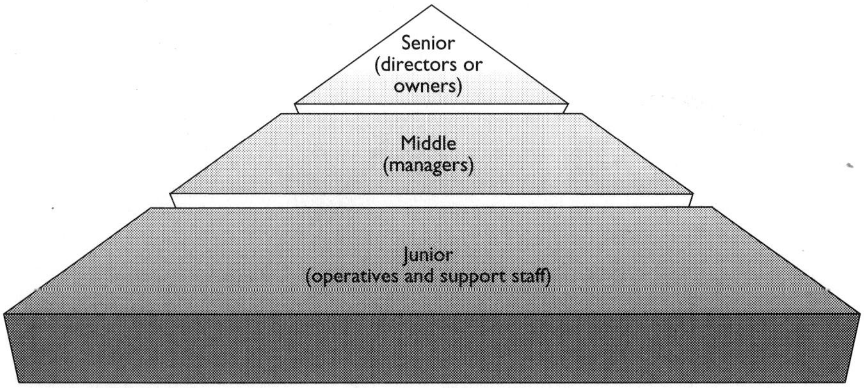

FIGURE 2.8 Levels of authority.

The relationship of different levels can be seen in *Fig. 2.8*. These levels refer to the authority, responsibility and type of job of personnel within each level, rather than length of service or any other criterion.

At the most senior level within the organisation are the **directors** of a private or public limited company, **executives** of state-owned organisations, and **owners** of sole trader businesses or partnerships. The most senior role in the organisation is that of the **chair** of the board of directors (the collective name for all the directors of a company), the **chief executive** or the owner. In a company, the role of chair of the board of directors is often incorporated with that of **managing director**. In a partnership, where there are several owners of the business, there may be a **senior partner** who takes on the same kind of role in relation to the other partners.

The duties of personnel at the most senior level of an organisation's hierarchy include:

- deciding the long-term goals of the organisation;
- setting short- and medium-term targets which will help the organisation to fulfil its goals;
- planning strategies for achieving the organisation's targets;
- deciding how to use the resources – human, physical and financial – of the organisation;
- making sure the organisation operates within the law.

Usually, the actual roles undertaken by individual senior personnel will depend on the size of the organisation. Small organisations have fewer senior personnel. Each will therefore be responsible for several areas of the organisation's operation. In a larger organisation, however, such as a public limited company or a large state-owned organisation, there will be more senior personnel, allowing each to specialise in one area.

FIGURE 2.9 The senior personnel of a large plc.

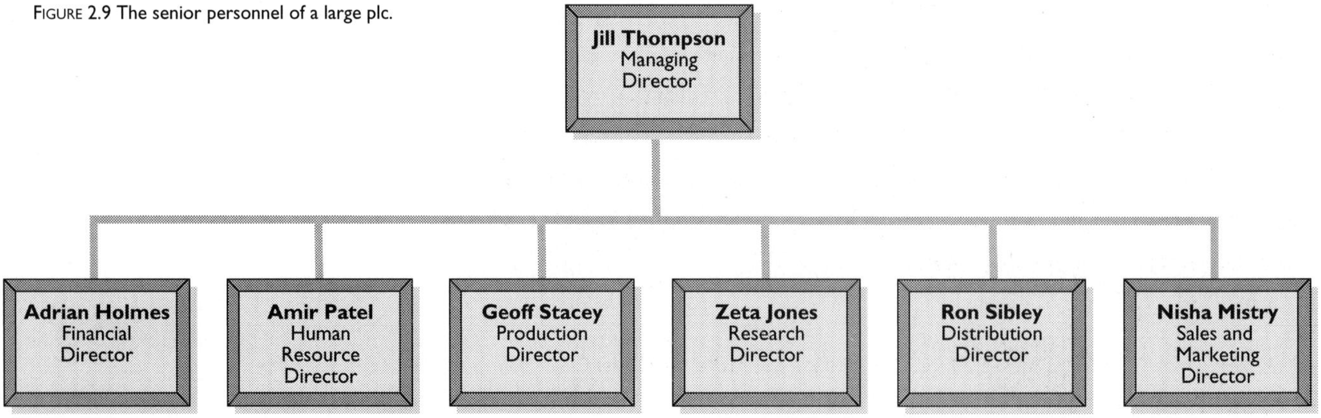

For example, *Fig. 2.9* shows the senior personnel of a large plc. The managing director is responsible for overall planning and for the running and performance of the company as a whole. Other directors, who report to the managing director, are responsible for planning and controlling the activities of their own departments and for setting targets for their own departments. A director must also communicate decisions and instructions from the board of directors as a whole to their own department, reporting back as appropriate.

ACTIVITY

Explain the difference in status and responsibility of the managing director of a large public limited company, such as ICI, and the owner of a sole trader business.

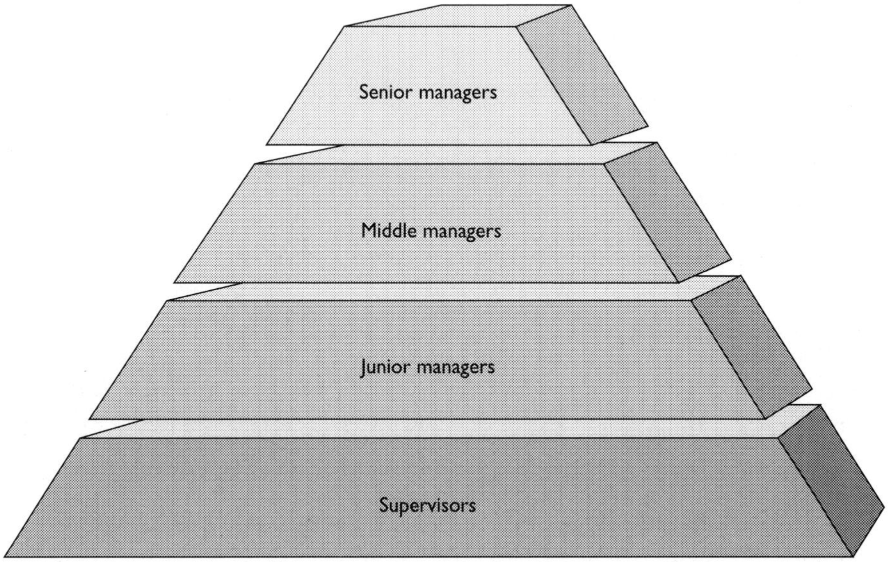

FIGURE 2.10 Levels of management.

At the middle level of an organisation's hierarchy are managers. As you have seen (p 125), there may be several levels of managers: senior managers, middle managers and junior managers (see *Fig. 2.10*). Senior managers are often the heads of departments, reporting directly to the appropriate director and responsible for the day-to-day running of their department. A senior manager may have one or more middle managers reporting to them. Junior managers may also assist each middle manager.

The duties of managers are to:

- undertake the day-to-day management, running and control of their department;
- communicate the instructions of their director to staff within the department and ensure they are carried out;
- allocate and manage the work of the staff in their department;

- ensure departmental targets are met;
- ensure standards of quality are maintained;
- identify and find solutions to everyday problems within the department;
- oversee the human resources management of the department, including recruitment, training and discipline; a manager will work with the Human Resources or Personnel Department in this;
- provide a communication link between the senior staff of the organisation and the staff of the department;
- liaise with other departments within the organisation;
- act as a spokesperson for the department.

A supervisor with his team.

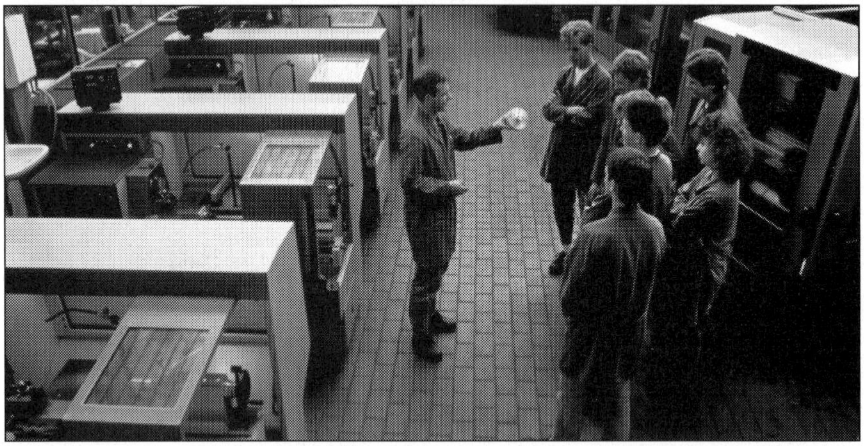

Supervisors are responsible for the activities of a small group of employees, known as a work group or team. Supervisors are sometimes considered to be at the bottom of the middle level of the organisational hierarchy and sometimes to be at the top of the junior level. This is because they are often regarded as senior members of the operative and support staff who form the work groups, rather than the first level of management.

Sometimes a supervisor does the same work as the employees in their work group or team. But the supervisor is also responsible for:

- ensuring employees in the work group carry out their work and instructions correctly;
- maintaining the output of the work group in terms of quantity and quality;
- supporting and advising members of the work group.

Supervisors are found in both manufacturing and service industries.

Where the supervisor is in charge of a team of production workers, they are often called a 'foreman'. The title 'supervisor' is more commonly used where the team provides a service. For example, an employee in charge of a team on a building site would be called a foreman. An employee in charge of a team of sales assistants in a shop, however, would be called a supervisor.

Supervisors usually make some lower-level decisions; for example, allocating particular jobs to members of the work group to ensure the day's production is completed. They are not normally involved in the overall management of resources or in deciding company policy.

At the most junior level of an organisation's hierarchy are **production operatives** and **support staff**.

Production operatives are employees who are directly involved in the production of the goods or services supplied by the organisation. For example, they operate machines and other equipment used to produce goods, assemble components, serve in shops, cut hair, and so on. They are not involved with decision-making except in so far as it affects their own jobs, but carry out instructions from their supervisors and management.

The support staff of an organisation are involved with the internal workings and administration of the organisation. They make it possible for the organisation as a whole, and individual departments within it, to operate effectively.

Support staff include employees such as security staff, cleaners, receptionists, maintenance staff and office support staff like computer operators, filing clerks, accounts clerks, administration assistants, and so on. Some support staff are important in supporting an organisation's external operations and relationships with its customers and clients. For example, customer support and customer service staff deal directly with customers. They help with any queries or problems customers have concerning the product or service provided by the organisation, dealing with refunds or returns, and so on. Customer service staff are frequently the first – and often the only – staff with whom a customer may come into contact.

QUICK response

Operatives and support staff are usually shown at the bottom of an organisational chart. Does this mean they are the least important members of the organisation? What does this say about drawing organisational charts as hierarchies?

ACTIVITY

In the activity on p 87, you constructed an organisation chart for your school or college or an organisation with which you are familiar. Using this, now identify the levels of job roles within the organisation.

THE BENEFITS OF TEAM MEMBERSHIP

On p 128, you looked at teams in relation to the role of the supervisor. However, teams are found at all levels in organisations. Teams bring benefits to individual employees and to the organisation by:

- helping them to achieve objectives and targets;
- developing an awareness of the needs of team members;
- improving the commitment of team members to the job role.

PEOPLE IN GROUPS

People are not solitary beings. They tend to come together in groups for several reasons, such as:

- to establish relationships with others;
- to gain recognition as a member of an identifiable group, both from other group members and from people outside the group;
- to exert influence, either within the group or on outside events and circumstances;
- to obtain the help of others in carrying out activities or objectives;
- to share in an activity.

Teams are groups whose members have joined forces to carry out a specific task or to achieve a common objective.

A team is a group of individuals who have joined forces to achieve a common goal.

ACTIVITY

Identify and describe three groups to which you belong. These may be connected with your school or college, work or leisure pursuits. To what extent do you think these groups are teams? Explain your answers.

TEAMS IN ORGANISATIONS

Just as being in a group is important to people as individuals, organisations need teams to:

- carry out tasks and procedures which would be impossible for one person working on their own;
- ensure the best use is made of the skills and experience of individual employees;
- help in the management of the organisation: a team working together can be managed far more easily than several individuals working on their own;
- help in the spread of information;
- increase the commitment and motivation of employees. Individual employees who feel they are part of a team are more likely to feel a commitment to, and work hard to achieve the success of, the team than they are to feel commitment to work for the success of a large impersonal organisation of which they find it hard to feel a part.

ACHIEVING OBJECTIVES AND TARGETS THROUGH TEAMWORK

Objectives and targets can be more easily achieved if the members of a team work together as a cohesive unit, rather than pulling in different directions, each trying to achieve their own ends. Each team will have three different types of objectives and targets.

1 **Organisational objectives and targets** are the long- and short-term aims of the organisation within which the team is operating. The team is formed to contribute, with other teams, to the overall achievement of organisational objectives and targets.

2 **Team objectives and targets** are those specific objectives and targets the team has been formed to achieve. How far it achieves

these objectives and targets is a measure of the success of the team.

3 **Personal objectives and targets**, often called **hidden agendas**, are the objectives and targets individual members seek to achieve through the team. Individual members often measure the success of the team against how far they achieve their personal objectives and targets.

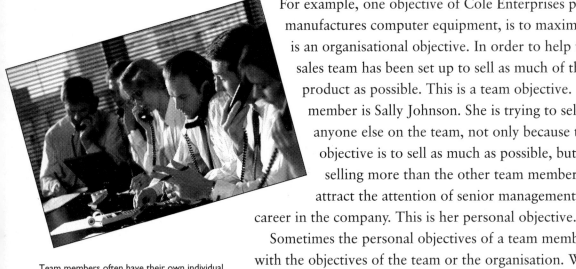

Team members often have their own individual objectives too.

For example, one objective of Cole Enterprises plc, which manufactures computer equipment, is to maximise income. This is an organisational objective. In order to help to achieve this, a sales team has been set up to sell as much of the company's product as possible. This is a team objective. One team member is Sally Johnson. She is trying to sell more than anyone else on the team, not only because the team objective is to sell as much as possible, but also because by selling more than the other team members she hopes to attract the attention of senior management and develop her career in the company. This is her personal objective.

Sometimes the personal objectives of a team member may conflict with the objectives of the team or the organisation. When this happens, the team leader must take action to resolve the conflict to ensure that the team and organisational objectives are achieved. In doing this, however, being aware of personal objectives is important. Unless team members have opportunities for achieving their own objectives and targets, their motivation and commitment to the team will decrease. This will lead to a decline in the effectiveness of the team.

ACTIVITY

Choose a team of which you are a member (this may be a team you identified for the activity on p 131). Identify the objectives of the team, and any personal objectives of the team members – including yourself. Is there any conflict between these objectives? How are any differences or conflicts resolved?

Clearly identified and accepted objectives are important factors in teamwork for several reasons:

- they establish criteria for the success of the team;
- they help in action-planning and decision-making;
- they provide a measure against which the progress of the team task can be monitored;
- they give purpose and direction to the team and its members;
- they provide a focus for the cohesiveness of the team, helping to develop the motivation and commitment of team members.

QUICK response

What feature of your GNVQ course is similar to the objectives of a team?

Approaches to achieving objectives and targets through teams include:

- shared goals, where all the members of the team understand, accept and assume joint responsibility for achieving team objectives and targets;
- helping team members to interact by listening and sharing their ideas. Team members should be encouraged to contribute fully to the activities of the team;
- sharing ideas, so that all team members are fully involved;
- ensuring that all team members support each other so that they all benefit from team membership.

ACTIVITIES AND TASKS

Employees at different levels in an organisation generally work in departments with a particular area of activity. Although they mostly work in teams within their departments, individual employees have specific tasks to undertake. These tasks contribute to the overall work of the team and the department.

HUMAN RESOURCING

Human resourcing is concerned with ensuring that the organisation has sufficient employees with the right skills. It is carried out by the Human Resources, or Personnel, Department, although managers in other departments do have some responsibility for the human resources of their own departments.

ACTIVITY

An important function of human resourcing is planning the future needs of the organisation. Make a list of all the factors you can think of that would need to be taken into consideration if you were asked to plan the human resource needs of your school or college for next September.

The main activities of human resourcing are:

- recruitment of new employees with appropriate skills and experience;
- training of employees to ensure that their skills are up to date and they can develop their careers;
- welfare, which is concerned with looking after the physical and emotional well-being of employees, including health and safety;
- salary and wages administration;
- ensuring that the organisation operates within the requirements of employment legislation, including issuing employees with contracts of employment (see p 113) and making sure they are treated fairly and equally (see p 122);
- keeping employee records, including records of pension contributions, sick pay and other benefits.

The Human Resources Department also plays a major role in advising the senior management of the organisation on pay, conditions of work and other employee-related matters. The department often has an advisory role in industrial relations and negotiations with trade unions.

PRODUCTION OF GOODS AND SERVICES

In a manufacturing organisation there is usually a separate Production Department which actually makes the organisation's goods. The Production Department is also responsible for monitoring the cost, usage and wastage of raw materials and components. The quality of the product must also be carefully monitored to ensure this meets the standards of the organisation and the requirements of customers. Sometimes the Production Department is involved in designing special tools and equipment which will produce the organisation's goods more efficiently and more cost-effectively.

The Production Department must also control the rate of production (that is the rate at which finished goods are produced) to ensure that sufficient goods are made, and kept in stock if necessary, to meet customers' demands. If too many goods are produced, however, these must be stored. Storing goods which are not required within a short time to meet customers' orders costs the organisation money, both for the storage of the goods and in terms of the cost of producing the goods for which no income will be received until they are sold.

An organisation which provides a service rather than goods does not normally have a Production Department. The service the organisation provides is produced by employees with specific skills and knowledge. They are often also involved in other areas of the organisation's operation.

ACCOUNTING

Accounting covers the management of the monetary or financial affairs of the business. This is usually the responsibility of the Company Accountant or Financial Manager, who may be at the head of an Accounts or Finance Department.

The Accounts Department sets the financial targets of the business. These are stated in a written budget, or forecast, normally covering a period of a year. Throughout the period of the budget, the department monitors the actual financial performance of the business against this. Any variances are reported to the senior management of the organisation so that appropriate action can be taken where necessary to ensure that the original financial targets are met.

QUICK response

Why is it important in business to set targets in financial terms rather than just in the numbers of goods or services to be sold?

The Accounts Department is also involved with calculating the costs and potential revenue (and therefore profit) of new projects.

It is the responsibility of the Accounts Department to pay invoices received in respect of expenditure incurred by the organisation, and to receive and bank money from the sale of the organisation's goods or services. Records of all financial transactions, including both incoming and outgoing payments, are kept. These are used to produce accounts (which are financial statements of the organisation's activities covering a specific period) and cash flow statements (which are records showing the inflow and outflow of funds to the organisation, and therefore show the actual cash the organisation currently has on hand and at the bank, which can be used to pay bills, wages and salaries, and so on).

ACTIVITY

One of the most important accounting records that is compiled in an organisation is the cash flow statement. Explain why this is so important and give reasons why it should be kept up to date.

Information for management is prepared in the form of reports and management accounts. In addition, the Accounts Department produces some financial information for government departments. This includes VAT returns (records of value added tax paid to other businesses and collected on behalf of Customs and Excise) and statutory financial accounts which must be submitted to the Inland Revenue after the end of each of the organisation's financial years.

Accounting is covered in more detail in Unit 4.

ADMINISTRATION

In larger organisations, administration is carried out by an Administration Department. The Administration Department is responsible for helping the smooth running of the organisation, including dealing with legal and insurance matters, buying office equipment, maintenance of offices, making planning applications, and so on. Services for other departments may also be provided by the Administration Department. These include photocopying, word processing and desk-top publishing, telephone and fax services, designing and printing forms, filing and keeping records in a central registry, organising meetings, arranging business travel, and so on. An efficient Administration Department is therefore essential, although in a smaller organisation many of these services will be carried out by staff in individual departments (for example, the Personnel Department may do its own word processing and photocopying, and keep its own records).

SELLING

Any business organisation which provides goods or services must sell those goods or services in order to make enough income to cover its costs. The methods used and the type of employees involved in the selling process depend on the type of organisation, the goods or services it produces and its customers.

A shop, for example, uses sales assistants to sell goods to customers, normally private individuals who come into the shop. The manufacturer who supplies the shop with the goods for resale to its customers probably has a team of sales executives who visit the shop and others like it to persuade them to buy the goods. Each sales executive may have an exclusive area – that is, all the shops which sell (or might sell) the organisation's goods in a certain area are considered to be customers of one sales executive. Similarly, businesses which produce machinery, raw materials and other goods and services, which are used by other businesses to produce their own goods, have sales teams who visit customers and potential customers in order to persuade them to buy the organisation's product. Some businesses which sell to the general public use teams of sales executives who visit potential customers in their homes. The sales executive normally makes an appointment to do this, and this method of selling is used extensively by, for example, insurance companies and banks selling financial services, double glazing manufacturers, and so on. Other businesses use salespeople who sell door to door, either from a catalogue which may have been previously delivered to the house (such as Avon and Betterwear), or from a mobile shop.

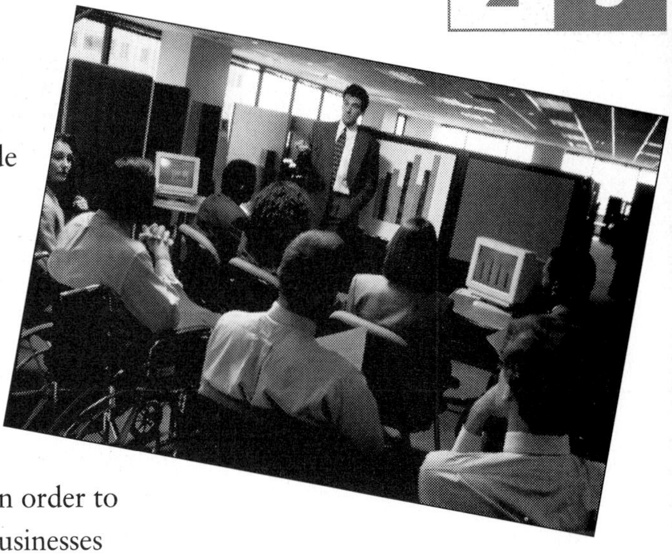

A sales executive may visit customers and make a presentation to persuade them to buy goods or services.

Whichever method of selling is used by an organisation, selling is a skilled job which is usually done by employees who have been specially trained. It is essential that any employee selling an organisation's products to customers is thoroughly familiar with the organisation and its products and is able to communicate effectively with the customers. Many larger organisations have a Sales Department whose sole activity is to sell to the organisation's customers.

It is not only profit-making business organisations in the private sector who need to sell their product. Many public sector organisations, such as schools and hospitals, receive funds from local and national government according to the number of clients they serve. These organisations therefore also have to 'sell' their services to potential customers. A head teacher showing their school to parents who are choosing a new school for their child is, in fact, 'selling' the services of the school to potential customers.

ACTIVITY

'Selling is the most important activity in an organisation.' In groups of four or five, discuss this statement, justifying your own position. Compare your findings as a class.

MARKETING

While it is the job of the Sales Department actually to sell an organisation's products to potential customers, it is the function of the Marketing Department to ensure that there are potential customers who know about the organisation and the products it supplies, and who want to buy those products.

For customers to want to buy an organisation's product, that product must be:

- the right product (that is, the product the customers want);
- at the right price (that is, at a price customers are willing to pay);
- in the right place (that is, available where customers want and expect to be able to buy the product);
- at the right time (that is, it should be available when there is a demand for it).

QUICK response

Why is market research important in business?

From this you will see that the emphasis is very much on providing what customers want. An organisation which does not strive to provide exactly what its customers want will find those customers buying elsewhere, from competitors who *do* provide what the customers want.

An essential activity of marketing is finding out exactly what it is that customers want, and how much they are prepared to pay for it. This is called market research and it may be done either from published records of trends in demand (**secondary research**), or by actually asking customers and potential customers what they want from a product (**primary research**).

Once the organisation knows what its customers and potential customers want, and produces a product which meets that want, it must make sure that customers and potential customers know about, and want to buy, its product. This, therefore, is the next activity of the Marketing Department, often called **promotion**. Promotion is carried out through advertising and other means.

The activities of marketing are covered in more detail in Unit 3.

DISTRIBUTING

An organisation which produces goods must deliver those goods to its customers, or to retail outlets if the goods are to be resold. Distribution may be carried out by post, road, air or sea, depending on the size and weight of the product and the location of the customer.

Large organisations have their own Distribution Department with their own vehicles, but in smaller organisations distribution may be an activity of another department such as the Production Department, using outside hauliers and other delivery systems. It is the responsibility of employees involved in distribution to ensure that the organisation's goods are delivered on time (that is, when the customer wants them or when they were promised) and undamaged. If the organisation runs its own vehicles, it must keep records of drivers and journeys. The number of hours which drivers may work – including the hours spent actually driving – have been established by law and must not be exceeded. Vehicles must be maintained and insurance and licences (vehicle licences and operators' licences, which allow businesses to operate commercial vehicles) kept up to date. The Distribution Department must also monitor the costs of fuel and vehicle maintenance and ensure goods are delivered by the most cost-effective route and method.

ACTIVITY

Restrictions such as drivers' hours do not apply to private motorists. Far more road accidents, however, involve private motorists than drivers of heavy goods vehicles. In view of this, as a group, discuss whether you think applying drivers' hours restrictions to operators of commercial vehicles is fair? Should drivers' hours restrictions perhaps also be applied to private motorists?

PROVIDING CUSTOMER SERVICE

Customers have needs, and all organisations must strive to meet those needs in order to sell their products. In addition to the need for the right product at the right price, customers have needs for:

- **information** about the organisation and the goods or services it provides;
- **assistance** in choosing goods and services which meet their requirements;
- **care and attention** in all dealings with the organisation;
- **refunds, replacements and after-sales service** as appropriate.

QUICK response

List three ways in which good customer service will lead to a high level of sales.

A business which meets these needs provides a high standard of customer service. The benefits of this will be customer satisfaction and a high level of sales.

The world of business today is becoming increasingly competitive, with organisations providing the same or similar products and all competing for the same customers. An organisation which does not offer a high level of customer service will lose customers to another organisation which does. Creating and maintaining a good impression and dealing efficiently with customers is vital. Providing customer service is therefore the responsibility of every employee. Many larger businesses, such as British Telecom and stores like Marks and Spencer, have dedicated Customer Service Departments with staff specially trained in dealing with customers, handling complaints or queries and developing good customer relations.

CLEANING

The cleanliness of premises where people work is emphasised by both health and safety and employment legislation. This includes keeping work areas free from dirt and debris which could cause a health hazard, and the cleaning of floors, walls and ceilings. Where food production or preparation is involved, the need for cleanliness is even more critical. A similar situation exists in hospitals, doctors' surgeries and anywhere where there is a danger of contamination.

All business organisations must employ cleaners. In some cases, cleaning is undertaken by an outside cleaning contractor (a firm which specialises in cleaning business premises), as this may be more cost-effective than for the business to employ its own cleaning staff. If hazardous substances are involved, as in the case of a chemical spillage, it may be necessary to obtain the services of a specialist cleaner with particular knowledge and skills in dealing with the hazardous substance.

SECURITY

A consideration of increasing importance for many organisations is security. This may be of:

- buildings, machinery and other equipment;
- stocks of raw materials and finished goods;
- money;
- employees;
- customers.

Many larger organisations employ security staff to maintain safety and security. Sometimes, however, as with cleaning, an organisation may employ an outside security firm. The range of activities includes:

- security guards patrolling sites and premises in order to prevent theft;
- uniformed or plain-clothes store detectives patrolling stores to prevent shoplifting;
- security staff monitoring the behaviour of employees to guard against internal fraud or theft;
- transporting large sums of money in armoured vehicles.

Some organisations need particular types of security staff, such as lifeguards in leisure centres. In certain areas, the need for security has grown with technological and other developments. Hi-tech products, such as computers and computer peripherals (like modems), have become targets for theft, as have newly developed products in other fields, such as drugs. A particularly disturbing development is the need for hospitals and similar establishments to provide security to protect their staff from assault and to guard against crimes such as baby snatching.

In all areas of activity, employees at different levels undertake individual activities and have specific tasks to carry out. Some employees, for example, actually produce the organisation's goods or services, input information on to a computer or do the filing, while others are concerned with managing the organisation, its employees and resources. Managing involves activities such as planning, decision-making, problem-solving, and setting and achieving targets. The actual tasks which employees carry out may be routine, day-to-day tasks, or non-routine tasks such as dealing with emergencies or accidents.

PRESENTING THE RESULTS OF AN INVESTIGATION INTO JOB ROLES

The portfolio assignment for this element asks you to make a presentation describing one job role and the activities and tasks undertaken by a person carrying out that role. Advice on making presentations was given in Unit 1, p 77. You should read this again before attempting the portfolio assignment.

PORTFOLIO ASSIGNMENT

This portfolio assignment builds on work you have done in previous activities and portfolio assignments, particularly the portfolio assignment for Element 2.1.

TASK 1

Select an organisation with which you are familiar and identify *three* job roles at different levels within that organisation. Write a summary describing each job role, its day-to-day activities and tasks. Explain how team membership increases the job holders' abilities to perform their job roles.

TASK 2

Choose one of the job roles selected for Task 1. Prepare a presentation describing the job role and the activities and tasks carried out by the job holder. In particular, you should describe how the person, either individually or as part of a team, deals with one routine problem-solving task and one non-routine task, such as an emergency or accident. Your description of dealing with the non-routine task should be illustrated with posters or signs giving instructions for dealing with the emergency or accident. You should keep a record of your presentation, including any visual aids, in your Portfolio of Evidence.

This portfolio assignment also presents an opportunity to gather evidence for the following core skills:

- Communication – take part in discussions; produce written material;
- Information Technology – prepare information; process information; present information.

PREPARING FOR EMPLOYMENT OR SELF-EMPLOYMENT

In Unit 1 (p 59) you saw that there are different types of employment, including:

- full-time;
- part-time;
- permanent;
- temporary;
- skilled;
- unskilled;
- self-employed.

In addition, you have seen that people work in different types of organisations:

- sole trader;
- partnership;
- private limited company;
- public limited company;
- franchise;
- co-operative;
- state-owned.

As there are so many different types of employment, it is important that you find out as much as you can about these and decide on the type of work that you would like to do. This will help you to prepare for employment in the future. We live in a competitive world, and this can be seen in the competition for jobs as much as in any other area of business. With careful preparation, however, you will have an excellent chance of finding an employment opportunity to suit you and of getting the type of job you want.

TYPES OF EMPLOYMENT AND SELF-EMPLOYMENT

PAID EMPLOYMENT

Most employment is paid employment – that is, the person in employment receives some form of remuneration in return for the work they do. The most usual type of remuneration is in the form of wages or salary.

People need paid employment to earn money to buy the things they need to live and the things they want in order to make life comfortable and enjoyable. Every day, people all over the world go out to work in jobs for which they earn a wage or salary. There is an almost infinite variety of paid employment. This can range from working as an administrative assistant in an office to being the managing director of a major international company, from nursing to being an airline pilot, from being an accountant to designing computer games.

Paid employment is found in both private and public sector organisations (see p 9). It may be full- or part-time, skilled or unskilled, permanent or temporary.

ACTIVITY

Start your preparation for employment or self-employment *now*. As a class, make a list of as many types of paid employment as you can. Put this on a noticeboard which your class can keep for information about employment and self-employment. Individually, identify types of paid employment you would like to do. Which do you think you could do? Keep your own lists in an 'Employment Planning' file, together with other material you gather or produce for later activities.

VOLUNTARY EMPLOYMENT

Voluntary employment is employment for which the employee does not receive any remuneration or payment. Sometimes the employer pays out-of-pocket expenses such as travelling costs or the cost of telephone calls.

Most voluntary employment is with local charities and involves working on local projects. In many areas there are volunteer bureaux which co-ordinate local charity work and recruit volunteers. The work can be skilled or unskilled, manual, such as building work or gardening for the elderly, or clerical and administrative, such as word processing or accounting.

Sometimes, voluntary work can be done abroad. Voluntary Service Overseas (VSO) is an organisation which recruits voluntary workers for various projects throughout the world. The types of workers they need are varied – from teachers, nurses and administrators to manual workers. Most projects last for one or more years.

Voluntary first-aiders may be seen at many public events.

Besides voluntary work for a charity, it is often possible to find voluntary employment with organisations such as schools and hospitals. These are often short-staffed, due to lack of funds, and welcome voluntary helpers. The type of work involved is usually unskilled, such as classroom helper or hospital porter. This is mainly because the skilled positions in these organisations require very specific knowledge and experience, normally only gained after a period of advanced study.

While voluntary employment does not pay a living salary or wage, and is not normally what people look for as their main employment, there are many reasons why a period of voluntary employment can be of great value in developing your career:

- Voluntary employment can provide a valuable opportunity for personal development.
- Many employers place a high value on voluntary work undertaken by a prospective employee as this shows enthusiasm and commitment to work.
- If suitable paid employment is not available, voluntary employment will help an employee to continue practising their skills (in particular, transferable core skills such as communication, application of number and possibly information technology), which means that a future employer, offering paid employment, will see that the employee has kept their skills up to date and has actively developed themselves rather than just waited for paid employment to come along. This is especially valuable if voluntary employment in the area in which paid employment is sought can be found, even though the actual job might be in a different kind of organisation

ACTIVITY

Find out what types of voluntary employment are available in your area. You can do this by contacting organisations such as hospitals, schools, the Citizens Advice Bureau and other voluntary bureaux and organisations. Make a list of opportunities for voluntary employment in which you would be interested and which you feel you could do.

SELF-EMPLOYMENT

Self-employment means working for yourself in your own business, either on your own or with others. Changing employment patterns in the UK over recent years have led to an increasing trend towards self-employment. To many people, self-employment is an attractive alternative to working for another employer. If your aim is to become self-employed, you can follow several routes to achieve this.

- **Joining a family business**: that is, a business which has already been set up by others in your family. Family businesses operate in all sectors of industry, and are often passed on from parents to their children. Farms have often been owned and worked by the same family for generations; shops and other small businesses have names like Mitchell and Son, or Sommers and Daughter; professional firms of solicitors or accountants may list their partners as Jones, Jones and Pritchett, where the second Jones is the daughter or son of the first.

Family-run businesses may be small corner shops or may grow into very large retail businesses over the generations.

Most family businesses are small, although this is not necessarily the case. It is not unusual for a successful family business to grow and become a large public company. In this case, of course, it will no longer remain a family business. If members of the family retain a large enough shareholding, however, they may keep control of the business. In this way, a son or daughter who starts working in a small family business may eventually become a director of a large public limited company.

ACTIVITY

Construct a table of small family businesses in your area, giving their type of organisation (such as sole trader, partnership, private limited company) and describing their activities, as follows.

Name of business	Type of organisation	Activities

- **Starting your own business:** If you have a particular skill or ability and can provide a service which is in demand, or can make something which customers want to buy, you may want to start your own business. Opportunities for starting your own business are almost limitless, but there are several questions you must ask yourself before committing yourself too deeply. 'How many people are likely to buy my product or service?' 'What competition already exists – and can I really compete with it?' 'How much will my product or service cost to produce and can I sell it at a price at which I will make a profit?' 'Is the market for my product or service growing or contracting?'

  In addition to questions such as these, you must ask questions about your own attributes and your suitability for self-employment. Are you self-motivated enough to make a go of your own business – if you are self-employed you will not have somebody else telling you what to do and when to do it. You will stand or fall according to your own efforts. Do you have the drive and confidence to go out and get customers for your product or service – and to persuade them to buy it? Are you good at organising yourself, and others if you are going to employ them? Do you have the administrative and financial knowledge and ability to run your own business?

  If you do not have some of these attributes yourself, it may be that you can employ someone who has, or perhaps go into partnership with them (in which case the business will be jointly owned – see p 19). For example, Narinder Jhesi wanted to start her own business designing and making saris. However, she knew that,

QUICK response

Make a list of as many things you could do to start your own business as you can think of. You will find other ideas in books on starting your own business in the library.

while she could design and make them herself, she did not have the administrative ability to run the business, and the thought of actually going out and selling her product to shops and other customers terrified her. She decided to form a partnership business with one of her friends from college, Lyndam Sharma, who had studied business. The partnership of Jhesi and Sharma is now one of the best known suppliers of saris in the Midlands and is renowned for the quality and design of their product.

- **Buying a franchise**: Another way of starting your own business and becoming self-employed is to purchase a franchise (see p 24). Rosemary Jefford is currently purchasing a franchise to run a Body Shop in South East London. In this way she is in control of her own business while enjoying the benefits of being part of a large and well-known organisation.

Of course, starting your own business costs money, and it can be some time before the business begins to make a profit. Finance for start-up costs, such as premises, equipment and raw materials, can often be obtained as a bank loan, although the owner of the business is normally expected to put some of their own money into the business at the outset. Capital is also required to bridge the period between starting the business and receiving the first income from sales. This can be several months, during which time the business is incurring expenses, such as rent and rates, raw materials, wages and salaries, and so on – all of which have to be paid out although no money is yet coming in. Insufficient funds at this time can put the new business out of business even before it has really got started – and even though, on paper, it may be profitable.

Finance is therefore one of the most important factors to take into consideration when thinking about becoming self-employed and starting your own business. Of course, there are many forms of self-employment which do not require much finance to start up. These types of businesses mainly involve the application of skills. They are carried on by one person working alone, such as plumbers, window cleaners, curtain and soft-furnishing makers, freelance photographers, writers and artists, consultants, and so on. A considerable amount of help and advice is available to people who wish to set up their own businesses. This is mainly provided through Training and Enterprise Councils (TECs). For example, Business Start-Up and other Enterprise Schemes not only ensure that people starting their own businesses have the basic knowledge needed to run a small business and are aware of the dangers and pitfalls, but also offer a grant of a weekly allowance for up to 15 months to help the new business to get through the period when it may not be making enough for the owner to draw any money for their personal use.

ACTIVITY

Investigate and gather information on the help that is available for people who want to become self-employed and start their own businesses in your area. A good place to begin your investigation is by asking your local Training and Enterprise Council (TEC – see p 154).

OPPORTUNITIES FOR EMPLOYMENT AND SELF-EMPLOYMENT

Opportunities for employment and self-employment may be found:

- locally;
- nationally;
- internationally.

Most people leaving school or college and looking for employment confine their initial job search to the area in which they live or to which they can easily travel. There are two main reasons for this.

- Wages and salaries are usually low when first starting work, so most young people cannot afford to move away from home or travel long distances to work.
- When you are just starting out it can be stressful to leave your family and friends or the environment where you feel secure.

Increasingly, however, people seeking employment are having to look further than their own area. The decline in manufacturing and other forms of industry in Britain (see p 37) means that opportunities for employment in some areas have been reduced dramatically. It may be necessary to move to a new area in order to find employment. In addition, employment opportunities for people with certain types of skills are better in some areas than others (this was discussed in Unit 1).

Since barriers to the free movement of labour between member states of the EU were removed, there have been more opportunities for employment abroad. A major barrier to working abroad is, of course, language. Such a barrier does not exist for British people wishing to live and work in English-speaking countries such as Australia, Canada and the USA. However, there are more restrictions on living and working in these countries than in countries in the EU.

The future will probably see an increase in the number of Britons working in Europe. Conversely, there is also likely to be an increase in the number of Europeans working in Britain. This means that competition in the employment market will increase both at home and abroad. The qualifications, skills and experience of potential employees will become more important to employers in selecting their employees.

FINDING OUT ABOUT EMPLOYMENT OPPORTUNITIES

QUICK response

Before you read this section, pause and think about your own plans for finding employment. Identify the areas where you feel you need help.

At first, investigating the jobs market and finding out about employment opportunities that will suit you may seem daunting. Where do you start?

It is important to remember that you do not have to 'go it alone' when planning your career or seeking employment. There are many people and other sources of information that you can go to for information and advice about employment and self-employment opportunities.

JOB CENTRES

Job Centres, which are part of the Department for Education and Employment and funded by the Government, can be found in most towns and cities. In these, trained personnel can help you to find local employment with firms who have notified the Centre of vacancies. The details of each vacancy are written on a card which is placed on a display board. People seeking employment go into the Job Centre and look at the jobs displayed to see if one is suitable. Besides local jobs, Job Centres have access to a national database of information about employment prospects. While Job Centres are not sources of careers guidance, they can help with making applications for jobs, and give advice and information about training schemes.

ACTIVITY

Visit your local Job Centre and ask about the services they offer people looking for employment. Look carefully at the vacancies and opportunities which are displayed. Write down the details of any which you think would be suitable for both a school or college leaver and for you in the future when you may want to develop your career further. Put copies of these details on the class noticeboard and in your own 'Employment Opportunities' file.

MEDIA

The media can be good sources of information about employment opportunities. Local and national newspapers have sections containing advertisements for jobs. Many national newspapers specialise in different types of employment on different days. It is a good idea to find out which papers specialise in the type of employment you are interested in and on which day. Specialist professional magazines are also good sources of information about employment opportunities in their own field. Study any professional magazines in areas of employment which interest you. Radio and television are also sometimes sources of information about employment opportunities. By following the business news on television and radio, the business sections of daily and Sunday national newspapers, and in magazines such as *The Economist*, you can often find out which companies are expanding or relocating in your area. If you contact these direct, you may find out about openings before they are advertised.

ACTIVITY

Look at the job advertisements in as many local and national newspapers (daily, Sunday and weekly) and magazines, including professional and special interest magazines, as you can (your school/college or local library will provide a good source for these). Find out which magazines carry advertisements, and on which days newspapers carry advertisements, for jobs you would be interested in and which would be suitable for you. Copy any advertisements which interest you.

At the same time, look out for items of news about local businesses or businesses which are moving into your area, which might provide suitable employment opportunities.

CAREERS OFFICES

Careers Offices are run by the local authority in most areas. They are staffed by specially trained careers officers who will provide guidance and advice on employment opportunities in the local area. Usually, they maintain contact with local employers and so are aware of current and forthcoming vacancies. Careers officers frequently visit schools and colleges to give guidance to students on the choice of a career.

ACTIVITY

If you have not already had a discussion with an officer from your local Careers Office – or you would like a further discussion – make an appointment with a careers officer. Keep a record of your discussion, and make sure you follow up any advice or leads given to you.

EMPLOYMENT AGENCIES

Employment agencies are privately run organisations. Their purpose is to find employees to fill vacancies which have been notified by employers. The employer pays a fee to the employment agency for this, but the service is normally free to applicants. Employment agencies can be found in the high streets of most large towns. You can

A high street employment agency.

find the addresses and telephone numbers of local employment agencies in *Yellow Pages*.

ACTIVITY

Make a list of the names and addresses of employment agencies in your area. Locate and mark these on a map of the area (you can also mark the location of the Careers Office and Job Centre). Visit as many of the employment agencies on your list as you can. If there are several employment agencies, it may be easiest to split them among several students. Find out what sort of employment opportunities each agency currently has on its books. You will probably be able to do this by looking at the advertisements in the agencies' windows or displayed outside. Mark on your list those agencies with opportunities which would suit you when you leave school or college. Copy out the details of any specific opportunities that interest you.

FEDERATION OF SELF-EMPLOYED

The Federation of Self-Employed is a national organisation which has been established to represent the interests of self-employed people. It provides advice and guidance on various matters including taxation and employment law. Although its primary purpose is to help people who are already self-employed, it is also a valuable source of information if you are considering starting your own business.

BANKS

All the major high street banks have small-business sections. Although their prime purpose is to obtain business for the bank, they do provide valuable information and advice on financial matters and constructing business plans. Most banks also have a range of booklets outlining their services for small businesses and containing information to help small businesses.

Many banks and other organisations offer help and advice to people wishing to start their own business.

TRAINING AND ENTERPRISE COUNCILS

Training and Enterprise Councils (TECs) also provide help and support to people wishing to start their own businesses. They will give advice on constructing a business plan, and, in cases where the business plan is approved, can provide financial assistance through a Business Start-Up or other enterprise scheme. As TECs have close connections with local businesses, they are also aware of local employment needs and can often give information about employment opportunities.

ACTIVITY

If you have not already contacted your local TEC, do so now. Find out what services, including opportunities for further training, they offer to school and college leavers seeking employment. Find out also about the help and assistance available for young people who want to start their own business.

CHARITABLE ORGANISATIONS

Information about opportunities for voluntary employment can be obtained by making direct contact with charities such as Voluntary Service Overseas (VSO) or the Red Cross. While most people who work for charitable organisations do so in a voluntary capacity, charities do have some paid employees. The Prince's Youth Business Trust is a charity established by HRH The Prince of Wales to help young people wishing to set up their own businesses.

Skills needed for employment and self-employment

Whatever type of employment you eventually decide to go into, you will need certain skills. A skill is something you can do. Once you have identified the type of employment or self-employment you want, you must analyse the skills that are needed for that type of employment or self-employment. This is so that you can ensure that you have the skills required both to enter and to progress in your chosen employment.

It is important that you identify the type of employment or self-employment you want as soon as possible so that you can analyse the skills needed. You can then compare these with the skills you have now. If you haven't the right skills now, you can begin acquiring them for when you start applying for jobs or setting up your own business.

You will need two types of skills:

- core skills;
- vocational or occupational skills.

Core skills

Core skills are *general skills* which you need for most types of employment. Core skills are also known as **transferable skills** because they apply to a range of employment opportunities and can therefore be *transferred* from one type of employment to another. The main core skills you will need are:

- **The ability to work with others**: As you have seen, being part of a team has benefits for both employees and employers: to be effective as a team member, it is important that you can work with others and contribute fully to the work of the team.
- **The ability to work independently**: Although working with others as part of a team is important, many jobs also require employees to work on their own, completing individual tasks which form part of their employment. Together, these individual tasks form the work of the team and of the organisation and an employee must therefore be able to work independently on their own tasks.

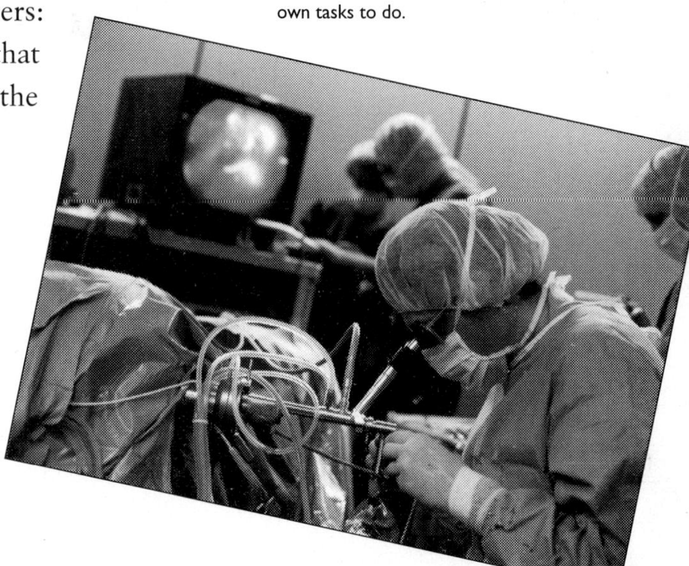

Within a team individual members still have their own tasks to do.

QUICK response

As you read through this section on core skills, make a list of examples which show how you have applied each skill at home, school, college or work.

- **The ability to manage time**: Time management involves more than just arriving at work on time and leaving at the end of the working day. Time management skills are needed to ensure that the most effective use is made of the time at work so that tasks are completed on time, maximum productivity is achieved and time is not wasted.

ACTIVITY

Time management is a skill that is valuable in many areas of life – including time spent at school or college. In groups of two or three, discuss how you could improve the way in which you spend your time at school or college. What techniques could you use, such as using a time diary to plan your day? How would better time management help you to achieve your goals?

- **The ability to make decisions**: Employees at all levels have to make decisions about what to do at work: how to carry out a task, what equipment or materials to use, what information is required, and so on. The higher the employee is in the organisation, the higher the level of decision to be taken. Decision-making is an essential skill for progressing in your chosen employment, and vital if you are considering self-employment (when there will be no one else to take the decisions for you).
- **The ability to solve problems**: In all types of employment there are problems to be solved. These may be routine problems which occur on a day-to-day basis (such as running out of a component used in production, or scheduling work so that tasks are done on time), or non-routine problems (such as failing to meet sales or profit targets). Most problems involve both planning and decision-making. As with decision-making, the higher the level of the employee, the more responsibility they will have for solving problems.
- **The ability to plan**: Planning is an essential skill which is closely connected with time management, decision-making and problem-solving. It is only through careful planning that the targets of the organisation will be met. Work planning is as important for an individual employee as it is for the organisation as a whole. Planning is one of the grading criteria for your GNVQ assessments.

- **Information-seeking**: In many areas of employment, you will need to find information to help you to carry out your task, and information-seeking is therefore a skill you should develop. Like planning, information-seeking is one of the criteria used in grading your GNVQ assessments.
- **Evaluating**: Another criterion used in grading your GNVQ assessments is evaluating your own work. An essential aspect of employment is maintaining quality of work. It is only by evaluating the work you have produced, comparing it with an established or anticipated standard, that you can ensure that the quality of your work is satisfactory.
- **Communication**: Whether working with others as part of a team, or working independently, an employee must communicate with others to receive instructions and orders from superiors and customers, to give instructions to subordinates and to pass information to subordinates, superiors, customers and others. Without effective communications, no organisation could function properly. The importance of effective communication skills is reflected in the fact that communications is one of the mandatory core skill units of the GNVQ you are studying.
- **Application of number**: Another mandatory core skill unit of your GNVQ is application of number. The application of numerical information is a part of virtually every type of employment, in that nearly all jobs require calculations to be made, measurements to be taken and so on.

ACTIVITY

Complete the following table giving examples of the application of number for each job.

Job title	Example of application of number
Chef	Calculating the quantities of ingredients used in cooking.
Shop sales assistant	
Plumber	
Architect	
Personnel assistant	
Landscape gardener	

- **Information technology**: In today's world, information technology is used throughout business. Its application can be seen on the production line in the factory, in computer-controlled machines and equipment, in computerised stock control systems, in accounting and management information systems and in many other areas of an organisation's operation. Many applications are now integrated so that information produced in one application is available for use in another. The ability to use information technology is therefore essential to current employment opportunities. Information technology is the third of the mandatory core skill units of your GNVQ.

VOCATIONAL OR OCCUPATIONAL SKILLS

Vocational or occupational skills are employment-specific skills which vary according to the particular type of employment you choose. The variety of occupational skills is as wide as the variety of jobs. For example, the skills required by an airline pilot are different to the skills needed by a chef. It is essential, therefore, that when you have identified the type of employment or self-employment you would like, you also identify the particular occupational skills needed.

Different jobs call for different skills.

ACTIVITY

In the activities on pp 144, 146, 151 and 153, you collected details of employment opportunities which would be suitable for you and in which you would be interested. For each one, identify and make a list of the core and vocational skills needed.

Most jobs which are suitable for school or college leavers as initial employment require a minimum of occupational skills to start, relying more on the core skills described above. Occupational skills can often be acquired through on-the-job training or further education while in employment, perhaps by day-release study (where an employer allows an employee time off during the normal working week so that they can attend college) or through further study at night school. Sometimes this additional study or training is paid for by the employer, but often the employee must pay for it themself. It is important, however, to continue developing and improving both core and occupational skills throughout your career.

IDENTIFYING YOUR OWN STRENGTHS AND WEAKNESSES IN RELATION TO SKILLS FOR EMPLOYMENT AND SELF-EMPLOYMENT

You have seen that whatever type of employment or self-employment you hope to enter, you must have:

- core, or general, skills which apply to all types of employment and self-employment;
- vocational, or occupational, skills which are specific to each type of employment or self-employment.

If you begin to develop the skills you need now, this will help you to achieve the type of employment or self-employment you want. In order to do this you must understand your own skills achievements and your own strengths and weaknesses in relation to the skills you need for employment or self-employment. This will enable you to build on your strengths and strengthen your weaknesses.

ACTIVITY

Using the list of employment opportunities and skills required from the last activity, construct a table identifying skills you have, those you need to develop, and how you can do this.

PORTFOLIO ASSIGNMENT

TASK 1
Arrange to interview three people in different types of employment. They may be people you know, such as family or friends, or may work in the same organisation, such as a tutor, administrative officer or librarian at your school or college. Interviews may be carried out individually or in groups. Write a record of each interview, describing how each person came to be in their current employment and the skills they need for their employment. Each record should state the name and job title of the person interviewed.

TASK 2
Identify three opportunities for employment or self-employment, locally, nationally and internationally, which would interest you and which you feel would suit you. Write a description of each opportunity and include copies of job advertisements, articles, careers information and other information you have collected.

TASK 3
Construct a chart showing the various core and vocational skills needed for employment and self-employment. In the chart, match your own skills and achievements against these, and show how you can develop skills as appropriate. You may use the table completed for the activity on p 159 for this task.

TASK 4
Using the chart you produced for Task 3 as a starting point, analyse your own strengths and weaknesses in relation to the skills you need for employment or self-employment. Make a table of these, as follows:

Strengths	Weaknesses

Write notes on how you feel you can build on your strengths and strengthen your weaknesses. Make an appointment to see a careers advisor from your school or college, or an officer from your local Careers Office, to discuss your strengths and weaknesses in relation to employment or self-employment. Make a record of the discussion, summarising what was said and who the discussion was with.

This portfolio assignment also presents an opportunity to gather evidence for the following core skills:

- Communication – take part in discussions; produce written material; read and respond to written materials;
- Information Technology – prepare information; process information; present information.

3
UNIT

Consumers and customers

CONTENTS

OUTLINE

In a market economy, consumers and customers create demand for products and services, which business organisations meet. Demand can lead to increased employment opportunities in order to produce these goods and services. In this unit you will look at consumers and customers as markets for businesses, and see the effect they have on competition and demand. You will also examine the individual needs and wants of consumers and customers and how these influence marketing activities, and the level of customer service that businesses must give.

After completing this unit you will be able to:

1 explain the importance of consumers and customers;
2 plan, design and produce promotional material;
3 provide customer service;
4 present proposals for improvements to

customer service.

THE IMPORTANCE OF CONSUMERS AND CUSTOMERS

All business organisations need consumers and customers for the products and services they provide.

- **Consumers** are people who use the goods and services provided by business organisations.
- **Customers** are people who buy and pay for the goods and services provided by business organisations.

We are therefore all consumers because we all use some goods and services. We are probably all customers, too, because we do buy some of the goods and services we use. However, we do not buy all of the goods and services we use and we do not use all of the goods and services we buy.

We use many goods and services we do not pay for – because they are bought and paid for by someone else. For example, the pen you use to make notes or write your assignments at school or college may have been given to you as a present. At home, you may produce work on a computer or watch television which uses electricity that is paid for by a parent or guardian.

We also buy goods and services we do not use. For example, we buy birthday presents for our friends and family – and maybe other gifts for boyfriends or girlfriends.

The distinction between consumers and customers is an important one. A business must know who the consumers of its products are and who its customers are. The manufacturer of an expensive perfume may produce perfume to be worn by women. The customers who actually buy the perfume, however, may be mainly men, who want to give the perfume to their girlfriends or wives.

ACTIVITY

Think about all the goods and services you have bought or used. Make two lists. On the first list identify all the goods and services, and the organisations which provided them, which you have used but not paid for yourself. On the second list identify all the goods and services which you bought but did not use yourself (in other words, which you bought for somebody else, possibly as a present), and the organisations which provided them.

THE EFFECT OF CONSUMERS ON SALES OF GOODS AND SERVICES

Consumers have a vital effect on sales of goods and services. They:

- create demand;
- cause changes in demand;
- stimulate the supply of goods and services to meet demand.

QUICK response

A consumer is ...
A customer is ...

Demand is created when people want something and are prepared to pay for it. If people want computers which can exchange messages electronically using telephone lines, and are prepared to pay for them, a demand will be created for such computers (or the hardware and software that enable existing computers to provide the facility).

Demand for a product or service stimulates the supply of that product or service by one or more business organisations. A business organisation, however, will only produce and supply goods or services if it knows that the income it will receive by selling them will exceed the costs of the business, at least in the long term.

In order to stimulate the supply of a product, therefore, the demand must be **strong**; that is, there must be enough consumers (or prospective consumers) who want the product and are prepared to pay a high enough price for it to cover the costs a business will incur in producing it. The stronger the demand, the more likely that sales will be high and that total income from sales will exceed costs by a greater amount. This will result in larger profits and other businesses may be tempted to supply the same product in order to share in those profits.

If demand is **weak**, on the other hand, there may not be enough consumers willing to pay a high enough price for the product to cover the costs of producing it. In this case, the demand is unlikely to stimulate supply of the product or service as sales will be low and total income from sales may not be enough to cover costs. The Government pays for many services which are considered essential, such as health and education, policing and defence, but which many individual consumers would be unlikely to pay for themselves.

Fashions change and so does demand for goods and services – in the early 1960s the Everly Brothers were just as popular as Oasis would become in the mid-1990s.

An important aspect of demand is that it does not remain the same. Goods and services which are in demand one year are forgotten the next. As you will see later in this unit, there are many reasons for this, including changes in taste and fashion. As consumers' tastes change, so demand for products and services changes. Clothes which were fashionable last year are no longer worn; pop groups which were number one a few years ago give place to the latest hit sounds.

Other changes in consumer demand lead to even more fundamental changes in the supply of goods and services. The availability of high quality recorded music on CD has led to a strong demand for CDs at the expense of traditional vinyl LPs. Record producers such as EMI and Decca, and shops such as WH Smith and HMV have therefore turned to providing recorded music entirely on CD or tape. Similarly, in the sphere of computers, the demand for faster processors has led to the supply of computers almost exclusively with 486 or Pentium processors. In some areas of high technology, new developments can bring about changes in consumer demand almost on a weekly basis.

ACTIVITY

In groups of three or four, identify and make a list of all the products you can think of that are popular now but were not so popular, and may not have been available, five years ago. Compare your list with the lists of other groups. Who has identified most products?

However great or small the change in consumer demand, and however quickly it changes, a business must be aware of, and respond to, the change. A business which continues to produce goods that are out of fashion, or which have not kept up with developments in technology, will lose sales of the goods it produces. Consumers will turn to other businesses which produce the goods they want *today*.

THE BUYING HABITS AND CHARACTERISTICS OF CONSUMERS

Although we are all consumers of goods and services, we have different buying habits. We buy:

- different types of goods and services;
- different amounts of the same goods and services;
- goods and services at different times and with different frequency.

For example, you might buy trainers for wearing to school or college, while your friend buys boots. You use your computer at home mainly for doing your assignments, only occasionally buying a computer game to play, while your friend is a computer games enthusiast and spends most of the money she earns working part-time at the supermarket on buying new games as soon as they are released. You use the bus every day, while your friend cycles, only using the bus once a week to get to town.

Our buying habits are influenced by our characteristics. It is important, therefore, for a business organisation to identify the characteristics of consumers of the products or services it supplies. By doing this, the business can ensure that the goods and services it provides are what its customers and consumers want. It can also plan its marketing and promotional activities, such as advertising, so that they are directed at the types of consumers who are likely to buy its goods and services (marketing and promotion are covered in detail on p 189). Even businesses which produce goods or services which are used by almost everyone, such as food or medical services, want to know the characteristics of consumers who use *their* products because individual business organisations may supply a particular section of the market (see p 46 for a definition of markets and market sectors).

ACTIVITY

Write short descriptions of the type of person you think would be a typical consumer of:

- **Sony personal CD players;**
- **Seven Seas multi-vitamin pills;**
- **the *Encyclopaedia Britannica*.**

As each person is unique, the characteristics of each person are also unique. The combination of characteristics of consumers is therefore potentially infinite. With an infinite range of possible consumer characteristics, it would be impossible for any business to identify exactly the characteristics of consumers of its own goods and services.

Fortunately, however, there are certain types of characteristics which are shared by all consumers, although the actual characteristic may be different. The main types of characteristics are:

- age;
- gender;
- geographical;
- lifestyle.

AGE

Consumers of different ages have different needs and use different goods and services. A business needs to know the ages of the consumers of the goods and services it supplies.

Consumers are identified as being in different age groups, or ranges. The actual groupings or ranges used depend on the goods or

QUICK response

Identify three goods or services that you buy now which you do not expect to buy in ten or 20 years' time.

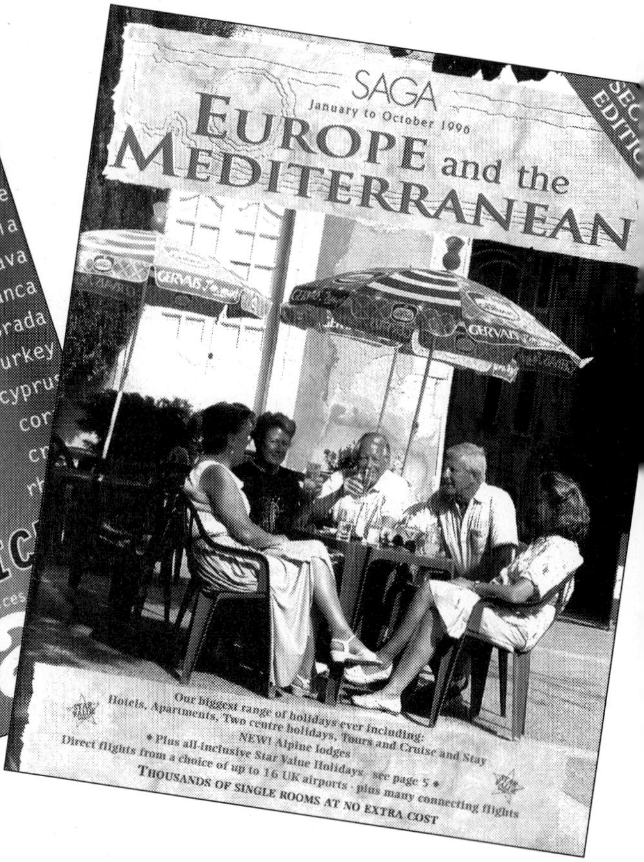

Specialist holiday companies aim to serve particular groups of consumers.

services being supplied. For example, an insurance company selling pension policies may be interested in consumers in the age range 25–65. They may also be particularly interested in consumers in the age range 25–35, as this is the age range when most new pension policies are taken out.

A specialist holiday company, such as Club 18–30, is interested in consumers within that age range (18–30) as only these people can use holidays offered by this company. Similarly, Saga Holidays offers holidays specifically for people over 50.

Other products, while not specifically aimed at one exact age group, may, in fact, appeal particularly to consumers in one age group. Sports cars, for example, are bought mainly by people in their mid-twenties to mid-thirties, although they are often owned and driven by pensioners who are still young at heart. Nevertheless, a sports car manufacturer's efforts may be best directed at the younger age group where there is the greatest scope for sales.

Overall, the age structure of the population affects the demand for many different goods and services as each age group has different demands.

GENDER

The types of goods and services consumers want are also influenced by their gender (whether they are male or female). This is evident in such things as the clothes they wear, the leisure pursuits they enjoy and the magazines they read. It is important for a business to know whether its product or service is used by women, men or both.

For example, a manufacturer of sports and leisure equipment who is bringing out a new range of aerobics steppers must know whether men or women are more likely to buy the steppers. This is not only so that advertising of the steppers can be directed mainly at men or at women in order to encourage sales (if the steppers are likely to be bought by women they would be more effectively advertised in a magazine such as *Woman's Weekly* than in a national newspaper such as *The Times*), but also so that they can be made appropriate to the consumer. Steppers for men need a stronger construction than steppers for women.

QUICK response

In Britain, an increasing number of women are pursuing a career rather than staying at home to look after the family. What effect do you think this has on demand?

ACTIVITY

As a class, discuss the kinds of goods and services bought and used by males and the types of goods and services bought and used by females. Which items fall clearly into one gender category? Which items are not so clear, although there may be a bias towards one gender category? Individually, write notes on your findings.

In some areas, the difference in consumer demand between women and men is clear. Where this is the case, products and services may be specially designed to be used by one sex. Examples are clothing and magazines. In other areas, however, the difference in demand is less obvious. The market for soap, for example, may be made up equally of men and women. However, if men like plain soap while women prefer scented soap, the soap manufacturers could miss out on a substantial number of sales if they make only scented soap.

It must also be remembered that some products which are used by one sex are often actually bought by the other. Ladies perfume, for example, is frequently bought by men to give to their girlfriends or wives. Ties, on the other hand, which are worn by men, are frequently bought as presents by women.

GEOGRAPHICAL

Buying habits are also affected by geographical factors. These may be:

- local;
- national.

Although the UK may seem relatively small in terms of geographical size, there are identifiable differences in buying habits between different regions. *Fig. 3.1* shows how household expenditure varies, both in terms of the total amount spent and the percentage spent on different types of goods and services.

Similarly, consumers in different countries have different buying habits. In 1991, for example, for every 1,000 inhabitants there were an estimated 434 television sets in use in the UK, compared with 556 in Germany and 76 in Ireland. This has obvious implications for a television manufacturer trying to sell in these countries.

Many factors affect local or national buying habits, including the age and gender structure of the population. Other factors are more closely linked to the geographical features of a region. The products and services required by consumers in a mainly rural area are different from those required by consumers in a large town. The proximity of lakes and rivers may give rise to demand for boats and sailboards or fishing tackle. In seaside areas there may be a demand for hotel accommodation, especially if there is a sandy beach.

Brighton seafront is lined with hotels.

Consumer demand is also influenced by government policies. In Britain, for example, the Government is encouraging a move towards consumers taking out their own private pension schemes and contracting out of the state scheme. Similarly, in health, the Government is encouraging individuals to take out private health insurance, so relieving the pressure on the National Health Service. One way of doing this is by offering a reduction in the amount of tax paid by those who take out private schemes.

ACTIVITY

Identify any geographical factors which influence the types of goods and services provided in your locality, or in another locality which you know well. Describe the effect these factors have on the types of goods and services which are in demand and are supplied.

6.2

Household expenditure[1]

United Kingdom

	1971	1981	1986	1990	1991	1992	1993 Indices/ percentages	1993 £ million (current prices)
Indices at constant 1990 prices								
Food	87	91	95	100	100	102	103	46,327
Alcoholic drink	74	95	100	100	97	94	94	24,395
Tobacco	136	121	101	100	98	94	91	10,829
Clothing and footwear	52	67	92	100	100	103	108	23,322
Housing	68	81	93	100	100	101	103	62,316
Fuel and power	86	94	103	100	108	106	109	14,618
Household goods and services								
Household durables	53	69	86	100	97	98	107	12,678
Other	66	68	84	100	99	102	106	13,482
Transport and communication								
Purchase of vehicles	51	59	82	100	81	77	86	18,046
Running of vehicles	47	65	84	100	99	98	101	30,460
Other travel	56	70	84	100	97	101	101	13,526
Post and telecommunications	33	63	80	100	100	101	107	7,592
Recreation, entertainment and education								
TV, video, etc	19	47	77	100	100	105	111	8,800
Books, newspapers, etc	101	97	92	100	95	96	99	5,462
Other	36	62	76	100	99	100	104	26,275
Other goods and services								
Catering (meals, etc)	55	58	72	100	93	91	93	34,746
Other goods	44	60	75	100	100	98	100	14,890
Other services	30	43	68	100	97	94	96	28,885
Less expenditure by foreign tourists, etc	48	72	94	100	86	89	97	-10,121
Household expenditure abroad	34	66	78	100	97	106	104	11,262
All household expenditure	59	72	85	100	98	98	101	397,790
Percentage of total household expenditure at current prices								
Food	*20.1*	*16.4*	*13.8*	*12.3*	*12.3*	*12.1*	*11.6*	46,327
Alcoholic drink	*7.3*	*7.3*	*6.9*	*6.4*	*6.6*	*6.3*	*6.1*	24,395
Tobacco	*4.8*	*3.6*	*3.1*	*2.5*	*2.7*	*2.7*	*2.7*	10,829
Clothing and footwear	*8.5*	*6.7*	*7.0*	*6.1*	*5.9*	*5.9*	*5.9*	23,322
Housing	*12.4*	*14.9*	*15.3*	*14.2*	*14.6*	*15.4*	*15.7*	62,316
Fuel and power	*4.5*	*5.1*	*4.6*	*3.6*	*4.0*	*3.8*	*3.7*	14,618
Household goods and services	*7.8*	*6.9*	*6.7*	*6.5*	*6.5*	*6.6*	*6.6*	26,160
Transport and communication	*14.3*	*17.2*	*17.5*	*18.3*	*17.3*	*17.3*	*17.5*	69,624
Recreation, entertainment and education	*8.8*	*9.4*	*9.4*	*10.0*	*10.0*	*10.1*	*10.2*	40,537
Other goods, services and adjustments	*11.4*	*12.5*	*15.6*	*20.0*	*20.0*	*19.9*	*20.0*	79,662
All household expenditure	*100*	*100*	*100*	*100*	*100*	*100*	*100*	397,790

1 See Appendix, Part 6: Household expenditure.

Source: Central Statistical Office

FIGURE 3.1 Household expenditure. Source: *Social Trends 25*, Crown copyright 1995.

LIFESTYLE

Consumers lead different lifestyles. The lifestyle an individual chooses is influenced by three main factors, each of which has an impact on demand:

- **Taste** – for example, for one colour rather than another. A consumer's taste influences everything they buy or use. It enables the consumer to decide between two products which are identical in every other respect.
- **Fashion** – for example, in clothes. New designs are produced on a regular basis, and many consumers want to own the latest design.
- **Preferences** – for example, for meat or vegetarian food, tea or coffee. Consumers' preferences can be influenced by taste or fashion – or by other factors such as care for the environment, a desire for health, and so on.

ACTIVITY

Write a short description of your own lifestyle. How is it influenced by your taste, fashion and your own preferences.

TRENDS IN CONSUMER DEMAND

On p 165, we said that consumer demand does not stay the same. Where demand changes over a period of time, it may be possible to identify a trend. Trends in demand may be identified by looking at patterns of sales of goods and services.

- If sales go up over a period of time, this indicates an increasing consumer demand.
- If sales go down over a period of time, this indicates a decreasing consumer demand.

QUICK response

If sales of a product go from 5,000 to 10,000 over a period of time, this indicates a ________ trend.

Trends in consumer demand can be identified for products in general, or of a particular type, and for products in particular. An increasing or decreasing trend in consumer demand for products in general, or of a particular type, indicates that demand for products of all types,

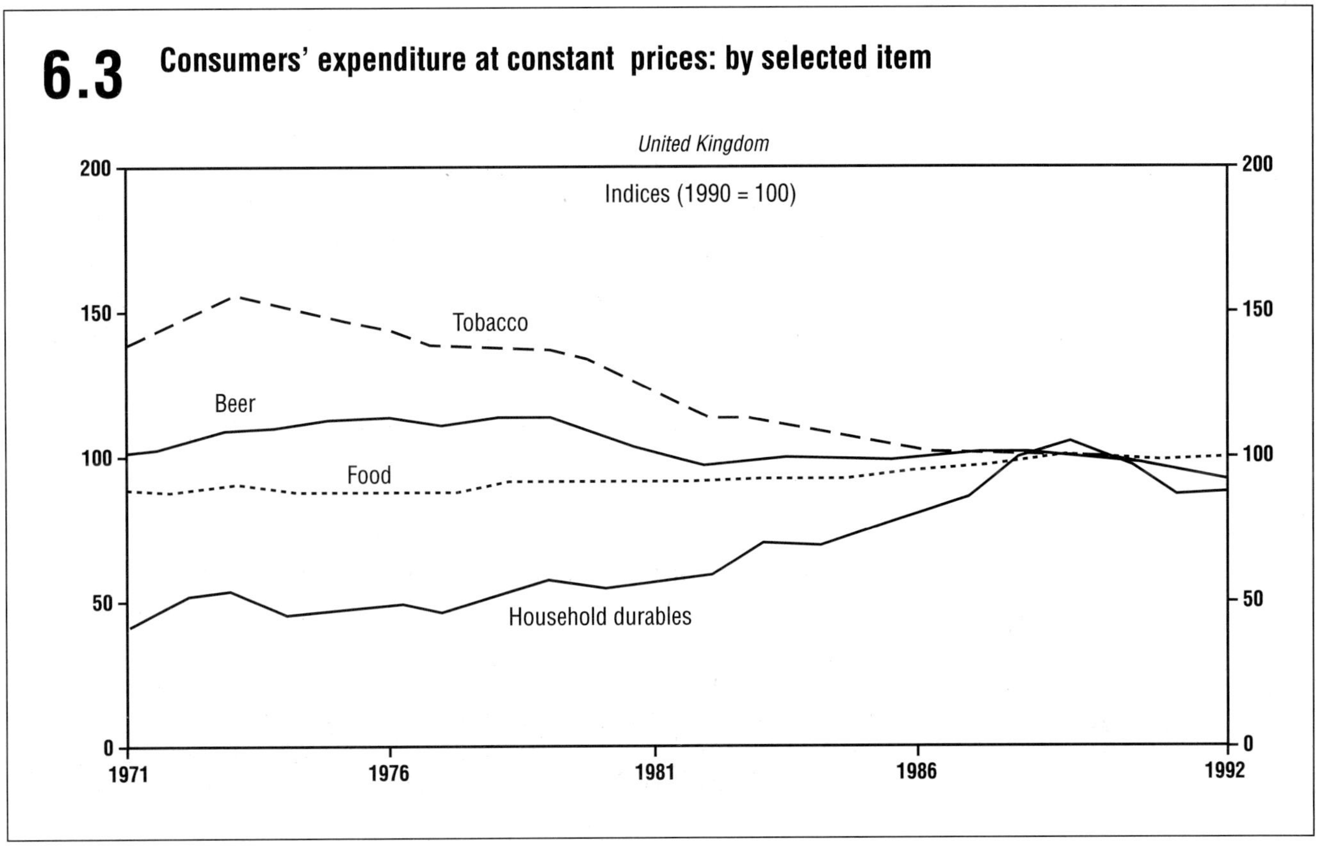

FIGURE 3.2 Consumers' expenditure from 1971 to 1992. Source: *Social Trends 24*, Crown copyright 1994

or of a particular type, is increasing or decreasing. An increasing or decreasing trend in consumer demand for a particular product indicates that demand for that product is increasing or decreasing.

For example, between 1971 and 1992, sales of tobacco products fell by 33 per cent, indicating a decreasing consumer demand for tobacco. During the same period, however, sales of household durables, such as televisions and refrigerators, nearly doubled, indicating an increasing consumer demand for household durables. *Fig. 3.2* shows trends in consumer expenditure on tobacco, household durables, beer and food during the period 1971 to 1992.

Trends such as these are important for businesses which supply products of the type covered. Manufacturers of household durables, such as Hotpoint and Electrolux, are interested in trends in demand for household durables. However, it is also important for a business to identify trends in demands for its own particular products.

During the period 1986 to 1996, for example, Ergon Manufacturing Limited, a small manufacturer of infra-red ovens, saw sales of its own products fall from £1,600,000 per year to £758,000 per year, allowing for inflation. This indicates a decreasing consumer demand for ovens manufactured by Ergon. Obviously, this is a situation Ergon must investigate as a matter of urgency – especially

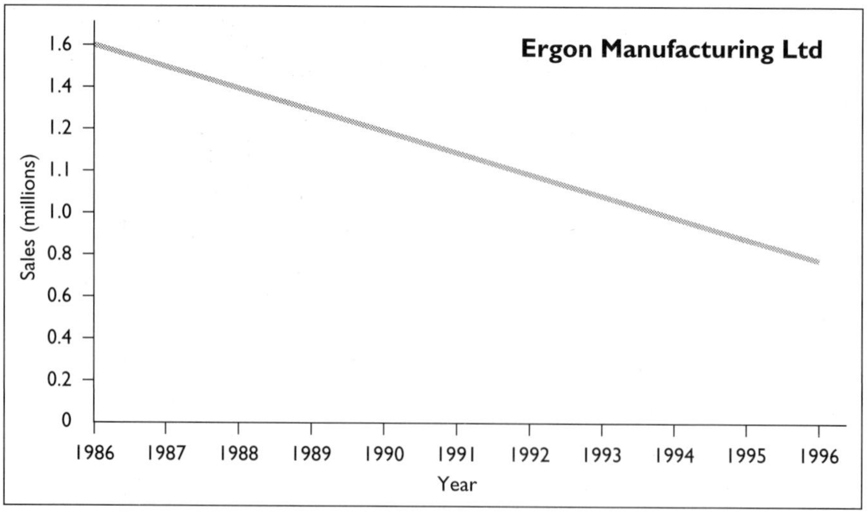

FIGURE 3.3 The decline in sales by Ergon Manufacturing is in contrast to the increase in demand for household durables.

in view of the fact that, as you can see from the graph in *Fig. 3.2*, overall consumer demand for household durables rose considerably during the period.

The trends you have looked at so far are based on past sales. There is a very good reason why the identification of trends in consumer demand is based on past sales, and this is because the only real information, or data, that is available is about the past – about what has actually happened. Trends may be:

- short-term – covering a period of six months to two years;
- long-term – covering a period of two to three years, or even longer.

The longer the period of the information indicating a trend, the more confidence a business can have that there is, in fact, a trend. If sales have risen steadily for two years, a business can be more certain that there is an increasing consumer demand than if sales have only risen for the past two or three months. However, the type of product involved will have a bearing on what can be considered a short-term or long-term trend in consumer demand. In the aeroplane industry, for example, where it takes years to develop and manufacture a plane, even five years may be considered short-term, while in the computer games industry, where new games are being developed and produced almost daily, six months may be considered very long-term for a product.

While the data on which the identification of trends in consumer demand is based are historical, the main purpose of identifying trends is to plan for the future. If trends in consumer demand can be projected into the future, a business can plan future production, raw materials usage, advertising, investment requirements, and so on.

If a trend in consumer demand can be identified in the past, it is possible to extend this into the future. Of course, there is no certainty that a past trend will continue but if a trend in the past has continued for a long time, there can be more confidence in the trend continuing. As with past trends, future trends may be short-term or long-term. There is more uncertainty as the anticipated trend is projected further into the future, however. This is because the further you look ahead, the more uncertain you are of what actual conditions will be like.

One way of calculating a trend in consumer demand, based on historical sales data, is to use a method called **linear estimation** (or **linear regression**). This method produces a graph of the trend in consumer demand which can be extended into the future. There are three steps to be followed:

1 Divide the data into two equal halves, arranged in time order.

2 Calculate the arithmetic mean (average) of each half.

3 Plot the two averages on a graph against the middle year in each half and join the two points.

This is called **two point linear estimation**, because only two points are plotted on the graph. The line produced can be extended to show future estimated demand.

For example, between 1986 and 1996 the annual sales of Perfect Office Supplies Limited are:

1987	£170,000
1988	£100,000
1989	£ 60,000
1990	£130,000
1991	£200,000
1992	£180,000
1993	£90,000
1994	£160,000
1995	£220,000
1996	£200,000

These figures fall into halves: 1987–1991; 1992–1996. You should note that there is an even number of data here, so the data fall easily into two halves. If there is an odd number of data, the middle item should be divided by two and one part included in each half.

QUICK response

Advertisements for unit trusts and other investments state that past performance should not be taken as a guide to future performance. Why do you think this is?

The average of the first half is found by:

£170,000 + £100,000 + £60,000 + £130,000 + £200,000 = £660,000 ÷ 5 = £132,000

The average of the second half is found by:

£180,000 + £90,000 + £160,000 + £220,000 + £200,000 = £850,000 ÷ 5 = £170,000

These averages are plotted on a graph against the middle year in each half (1989; 1994) to produce a graph as shown in *Fig. 3.4*. The line of the graph (called a **trend line**) can be extended to show anticipated demand in any future year *assuming the past trend in sales continues unaltered.* You should note, however, that as the tend is an average trend, the demand shown for future years is also an average anticipated demand. Anticipated future demand may be decreasing as well as increasing.

ACTIVITY

The following table gives the sales figures of Brentwood Windows and Glass Limited for the ten-year period 1986–1995.

Year	Sales in £'000
1986	1,560
1987	1,736
1988	1,750
1989	1,663
1990	2,012
1991	1,997
1992	2,018
1993	2,023
1994	1,749
1995	1,843

- **Construct a graph showing a trend line for the sales.**
- **Identify whether this indicates an increasing or decreasing trend in consumer demand.**

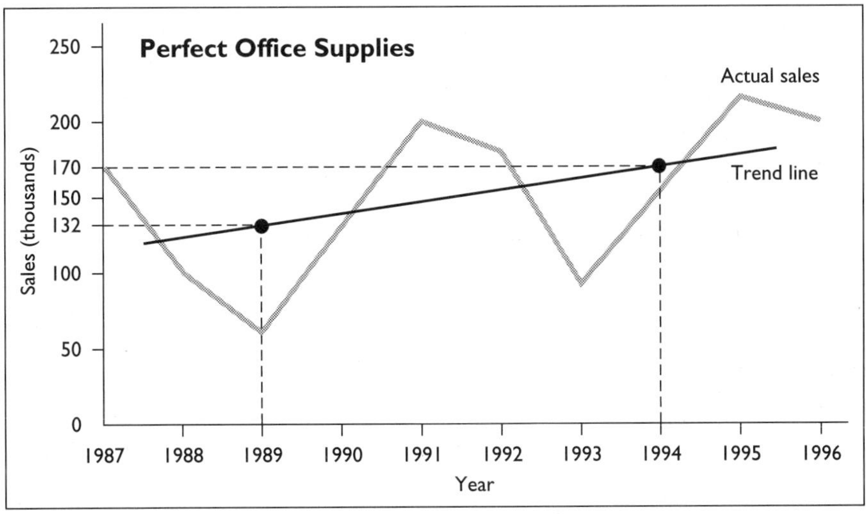

FIGURE 3.4 A graph showing the trend line of sales for Perfect Office Supplies.

INFORMATION ABOUT TRENDS IN CONSUMER DEMAND

There are many sources of information about trends in consumer demand for a business organisation to use. Information can be obtained directly from individual consumers themselves, either through observation of their buying behaviour or by conducting a survey – actually asking their opinions, perhaps using a questionnaire. There are, however, many published sources of data which a business might use. These include:

- articles, reports and news items in the business pages of national and international newspapers and magazines, including trade and professional magazines;
- economic and statistical publications of government departments, including *Social Trends, Family Expenditure Survey, Economic Trends, British Business, Population Trends, General Household Survey, Department of Education and Employment Gazette*;
- publications of Eurostat, the Statistical Office of the European Union, including a yearbook of *Basic Statistics*.

USING GRAPHICS TO ILLUSTRATE TRENDS

The raw data (singular datum) which are used to identify trends are figures. In order to calculate a trend, these are normally presented in the form of a table, as in *Fig. 3.5*.

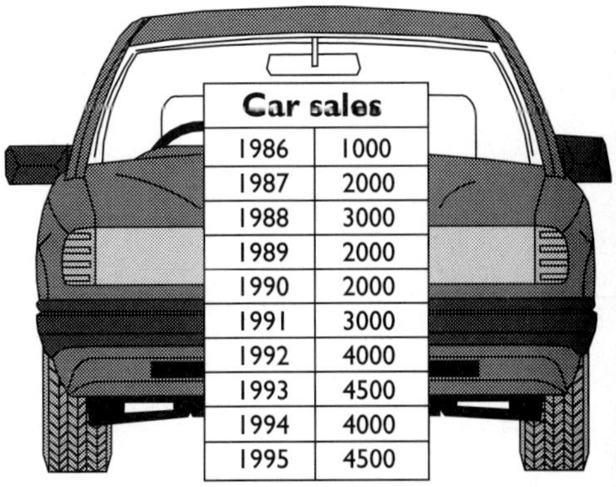

Car sales	
1986	1000
1987	2000
1988	3000
1989	2000
1990	2000
1991	3000
1992	4000
1993	4500
1994	4000
1995	4500

FIGURE 3.5 Car sales at a garage between 1986 and 1995.

However, tables often contain a lot of data and can be confusing or difficult to understand. It is often not easy to see whether the figures represent a trend or not, as figures frequently go up and down.

In order to enable a trend to be seen more easily, graphics are often used to represent the appropriate data and to illustrate a trend. The three types of graphic normally used to illustrate a trend are:

- pictograms;
- line graphs;
- bar charts.

PICTOGRAMS

In a pictogram, quantities are represented by pictures or symbols. For example, the table on p 177 gives the sales of cars by a garage during the period 1986 to 1995. In a pictogram, the numbers of cars sold would be represented by pictures of cars, as in *Fig. 3.6*. In this example, each picture represents 1,000 cars sold.

When using pictograms, each picture must be clear and simply drawn. The quantities represented by each picture should be given in a key to the pictogram. Obviously, each picture should represent the item.

FIGURE 3.6 A pictogram of the car sales shown in *Fig. 3.5*

The main disadvantages of pictograms are:

- it can be difficult to find a picture to represent some items (how do you represent 'other items' in *Fig. 3.6*?);
- pictograms can only really be used to represent quantities in multiples of 10, 100, 1,000 and so on. Therefore, it is difficult to represent accurately quantities of 18, 68, 862, and so on;
- a pictogram can only represent quantities of one commodity;
- a pictogram cannot be used to calculate future trends.

ACTIVITY

Using suitable pictures, construct a pictogram representing the following sales of CDs by a high street retailer. Make sure you give your pictogram a key.

Month	Number of CDs sold
April	2,000
May	4,000
June	5,000

LINE GRAPHS

Line graphs have already been used to illustrate trends in this unit (see p 177).

A graph consist of a horizontal axis, called the *x* axis and a vertical axis, called the *y* axis. Generally, graphs are used to show the relationship between two variables: an independent variable, and a dependent variable. The value of the dependent variable depends on the value of the independent variable. The value of the independent variable is plotted against the *x* axis, and the value of the dependent variable is plotted against the *y* axis. Therefore, the value of *y* can be said to depend on the value of *x*.

In constructing a graph illustrating a trend, we are constructing a graph of a series of values over time. Time is plotted on the *x* axis. The garage car sales shown as a simple table on p 177 are shown as a graph in *Fig. 3.7*.

QUICK response

If you constructed a graph of sales in each month over a year, you would plot months on the __- axis and sales on the __- axis.

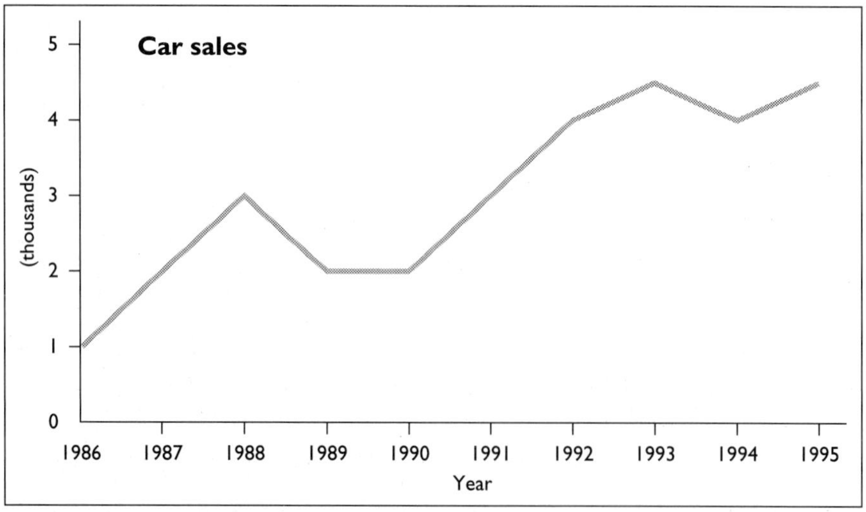

FIGURE 3.7 The car sales from *Fig. 3.5* shown as a graph.

The advantages of using graphs to illustrate trends are:

- they are accurate and use the exact data;
- more than one commodity can be shown on the same graph;
- they are easy to understand and clearly show any trend;
- they can be used to estimate the future effects of a trend.

If a graph shows a trend, it is possible to extend this into the future. However, the line of a graph constructed from actual data is rarely straight. Before any future projections are made based on a graph, therefore, the line of the graph must be straightened. In other words, a **trend line** must be added.

The easiest way of doing this is to add a **line of best fit**. This can be drawn by eye, by carefully examining the points on the graph and drawing a straight trend line so that the points are equally distributed above and below the trend line. This may not be accurate, however, and it may be better to calculate the trend line by using a two point linear estimation, as described on p 175. You can then extend this to show the future effects of the trend – *assuming the past trend in sales continues unaltered.*

BAR CHARTS

A bar chart is one of the commonest methods of illustrating data and trends. Bar charts are constructed along the same axes as graphs, but the values are shown in the form of bars, and the length of each bar shows the value of the corresponding data item. Bar charts are clear and easily understood ways of representing past data to show trends, but they cannot be used to calculate future trends.

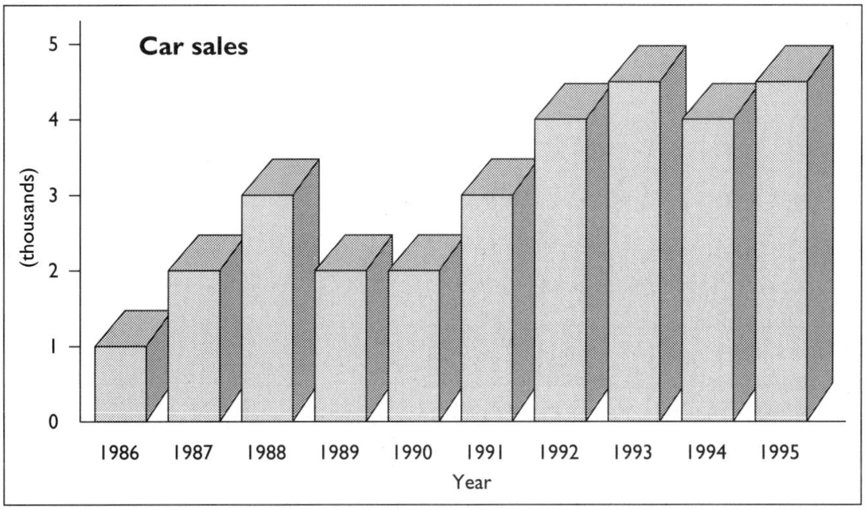

FIGURE 3.8 A bar chart of the car sales shown in *Fig. 3.5.*

ACTIVITY

Construct a bar chart of the sales of CDs given in the table used in the last activity on p 179.

Many computer spreadsheet programs have facilities for generating graphs and bar charts, although few will calculate trend lines. You should obtain access to a program which can generate graphs or bar charts, find out how this works and practise using it. You should, however, also be able to construct graphs and bar charts manually, and also calculate a trend line.

CAUSES OF CHANGE IN CONSUMER DEMAND

You have seen that consumer demand changes over time, and that it is important for a business organisation to identify changes in demand for the goods or services it produces. A business which does not respond to changes in consumer demand will soon find that the goods or services it supplies are no longer what its customers want.

However, a business must not only identify trends in demand, it must know why changes in consumer demand occur. Some changes in consumer demand are due to changes in the general characteristics of consumers themselves, including changes in the following factors:

- age distribution in the population;
- gender differences and distribution;
- geographical factors;
- preferences for different lifestyles.

However, other factors also influence consumer demand.

Disposable income

A person's disposable income is the money they have to spend on goods and services. This is the amount left out of their earnings after income tax, National Insurance and certain other necessary expenses (such as the cost of housing) have been taken into consideration.

Obviously, consumer demand for goods and services is very much influenced by the amount of money consumers have to spend on those goods and services. This, in turn, depends on:

- earnings;
- the cost of living.

QUICK response

What are the current Retail Price Index and Inflation Rate?

Each month, the Government measures increases in the cost of living by calculating the **Retail Price Index** (RPI). This is not a money value, but an index number which shows the percentage change over time. January 1987 was chosen as the base month and year, against which other periods would be measured.

On a particular day each month, approximately 130,000 prices, covering about 600 goods and services, are obtained from a sample of retail outlets. The goods and services involved, called a 'basket' of goods and services, are the same each month, in order to provide a uniform basis for comparison. They are goods and services on which households spend a significant proportion of their income. If it is felt that a particular item is no longer relevant, the make up of the 'basket' can be changed at any time, but for purposes of comparison this involves the recalculation of previous monthly figures. The base month and year for comparison can also be changed if necessary.

The resulting prices for a given period are weighted according to their importance to household expenditure and the total value divided by the value for the base period. The index number for the period is then found by multiplying this by 100. In January 1987 the Retail Price Index was 100. If the Retail Price Index is recalculated for a subsequent month and found to be 120, this means that retail

5.4

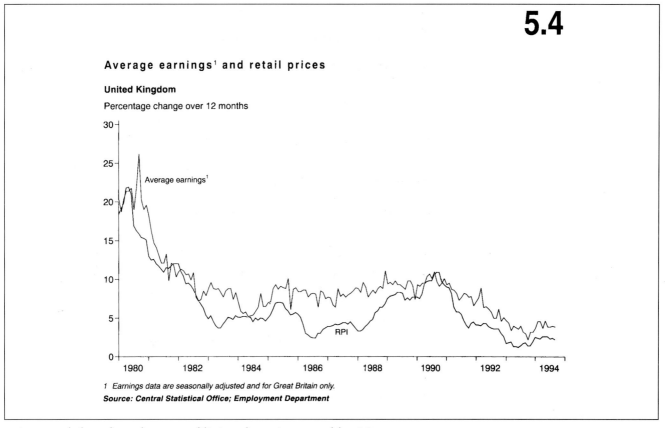

Average earnings[1] and retail prices

United Kingdom

Percentage change over 12 months

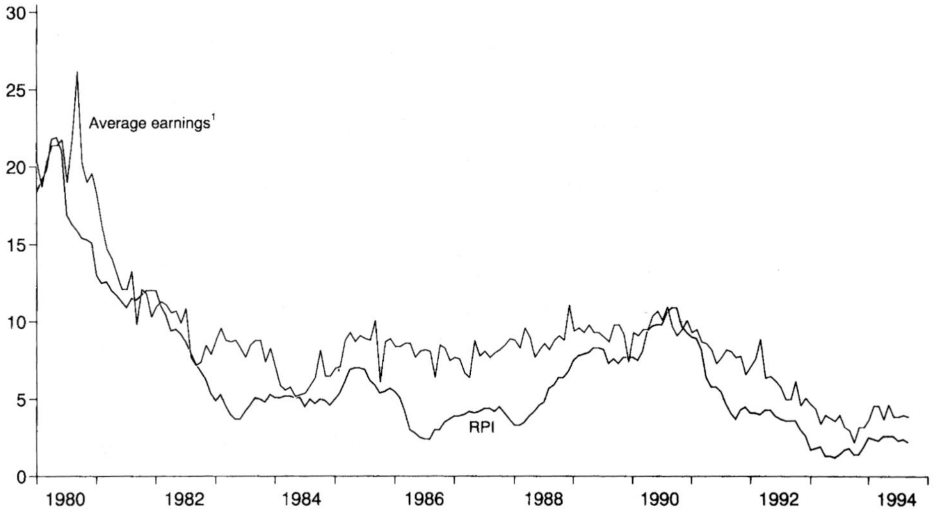

1 Earnings data are seasonally adjusted and for Great Britain only.

Source: Central Statistical Office; Employment Department

FIGURE 3.9 Average earnings and retail prices between 1980 and 1994. Source: *Social Trends 25*, Crown copyright 1995.

prices, and therefore the cost of living, have increased by 20 per cent since January 1987.

In order for there to be an increase in consumer demand, the average level of earnings must rise faster than the cost of living. If the cost of living increases by 5 per cent in a given year, for example, and the average earnings of consumers also rise by 5 per cent, consumers will be no better off. If, however, the average earnings of consumers rise by 6 per cent, while the cost of living rises by 5 per cent, consumers will be able to buy more goods and services (although some of the additional earnings will be deducted as income tax and National Insurance). This means that there is scope for an increase in consumer demand.

Fig. 3.9 shows the percentage change over 12 months of both average earnings and the Retail Price Index between 1980 and 1994.

CONFIDENCE TO SPEND

Consumers having more money to spend on goods and services will only lead to an increase in consumer demand if they want to spend their money on those goods and services. They must be confident that they will not require their money for other purposes.

Consumer confidence to spend is particularly affected by changes in economic certainty and the level of employment. If the economic future is uncertain, interest rates, including mortgage interest rates, are high and people are unsure of their own jobs and future, confidence to spend on goods and services will be low. Consumers will be more inclined to save their money, putting some by for 'a rainy day', just in case. Demand will therefore also be low. If the economic future is bright, on the other hand, and people are happy that their own futures and jobs are secure, the need to save for a rainy day will not be so great. Confidence to spend more on goods and services will be higher, resulting in greater consumer demand.

CHANGING WANTS AND NEEDS

We often use the words wants and needs as meaning the same thing. How often do you say that you need a new T-shirt, or you need a new CD by your favourite group, when what you really mean is that you want those things?

- A need is something we must have in order to sustain life and well-being, such as food, housing and clothing.
- A want is something we would like in order to make life more enjoyable or easy, such as a personal stereo, a computer or a holiday.

Often, what we choose to satisfy our needs is influenced by our wants. You many need a drink to satisfy your thirst, but you buy a can of cola because that is what you want.

Changes in the characteristics of consumers, such as age, gender and lifestyle, affect their wants and needs. In Britain, for example, the average age of the population is increasing. As they grow older, people tend to need more medical care. This has obvious implications for demand on the health services. In addition, as people grow older they have more leisure time. Improvements in medical care have meant that older people remain active longer. An aging consumer population is therefore likely to increase demand for leisure services – and for pension policies and other forms of investment which will provide the money to enjoy retirement.

ACTIVITY

As a group, discuss how your own needs have changed over the last five years, due to growing older. Individually, make notes on your findings.

ADVERTISING

Business organisations can bring about changes in consumer demand through careful advertising of goods and services. Advertising is a form of promotion and is discussed in detail on p 191.

The objective of advertising is to persuade consumers that they want the product or service advertised, or that it is fashionable and 'the thing to have'. If an advertisement is successful, consumer demand for the product advertised will increase. Advertising can be used to create demand for a new product, or to increase demand for an existing product, perhaps by changing the way consumers perceive that product.

THE IMPORTANCE OF CUSTOMERS

While every business must understand who are the consumers of its products, and be aware of consumer demand so that it

QUICK response

What will happen to a business which fails to attract customers?

can ensure that the goods and services it provides are those that consumers want, it is the actual customer who is most important. It is the customer who buys and pays for the goods and services of business organisations, and so provides the income of the business.

Without sales, a business would receive no income. It would have no money to pay its expenses. As you have seen (p 11) the profit of a business is the amount left out of income once all the expenses of the business have been paid. Even if a business does not make a profit, it cannot carry on for long if the income it receives from sales of its goods or services does not equal its expenses. Income, profit and the very survival of a business all depend on sales.

A business must therefore attract customers who will actually buy and pay for the goods or services it provides – regardless of who is the final consumer. If most after-shave is bought for their husbands and boyfriends by women doing the weekly shopping, a manufacturer of after-shave must persuade women, rather than men, to buy its product.

The objective of a business must be not simply to sell its product once, but to go on selling. There are, however, only a finite number of customers for the products of any business. In order to keep selling, therefore, a business needs repeat sales. For example, some years ago a business was started in America which sold small stones as pets. There were many advantages of having a stone as a pet: they don't need much care; they don't need feeding; you can talk to them without them answering back, and so on. At first the idea caught on and the business was successful. However, most customers were happy with their initial purchase and, as stone pets do not die, once the initial demand for stone pets was satisfied, there were no repeat sales. The company which sold them has now gone out of business.

As well as being the source of income and profit for a business, customers are also a source of information. You have seen that consumer demand influences what goods and services are provided by business organisations. Consumer demand changes, however, and businesses must change the goods and services they provide to meet changes in consumer demand. Customers provide valuable information for businesses about the range and quality of the products and services they provide.

Obtaining information from – and about – customers is called **marketing research**. This can be carried out by:

- conducting a survey of customers and potential customers either by observation or questioning, perhaps using a specially constructed questionnaire;

- analysing customer records (such as sales records and records of enquiries, complaints and so on) already held by the business.

Methods of marketing research are described on p 227.

Information about customers and customer behaviour will provide a basis for decisions on changing the range of products and improving the quality of goods and services a business offers.

PORTFOLIO ASSIGNMENT

For this portfolio assignment you will research demand for goods and services. In order to complete this assignment you will need access to some of the sources of information about consumer demand and trends in demand mentioned in the text.

TASK 1

Choose one type of good and one service to investigate. Write a summary describing how consumers both create, and bring about changes in, demand for these. In particular, you should show how the behaviour of consumers stimulates the supply of your chosen good and service.

TASK 2

Identify three groups of consumers with different characteristics or combinations of characteristics. For example, you may base your consumer groups on age, gender, income, or a combination of these. Describe the characteristics of the consumer groups you have identified and show how these have brought about changes in their buying habits over the past two to three years.

TASK 3

Select three products into which you can research trends in demand. The products you select may be either goods or services. Describe the products and investigate demand for them over the past ten years. Identify trends in demand and produce a graph to show these. You may produce your graph manually or on a computer. Calculate likely demand over the next two to three years. Write notes explaining why the changes in demand for each product have taken place.

TASK 4

Choose a business organisation you know well. Briefly describe the type and purpose of the organisation and explain how its customers are an important source of income, repeat business and information.

This portfolio assignment also presents an opportunity to gather evidence for the following core skills:

- Application of Number – collect and record data; interpret and present data;
- Communication – produce written material; read and respond to written material;
- Information Technology – prepare information; process information; present information.

Planning, Designing and Producing Promotional Materials

All business organisations must promote themselves and the goods or services they provide if they are to sell these in sufficient quantities. Promotion has two main purposes. By promoting its goods or services a business organisation aims to:

- create an awareness in customers and consumers of both the business and of the goods or services it provides;
- create a demand for those goods or services by persuading customers and consumers that they want the product or service being promoted.

Types of promotion

There are four main types of promotion which businesses use to market their goods and services:

- point of sale;
- advertisements;
- sponsorship;
- competition.

Point of sale

Point of sale is a type of promotion which is carried out in the place where the product or service being promoted is sold. For example, point of sale promotion of the latest book by a well-known author is carried out in bookshops, while point of sale promotion of holidays is carried out at travel agents. Some methods of point of sale promotion are appropriate only to specific types of goods or services, such as author book signings in bookshops. Other methods, however, can be applied to the promotion of different types of goods and services. The most common methods of point of sale promotion are:

- displaying the product in special display stands designed to attract the attention of potential customers, such as displays of the latest video release in supermarkets;
- special offers, such as three packs for the price of two, or giving an extra amount of the product free;
- giving free gifts with purchases of a product, or money-off vouchers towards further purchases;
- cut-price trial packs;
- displaying posters advertising the product;
- other materials describing the product or service, such as brochures and leaflets.

ACTIVITY

Investigate a local supermarket or department store. Identify and make a list of all the point of sale promotional material displayed. What promotional materials are used? How effective do you think they are?

An advantage of point of sale promotion is that it is relatively inexpensive because it does not involve huge advertising campaigns and is most likely to reach the type of consumers who will buy the product – people in a supermarket can be considered potential customers for the goods it sells.

Petrol companies have long relied on point of sales promotions based on customers collecting vouchers or 'points' which can be exchanged for free gifts. At certain times of the year, principally January and July, shops and stores hold 'sales'. The shops and stores promote these with posters in their windows and inside, making it clear to potential customers that there are bargains available and which products are reduced in price. Many retail businesses also recognise the importance of point of sale promotion by creating special window and in-store displays at Christmas and other times.

Point of sale promotion is often intended to encourage 'impulse buying' – that is, to encourage customers to buy a product they might not have thought of buying – or more of a product than they would normally have bought. To be effective, it must be eye-catching, gain the interest of customers and persuade them to buy.

ADVERTISEMENTS

Advertisements are the most common form of promotion. They are all around us: as posters on billboards and elsewhere; on television and radio; in newspapers and magazines. A business wishing to advertise its goods or services can choose an expensive national advertising campaign or an inexpensive campaign which will only reach a limited potential market. However, an effective campaign will be carefully targeted at the type of consumer likely to purchase the product being advertised, taking into consideration characteristics such as age, gender, geographical location, lifestyle, and whether the customer is an individual or another business.

- **Posters:** Some posters are huge advertisements put on large billboards in public places such as in towns, at railway stations and on bus shelters. Other posters are smaller – often advertising a local event such as a pop concert or a fair. They are mainly seen by people in passing, and must therefore catch the attention of passersby. Their message must be simple and conveyed at a glance.

  The advantages of posters are that they are inexpensive, relatively long-lasting and may be seen several times by people who pass them regularly, reinforcing their message. Disadvantages are that they will be seen by many people who are unlikely to be interested in what they are promoting, thus reducing the effectiveness of the promotion, and that most people take little notice of posters that they pass.

- **Television and radio**: Television advertising can be one of the most effective forms of promotion. As it consists of both sound and vision, television advertisements are easily remembered, particularly when the sound is a catchy tune or even a well-known pop song.

  A peak-time advertisement on national television can be seen by millions of viewers. It is, however, very expensive to produce and show. National television advertising is only really appropriate to national businesses providing goods and services which are bought by a wide range of people. Television advertisements can also be shown regionally. This reduces the cost but also the audience.

Advertising on radio is cheaper and can be more selective in the audience at which it is aimed. Listener profiles can be made which are fairly detailed descriptions of the type of consumer who listens to a particular programme.

When placing an advertisement on television or radio, a business must decide what types of consumer will watch or listen to a particular programme. Timing is also important. For example, advertisements for toys are shown during programmes aimed at children, before six o'clock on weekday evenings, and during the day at weekends. Opportunities for advertising on television have greatly increased with the introduction of satellite and cable stations, while the development of relatively small local community radio stations has provided opportunities for local businesses to advertise.

The main advantages of television and radio advertisements are that they reach an extremely wide audience and, combining sound and visual images, can be very effective. Repeat transmissions can reinforce the message. Disadvantages are that they are the most expensive forms of advertising, and the advertisement only lasts as long as the transmission – perhaps 30 seconds. The message of the advertisement must therefore be conveyed in this time. In addition, advertisements can only be very broadly targeted, and are therefore most appropriate for products with wide appeal.

ACTIVITY

Watch the advertisements in a commercial break on one of the commercial television stations. Make a list of all the products advertised. How many advertisements are repeated during other commercial breaks in the same programme?

- **Newspapers and magazines**: Advertisements in newspapers and magazines are long lasting. They can be read and re-read, cut out and filed for future reference if required. A newspaper or magazine advertisement can therefore contain much more information than posters or advertisements on television or the radio. National daily and Sunday newspapers reach a wide audience, although not as wide as television, but advertisements in these newspapers can be expensive, especially if they are large.

An advantage of advertising in newspapers and magazines is that an advertiser can target consumers with specific characteristics and interests, by choosing local newspapers, national and local general interest magazines such as *Reader's Digest* and *Suffolk Life*, or special interest and professional magazines such as *Camping Magazine* and *Accountancy*.

SPONSORSHIP

Many businesses promote themselves and their products by sponsoring events and people. This is mainly in the field of sports, although sponsorship of arts events, in particular concerts and exhibitions, is common. The sponsorship is normally in the form of money in return for which the name or logo of the business is prominently displayed on promotional material for the event, such as posters and programmes, where it will be seen by spectators, for example around a football pitch, or on the clothing and equipment of participants in the event.

Normally, a business will sponsor an event with which it is connected in some way, or which conveys an image with which the business wants to be associated. For example, motor racing is largely sponsored by car manufacturers and other businesses which want the high profile and glamour associated with the sport.

Some businesses also sponsor events in the field of human endeavour, such as Ffyona Campbell's expedition on foot through Africa which was sponsored in the form of cash and goods by many organisations, including Hi-Tec Sports, Sabona, and Ever Ready. Events such as this produce only a limited amount of promotional opportunity but are felt to be worthwhile because they help human achievement.

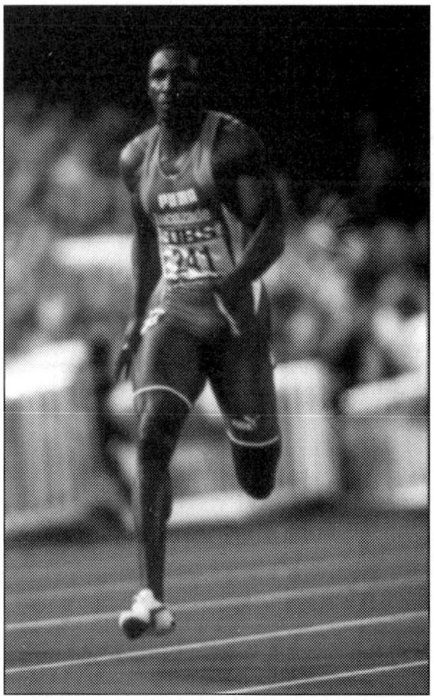

Many top athletes are sponsored by businesses.

ACTIVITY

Study the sports or arts pages of a national newspaper. Make a list of all the sponsored events or personalities that you can identify. What are the sponsoring organisations? Select two sponsorships and write notes on how you think each sponsorship promotes the sponsoring organisation.

COMPETITIONS

This form of promotion is based on persuading consumers to purchase a product by offering a valuable prize in a competition. The competition is normally free to enter, and in some cases you do not actually have to make a purchase first. Daily newspapers, particularly the tabloids such as *The Sun* and *Daily Mirror* regularly offer free bingo or lottery-type competitions with large cash prizes in order to attract customers. The *Reader's Digest* is well known for the prize draws it offers, for which free entry is sent to a large number of consumers throughout the country. Competitions are by no means restricted to promoting newspapers and magazines, however, and many businesses have realised that sales of their goods or services can be increased by offering customers the chance of winning a prize.

CONSTRAINTS ON THE CONTENT OF PROMOTIONAL MATERIALS

Businesses promote their goods and services in order to influence consumer perception of them and to increase demand. However, there are certain constraints on what can be put in promotional materials. These constraints are intended to protect consumers from being misled by unscrupulous businesses making exaggerated and unwarranted claims for the goods and services they provide. They also ensure that the content of promotional materials is not offensive to consumers. Some constraints on the content of promotional materials are voluntary, and contained in agreed codes of practice. Other constraints are enforceable in law, being covered by Acts of Parliament.

VOLUNTARY CONSTRAINTS

The principal codes of practice which govern the content and use of promotional materials are:

- the British Code of Advertising and Sales Promotion Practice;
- the codes of practice of the Independent Television Commission and the Radio Authority.

The British Code of Advertising and Sales Promotion Practice is supervised by the Advertising Standards Authority which monitors all advertising and promotional material, apart from that on television and radio. It works on the principle that all promotional material should be 'legal, decent, honest and truthful'. The authority will ask an organisation to alter any material which does not comply with this principle.

Advertisements on television and radio are covered by the codes of practice of the Independent Television Authority (television) and the Radio Authority (radio). Advertisements must be approved by these bodies before they are broadcast and may be changed or rejected if considered unsuitable. In the main, the codes of practice for radio and television advertising are similar to those established by the Advertising Standards Authority, although special conditions apply to certain products such as alcohol and cigarettes.

ASA

The Advertising Standards Authority monitors all advertising and promotional material.

LEGAL CONSTRAINTS

The main laws which govern the content of promotional materials are:

- **The Trades Descriptions Act 1968** – which makes it illegal to falsely describe a product or service in any way.
- **The Sale of Goods Act 1979** – which sets out the responsibility of a business which sells goods towards the buyer. It is the seller, rather than the manufacturer, who must deal with any complaints the buyer may have. The Sale of Goods Act was extended by the Supply of Goods and Services Act 1982 to state that goods sold must be of saleable quality and fit for their purpose and any other purpose which the seller has confirmed. Goods must also be as described in any promotional material on packaging and in any statements made by the seller.
- **The Consumer Protection Act 1987** – makes it a criminal offence to mislead consumers about the price of goods, including special offers and price reductions in sales. This is reinforced by the Code of Practice for Traders on Price Indications, published by the Department of Trade and Industry. The Act also makes it a criminal offence to supply goods which do not meet general safety standards.

QUICK response

The difference between voluntary and legal constraints on the content of promotional materials is ________.

STANDARDS

An important aspect of voluntary and legal constraints is that they seek to apply standards. Codes of practice are standards of behaviour, and those of the Advertising Standards Authority, the Independent Television Authority and the Radio Authority try to set and reinforce standards in the content of promotional materials, including advertisements on radio and television.

Offices of the Trading Standards Department are run by local authorities, and can be found in all major towns. The job of the Trading Standards Department is to promote a fair and safe trading environment for consumers and businesses. Some of the activities of the department are:

- checking that goods sold are of the correct (advertised) weight or measure;
- testing that the composition and labelling of food meet legal requirements;
- regularly testing that products meet safety requirements, and removing dangerous goods from sale;
- vetting credit advertisements and documentation to make sure they are truthful and contain information required by law;
- enforcing legislation which requires prices to be displayed and outlaws misleading bargain offers;
- taking action against sellers of counterfeit or pirated items;
- checking that any descriptions applied to goods and services are true;
- investigating complaints by consumers;
- providing advice on the rights and responsibilities of businesses and consumers when buying or selling goods or services.

ACTIVITY

Constraints, legal and voluntary, and standards are imposed in order to protect the consumer. As a group, discuss whether you think these constraints are necessary safeguards or a restriction on the freedom of people and organisations.

PLANNING PROMOTIONAL MATERIALS

QUICK response
Name the four main types of promotion.

If they are going to be effective, promotional materials must be carefully planned. This involves:

- clarifying the objectives of the promotion;
- deciding on the types of promotional materials to be used;
- identifying and obtaining resources required.

The objectives of promotions are examined in the next section. The decision as to what types of promotions and what promotional materials to use – point of sale, advertisement, sponsorship or competition – will largely depend on their purpose. Whatever the purpose of the promotion, and whatever the promotional materials selected, resources will be required.

Resources for promotional materials fall into five general categories.

1 **Time**: Time is needed to plan, design and produce the promotional materials, carry out the promotion and evaluate its effectiveness. In some cases, for example when additional sales are needed for the business to survive, time is of the essence. On other occasions, such as seasonal promotions for Christmas and Easter, or promotions of summer holidays in January, the promotional material can be planned months in advance.

   Businesses have a limited amount of time to allocate to the various activities they undertake. The longer there is to plan and produce promotional materials before the promotion starts, the easier it will be for a business to allocate time for this out of its own resources. If a business organisation cannot spare time to undertake the planning and production of promotional materials itself, it can use an outside marketing, advertising or promotion agency.

2 **People**: Similarly, in order to prepare its own promotional materials, a business needs people who are available to produce those materials (that is, who are not too busy with other activities from which they cannot be diverted). It must also have people with the right skills. For example, producing artwork for a poster may involve people with artistic skills, photographic skills and possibly skills in producing computer graphics. When planning promotional materials, therefore, it is important to plan for people

with the right skills to be available. If there is no one in the organisation with these skills, again, the preparation of the promotional materials can be passed to an outside agency.

3 **Materials and equipment**: No promotional materials can be produced without the appropriate materials and equipment. Designing a poster requires paper, pencils, paints, brushes and other artist's equipment, including a drawing board. If a photograph is to be used, a camera and film must be available – as must facilities to process the film. A computer with a desk-top publishing package may be needed to plan the layout of the poster and produce any lettering. If more than one copy of the poster is to be produced, copying or printing facilities are required, together with sufficient paper to make the copies.

A brochure requires many of the same types of materials and equipment, but items such as paper and printing facilities will be different. When planning promotional materials, items such as staples and drawing pins, stamps and envelopes for sending brochures through the post, or display boards and stands for posters and other materials must not be forgotten.

ACTIVITY

You have been asked to prepare a point of sale promotional display of the GNVQ Intermediate Business course at your school or college. Make a list of the different materials and equipment you will need for this.

4 **Cost**: Obviously, all of the above cost money. If these resources are already available, then the real cost is the alternative use which might have been made of them. This is particularly the case with time and people. Resources that are not available will have to be bought and paid for. If the promotional materials are not to be prepared in-house, the services of an outside agency will have to be paid for.

If the type of promotion is a sponsorship, the cost of the sponsorship must be added to any other promotional materials used in conjunction with the sponsorship. Where a competition is involved, the cost of the prizes must be taken into consideration. Cost is perhaps one of the most important factors in planning promotional materials.

THE PURPOSES OF PROMOTIONAL MATERIALS

The prime objective of all promotional materials is to communicate a message to an audience. Good promotional materials communicate the right message to the right audience.

In order to achieve this, the business carrying out the promotion must first decide what message it wants to communicate and at whom the message is aimed. The purpose of the message may be:

- to create sales;
- to influence customers' perception;
- to provide information.

An advertisement intended to create sales.

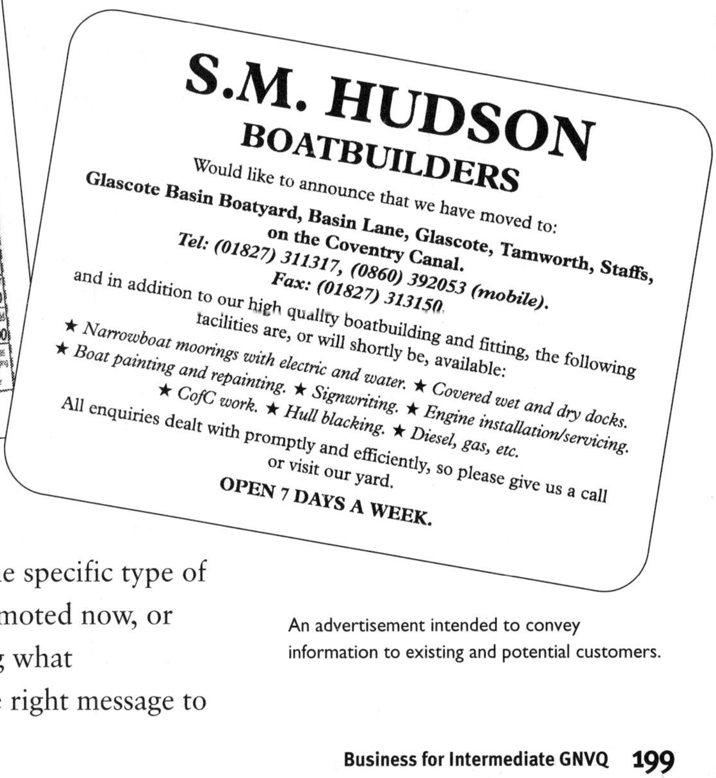

An advertisement intended to convey information to existing and potential customers.

The audience at whom the message is aimed is the specific type of customer who buys the goods or services being promoted now, or who may buy them in the future. When considering what promotional materials are most likely to convey the right message to that audience, a business organisation must consider how the intended audience can most effectively be reached.

QUICK response

Where might a business producing fitted kitchens advertise its product?

- A large supermarket chain with stores in major towns throughout the UK will choose to advertise on national television in order to reach as wide an audience of potential customers as possible.
- A new restaurant may decide to deliver leaflets through the doors of local houses because its customers are likely to live in the immediate neighbourhood, at least until the reputation of the restaurant is well established.
- A manufacturer of walking boots and outdoor clothing is likely to place an advertisement in a magazine such as *Camping Magazine*, and may also use point of sale promotional material such as posters and special displays in camping shops.

Choosing an inappropriate medium for the promotion can be a waste of effort and money. For example, there is little point in the organisers of a car boot sale mailing a leaflet to households nationwide, as only a very small percentage of those receiving the leaflet would be able to go to the sale. Similarly, a manufacturer of light aircraft would be more likely to reach potential customers by advertising in a specialised magazine such as *Flight International* than in a national newspaper such as the *Daily Mail*.

ACTIVITY

You work in the Marketing Department of Oak Designs Limited, a small firm of furniture makers, specialising in oak period designs. Your company wants to promote its furniture to potential customers. Identify and make a list of appropriate media in which it can advertise.

The promotional materials chosen to convey the intended message must also take account of the purpose of the message, the type of goods or services, and the organisation.

- If the purpose is to create sales, a travel agent will use point of sale display material to attract customers, and possibly advertise or distribute leaflets in a local newspaper. A supplier of business office equipment will produce a glossy catalogue which it will distribute to potential customers in the area. The supplier may follow this up with calls by sales executives and the delivery of leaflets containing special offers.

- If the purpose is to influence customer perception, perhaps by improving the image of an organisation or the product it provides, an advertisement on national television may reach the widest audience and have the greatest impact. If the customers are other businesses, however, a quality brochure mailed direct to existing and potential customers may be more appropriate.
- If the purpose is to provide information a brochure or catalogue which customers can read at their leisure and retain for future reference may be the most suitable method.

Customers usually have a perception of business organisations and the goods and services they provide. Promotional material should reflect that image. However, a popular image can be modified. For many years the popular image of Lucozade was of a drink for convalescents. As a result, sales were not as high as the manufacturer, SmithKline Beecham, believed they could be. By promoting the drink nationally as a health drink, rather than just a drink for convalescents, and using well-known sports personalities such as Daley Thompson and Linford Christie, the popular image of the drink has been successfully changed. This has brought an increase in sales and an improved market position.

DESIGNING AND PRODUCING PROMOTIONAL MATERIALS TO PROMOTE GOODS AND SERVICES

As you have seen, the basic purpose of promotional material is to communicate a message to an audience. In order to communicate the message effectively, the promotional materials must be designed to promote a response in the customer. Marketing professionals use the acronym AIDA to describe the sequence of response promotional materials must evoke. They must:

- get the Attention of potential customers;
- hold their Interest;
- create a Desire for the product being promoted;
- stimulate Action to buy the product.

ATTENTION

The first thing the promotional materials must do is to get the attention of the target audience. Obviously, to do this the materials must be placed where they will be seen by potential customers – whether this is on national television, an advertisement in a specialist magazine, a glossy brochure distributed to other businesses, a sponsored sportsperson or another method of promotion. Promotional materials must also stand out and make potential customers notice them.

Consider the advertisements you see on television, or the 'junk mail' that comes through the door. What makes you take notice of one advertisement, while another goes by without you realising it? Or what makes you look at one piece of 'junk mail', while you throw the rest unopened into the waste paper basket?

Advertisers can attract the attention of potential customers by using:

- bright, bold colours;
- attractive, eye-catching design of materials;
- striking illustrations – whether attractive, appealing or shocking;
- images which can be instantly recognised and associated with the product or organisation;
- bold headlines or slogans;
- good quality paper and printing for brochures and leaflets;
- well-known celebrities – either in illustrations endorsing the product, or through sponsorship;
- familiar or easily remembered music in television or radio advertisements.

QUICK response

Think of an advertisement which has caught your attention recently. What was it about the advertisement that caught your attention?

INTEREST

Grabbing the attention of potential customers is the first step. Next the promotional material has to build on this by holding their interest long enough for the message to be conveyed. The actual content of the promotional material should be:

- appropriate to the product and the potential customer;
- relevant to the audience, so that it points to a way of meeting a need or resolving a problem;
- interesting and enjoyable;
- informative.

Desire

The content of the promotional material must also make potential customers actually want the product being promoted. For example, the product might be shown as:

- meeting a need that the potential customer has;
- cost-effective;
- attractive;
- efficient;
- meeting other needs as well;
- the latest thing, for example in terms of style or technology.

Action

Finally, the promotional material must encourage potential customers to take the necessary action to buy the product – and so become *actual* customers.

Buying the product must therefore be made as easy as possible. Point of sale promotional material does this by enabling customers to buy the product where and at the time they see the promotion. This can encourage impulse buying – where customers buy a product as a result of seeing the promotion, rather than because it was what they wanted anyway. Examples of this are displays of videos in supermarkets which are intended to persuade customers to purchase the video in addition to their normal shopping.

Advertisements in newspapers and magazines can encourage prospective customers to purchase the product by including a tear-off reply coupon or freephone telephone number which can be used to order or obtain more information about the product. Payment can be easily made over the telephone using a credit card. Other products may be well known, so that prospective customers know where to purchase them. Even advertisements for products like cars, however, can encourage customers to purchase by offering credit terms (sometimes free) or another payment plan. A car advertisement can include a reply coupon to request further information in the form of a glossy brochure. Such requests can be passed to local dealers who will follow up the brochure with a telephone call in an attempt to make a sale.

ACTIVITY

Look through a magazine or the colour supplement of a Saturday or Sunday newspaper. Select one advertisement to study. Identify how your chosen advertisement meets the requirements of AIDA.

EVALUATING THE SUCCESS OF PROMOTIONAL MATERIALS

Effective promotional materials cost time and money. Ineffective promotional materials waste time and money.

It is important, therefore, to evaluate the success of promotional materials. Evaluation is important for two main reasons:

- To consider whether the promotional materials achieved their objectives or if further promotional activity is required.
- To consider whether they could be improved in any way, and if so how.

All promotional materials should be evaluated against their stated objectives. As you have seen (p 199) the principal objectives of promotional materials are:

- to communicate a message to an audience;
- to create sales;
- to influence customers' perception;
- to provide information.

An evaluation of the effectiveness of promotional materials will therefore ask questions such as:

- 'Did the materials attract the attention of potential customers?'
- 'Did they get the message across to the target audience?'
- 'Have sales of the product increased?'
- 'Did the promotional materials attract new customers and help to retain existing ones?'
- 'Did they portray an appropriate image?'

- 'Has consumer perception of the product and the organisation improved as a result of the promotion?'
- 'Is there increased awareness of the product and the organisation?'

Answers to these questions may be found by:

- carrying out a survey of customers and potential customers, by interviewing them or completing a questionnaire face to face, by telephone or by post;
- examining the organisation's records of sales, product enquiries, customer records and so on;
- asking sales staff for their opinion of the response to the promotional materials.

A positive response to questions such as these indicates that the objectives have been achieved and the promotional materials were successful. Care must be taken, however, to ensure that other factors are excluded from the evaluation. For example, using sales figures alone in evaluating promotional materials could be misleading if increased sales could be a result of seasonal variations – such as increased sales at Christmas. In this case, allowance must be made for the normal anticipated seasonal variation.

QUICK response

If a business found that its advertising campaign was not having the desired effect on sales, what could the business do?

CASE STUDY

The Vale range

Belvoir Fruit Drinks Limited is a medium sized company based near Grantham in Lincolnshire. A consortium of four farms established the company in 1975 to market fruit juices produced by the farms. They sold these mainly through major high street supermarket chains. The Vale range of drinks quickly became established and, by 1985, sales had reached £25 million a year.

It was soon apparent, however, that the company was unable to maintain such a high level of sales. By 1990, sales had dropped to less than £15 million. This decline caused considerable concern and, in view of the investment which had gone into the company over the past 15 years, the directors called for an immediate review of the situation.

Market research revealed that:

- The main customers for the Vale range were mothers buying fruit juice for their young children as part of the weekly shopping.
- There was a growing market for fruit drinks seen as 'healthy', which were bought by customers in their late twenties upwards as part of a trend towards a healthier lifestyle.
- There was a trend towards buying fruit juices in cartons rather than in traditional glass or plastic bottles as used by the Vale range.

As a result, Belvoir Fruit Drinks Limited decided to try to revive flagging sales by breaking into the growing market for healthy fruit drinks. The company reduced the sugar content of its fruit juices and changed from bottles to cartons. In 1992, the company embarked on a promotional campaign designed to change public perception of their product and to increase sales. The following methods of promotion were used.

- **Advertising**: a series of television advertisements was produced by a firm of marketing consultants. This was intended to raise the Vale range of drinks in the awareness of the public and to emphasise its energy- and health-giving aspects. Vale fruit juices were also shown as refreshing drinks for any occasion.
- **Point of sale**: the television advertising was reinforced by attention-grabbing point of sale marketing in supermarkets and also in health-food shops which were seen as an important new outlet for the drinks.

By 1995, sales of the Vale range had topped £30 million. The latest research by the company suggests that the brand is better known in some areas than others but that, generally, they are seen as healthy, energy-giving drinks rather than just children's fruit juices. The new packaging also appears to be helping to increase sales too. Shoppers in supermarkets are more likely to put half a dozen cartons into their shopping trolley to take home than to buy bottles which are heavy and bulky.

PORTFOLIO ASSIGNMENT

For this portfolio assignment you will look at different types of promotion and the constraints placed on business organisations. You will also produce your own promotional materials for a product or service, which could be an event, and evaluate their effectiveness.

TASK 1

Identify three types of business promotion, including an advertisement and a sponsorship. For each method, describe one product which is promoted using that method, and the content of the promotion. Explain the purpose of each promotion and how the content is constrained by the Consumer Protection Act and the Advertising Standards Authority.

TASK 2

This task should be completed in groups. Prepare a plan for producing material to promote a product or service. This could, for example, be an event at your school or college, a service provided by your school or college, such as the library or refectory, or a product sold at your college shop. Your promotional material could include posters, leaflets, videos and audio tapes, and may be computer-generated. Your plan should explain the purpose of the material and contain estimates of resources required, including costs.

TASK 3

Produce the promotional materials in your plan and use them to promote the product or service. You will need to keep the promotional material, or a copy or photograph of it, in your Portfolio of Evidence.

TASK 4

Write an informal report evaluating the effectiveness of the promotional materials you produced. Include an appendix explaining the part you played in carrying out Tasks 2, 3 and 4.

This portfolio assignment also presents an opportunity to gather evidence for the following core skills:

- Communication – take part in discussions; produce written material.

PROVIDING CUSTOMER SERVICE

The world of business today is a competitive world. The number of business organisations trying to sell the goods and services they produce is growing faster than the number of customers to sell them to. To attract and keep customers, businesses have to offer more than just a good product which does what it is supposed to. They have to offer something called **customer service**.

Customer service means ensuring that the customer is happy. It means putting the needs of the customer first. Above all, it means providing what the customer wants, not only in terms of the product, but in:

- dealing with enquiries;
- handling complaints;
- making refunds;
- helping the customer to purchase the product by arranging credit terms or other easy payment methods as appropriate;
- ensuring that the product is the right one for the customer and meets their needs.

Customer service is a vital part of the relationship between customers and businesses. It is often the factor which makes a customer buy from one organisation rather than from another. If a business provides poor customer service, it will lose customers to a competitor who provides good service, even though the product is the same. The survival of a business may therefore depend on its customer service.

Providing good customer service is the responsibility of everyone who works in the business. This is so whether they have direct contact with the customers or not. A salesperson may be in direct contact with the customer, but an accounts clerk, for example, is responsible for seeing that the invoice the customer receives is accurate and that payments made by the customer are correctly dealt with, thus avoiding customer complaints and frustration with the business.

QUICK response

Before reading this element, note down why you think it is important for a business to attract and keep customers.

ACTIVITY

As a class, discuss the type of service you expect as a customer of a shop or other retail outlet. Agree a definition of customer service.

CUSTOMERS AND CUSTOMER NEEDS

Not all people who may be considered customers of an organisation are immediately recognised as such. For example, customers may be:

- paying or non-paying;
- external or internal.

Consider the following:

- A person who buys a ticket for a disco run by EME Enterprises Limited is a paying external customer of EME Enterprises.
- A National Health patient in The Queen's Medical Centre in Nottingham is a non-paying external customer of The Queen's Medical Centre.
- A member of staff who works at EME Enterprises as a security guard and wants a new uniform is an internal customer of EME Enterprises.

A paying customer is therefore a person or organisation who buys and pays for the goods or services of an organisation. A non-paying customer is a person who is provided with goods or services by an organisation but who does not pay the organisation for them. An external customer is a person or organisation who is provided with goods or services by another organisation which is separate from the customer. An internal customer is an employee who is provided with goods or services in the course of their work by the organisation which employs them. An organisation which is part of a group and which receives goods or services from another organisation within that group can also be considered as an internal customer.

Whether a customer is paying or non-paying, external or internal, they have the right to expect the same high standard of customer service. The needs of customers which customer service seeks to meet fall into seven basic categories.

1 **To make a purchase**: Customers wishing to make a purchase are the lifeblood of a business, and everything should be done to make this as simple as possible. Assistance should be given in helping the customer to choose a product which meets their needs. Accepting payment in cash, by credit or debit card, or by arranging hire purchase, can give help in paying for the product. Additional services, such as delivery of the product, extended warranties and after-sales service, are also services which can help to attract new customers and retain existing ones.

2 **To obtain information**: Often, prospective customers require information about a product before committing themselves to buying it. Information about the organisation, its products or services, prices, suitability for different purposes and available alternatives helps customers to choose a product from one supplier rather than another. Some organisations also provide more general information about types of products and matters such as environmental issues which are of concern to consumers. Waitrose, for example, provides a range of leaflets on nutrition, healthy eating and other matters. A business should identify the kinds of information prospective customers would like and ensure that this is freely available for customers to take away with them to study at their leisure.

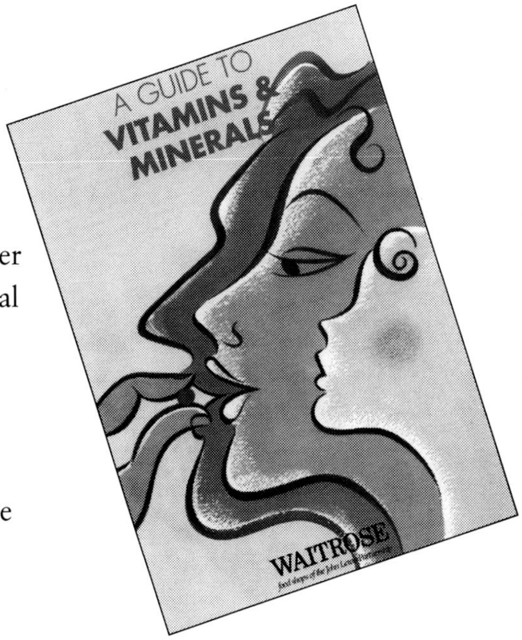

Many organisations provide information on health or environmental concerns.

ACTIVITY

Choose a product, such as a camera or a CD player, which you would like to investigate. Visit two or three retailers who supply your chosen product and enquire about it as if you were a prospective customer. Obtain all the information you can. Afterwards, write notes about the quality of customer service each retailer gave in supplying information.

3 **To obtain a refund**: Almost inevitably there will be times when a product or service supplied to a customer is not satisfactory. This may be because it is faulty, or does not meet the customer's

requirements. In either case the customer will probably want a refund. If the refund is given promptly and without undue fuss, the customer will be satisfied and likely to remain a customer. If the refund is given grudgingly and the customer is made to feel uneasy, they will probably take their custom elsewhere in future.

> **QUICK response**
>
> **If you sold a customer goods which proved to be faulty, would it be better to give a refund or to exchange the goods? Why?**

4 **To exchange goods**: An alternative to giving a refund is to exchange the goods if the customer is willing to accept a replacement. If the goods originally supplied were faulty, then they can be exchanged for goods which are in sound condition. Goods which do not fulfil the purpose for which the customer wants them should be exchanged for alternative goods which do. Many larger retail stores, such as Marks and Spencer and Littlewoods, will automatically exchange goods which customers return, or give refunds if preferred.

5 **To make a complaint**: Unfortunately, satisfying every customer all the time is impossible, and some dissatisfied customers will make complaints. Complaints should be dealt with speedily, efficiently and courteously. There should be a set procedure for dealing with complaints, and all staff in an organisation should be familiar with this. Customers whose complaints are dealt with in such a manner may well remain customers once their complaints have been sorted out to their satisfaction. Customers who feel the need to complain and are then dissatisfied by the way their complaint is handled will, in future, take their custom elsewhere.

6 **Special needs**: Many customers have special needs, and these should be given particular attention. Children, for example, may need help in expressing themselves and deciding what they want. They may also find it difficult to handle money. Parents with children, perhaps in a push chair, have to consider their child first, and may themselves need special attention. Elderly people are sometimes unsure of themselves and may need help climbing stairs, or need a chair to sit on. Many customers have physical disadvantages and need physical assistance. Ramps for wheelchairs to gain access to premises are one way in which a business organisation can provide customer service for the disabled. Induction loops can help the hard of hearing. Foreign customers may not understand English well or need help in expressing themselves. Other customers may be particularly shy or nervous and need time, understanding and encouragement. By providing these kinds of services for people with special needs, a business

Some customers have special needs.

can attract many customers who will be happy with the service they receive and remain loyal.

7 **Ethical standards**: All customers expect, and are entitled, to be treated fairly and with respect. All business activity should be conducted both within the law and according to high ethical standards. Even in the cut-throat world of business today, a business which conducts its activities according to ethical standards will win the respect and loyalty of its customers and also attract new ones.

TYPES OF CUSTOMER SERVICE IN AN ORGANISATION

The individual needs of customers and the methods of providing customer service are different for different types of business. Levels and methods of providing customer service vary even between organisations providing the same goods and services. Types of customer service range from simple notices in shop windows stating opening hours to customer service staff specially trained to deal with customers' enquiries, requests for exchanges or refunds and complaints. Most business organisations keep up-to-date records of their customers, including details of their purchases. In some major stores and supermarkets with electronic tills, customer records are updated automatically when each purchase is registered on the till. Other methods of providing customer service include measures to reduce the time taken for customers to be served; providing leaflets and information about products, their effect on health or on the environment, and about the business itself; improved access to premises and facilities for customers with special needs; and even training staff to greet customers with a smile and a friendly gesture, to make them feel welcome and valued by the business.

ACTIVITY

Select a business organisation with which you are familiar or to which you have easy access. For example, you may choose a local department store, a public library or leisure centre, or even your school or college. If you work part-time in the evenings or at weekends, you may choose your employer. Visit the organisation you have chosen and identify ways in which it provides customer service. Write a summary describing the customer service provided by your chosen organisation. Keep this in your portfolio of evidence. It forms an important part of the evidence you will produce for this element.

TYPES OF BUSINESS COMMUNICATIONS WHICH MEET THE NEEDS OF CUSTOMERS

Meeting the needs of customers and providing customer service involves communications. Communications is one of the core skills you are studying as part of your GNVQ course. Here, we shall cover some aspects of how communications are applied in business.

There are two main types of communications in which you must develop skills:

- oral communications – that is, through speaking and listening;
- written communications – that is, through letters, memos and other forms of written material, some of which may be printed.

ORAL COMMUNICATION

Whenever you speak to somebody, or somebody speaks to you, you are using oral communication. It is the most common form of communication, and the one with which we are all most familiar. Most oral communication takes place either face to face or over the telephone.

When you go into a shop and ask the sales assistant for a pair of jeans, you are using face to face oral communication. If, when you get home, you find the jeans are faulty, you may telephone the shop to let the assistant know that you will bring them back next week and expect to exchange them for a perfect pair.

Although we all talk to people every day, being able to use oral communication effectively is a skill which must be learned and practised.

Some points about oral communication which you should bear in mind are to:

- speak clearly;
- check that your listener understands what you are saying;
- use words which are appropriate to the situation – do not use colloquial expressions or swear words when speaking to customers;
- be polite and formal, but do not be cold; try to put the customer at ease;
- watch carefully for any non-verbal clues as to what the other person is actually thinking – these can sometimes be at variance with what they are saying;
- listen carefully to what the other person says to you – and allow them time to say it;
- be confident and helpful;
- if you cannot deal with a problem, say so – do not waffle or make excuses: pass the problem on to someone else who can deal with it.

Watch carefully for non-verbal clues as to what the other person is actually thinking!

ACTIVITY

For this and the next activity you should form pairs. The activities consist of two situations in each of which one of you should role play the customer and the other the person dealing with the customer. The one playing the customer in the first situation should play the person dealing with the customer in the second situation. In each situation you should decide exactly what you are going to say before acting out the role play. A 'witness statement' or 'record of observation' should be completed by your tutor to confirm that they have observed you. They may add their own comments and evaluation to this. It is also helpful if the role play can be recorded on video which can be used as evidence.

Situation 1
This takes place in a shop which sells gas cookers. The customer came into the shop last week and purchased a gas cooker. Delivery of the cooker was promised within two days but the customer is still waiting. The customer has returned to the shop to find out why the cooker has not yet been delivered and what is happening. The person serving the customer this time knows nothing about the matter but takes all relevant details and promises to telephone the customer later that day to confirm when delivery will be made.

Situation 2
This takes place in a bookshop. The customer wants to buy a particular book. The person serving the customer explains that the book is not in stock but can be ordered. He or she takes details of the book and the customer, promising to telephone when the book is in.

Using the telephone is more difficult than speaking face to face, and many people are uncomfortable about making telephone calls.

One of the main problems with telephone communications is that when you talk to someone on the telephone you cannot see their response or facial expressions. It is especially important, therefore, to listen carefully to what the other person is saying – and the way they say it. Note their tone of voice and the words they use.

The telephone can be an important tool in meeting customers' needs but, as with all forms of communications, you need to know how to use it effectively.

- If the telephone rings, answer it promptly – a sale can be lost if a customer gets fed up with waiting.
- When you answer the telephone, be polite and helpful – even if you have an irate customer making a complaint on the other end.
- Write down the important points of the conversation as the caller makes them so that you can refer to them later (it is useful to keep a pen and paper near the telephone for this).
- If you cannot deal with the call, pass it to someone who can (make sure you know how the telephone system works and how to transfer calls).
- If you cannot deal with a call then and there, or cannot transfer it, write down the caller's name and telephone number and promise to call back – if possible, arrange a time for this.
- If you do promise to call someone back, or arrange for someone else to do so, make sure the call is made.

QUICK response

When speaking on the telephone, your manner and tone of voice are especially important because ________.

ACTIVITY

This activity follows on from the last activity. It involves simulated telephone calls in which the person who served the customer in the last activity now telephones the customer. If dummy telephones are not available, the simulation can be performed by talking to each other with a barrier between you so that neither person can see the other. In each situation you should decide exactly what you are going to say before acting out the role play. A 'witness statement' or 'record of observation' should be completed by your tutor to confirm that they have observed you. They may add their own comments and evaluation to this. It is also helpful if the role plays can be recorded on video or audio tape which can be used as evidence.

Situation 1

The person who dealt with the customer has found out that the cooker was not delivered because the driver was ill. They telephone the customer as promised to apologise and to tell them that the cooker will be delivered next Tuesday if this is convenient. The sales assistant asks for directions to the customer's address.

> **Situation 2**
> **The book ordered by the customer is now in stock at the bookshop. The person who served the customer therefore telephones the customer to inform them of this. The customer asks for the book to be posted and gives their name and address when asked.**

WRITTEN COMMUNICATIONS

The most common types of written communications you will have to deal with are letters and memos. Letters are used for written communications with people and business organisations outside the organisation you work for. Memos (short for memoranda) are used for written communications with other people who work in the same organisation. Business letters and memos are more formal than the letters you write to your friends, although they basically serve the same purpose – to communicate a message. Examples of business letters and memos are shown in *Fig. 3.10* and on p 219.

HiTown Interiors Limited

☎ 0115 867432

79 King Street Leicester LE1 9YZ

P J Decorators Ltd
18 Maid Marion Way
Nottingham
NG2 7JY

Our Ref: JN
Your Ref: 9763

20 February 1996

Dear Sir or Madam

Re: Your Order Number 9763

Thank you for your above order for quarry tiles, received today. We are pleased to confirm that the tiles are in stock and will be despatched from our warehouse early next week. Should you have any queries relating to this order, please contact the undersigned.

Yours faithfully

FIGURE 3.10 A business letter.

FIGURE 3.11 A business letter and two memos.

Williams Homes plc
30 High Street Camberley Surrey
Telephone 01276 69341

Miss J Stevens
27 Field Road
Epsom
Surrey

Our Ref: ST

19 September 1996

Dear Miss Stevens

Thank you for your recent application for the post of Sales Negotiator with Williams Homes Limited.

Would you please attend for interview at this office on next Tuesday, 25 September, at 3.00 pm.

Yours sincerely

Sara Thomson
Personnel Manager

HiTown Interiors Ltd
Memo

Date 20 February 1996

From J Nicholls, Sales Manager

Subject P J Decorators, Nottingham

To Mrs Y Johnson, Warehouse Manager

As you know, P J Decorators is a new customer. Although their first order for quarry tiles is relatively small, I feel that they are trying us. Future orders from this customer could be very profitable.

I am concerned, therefore that nothing should go wrong with this order. Please keep me informed of progress, and if there are any difficulties with delivery early next week, let me know in order that I may contact the customer.

Williams Homes
memo

Date 26 September 1996

To Trish Parker, Training Officer

From Sara Thomson, Personnel Manager

Subject Training

Just to remind you that following the interviews yesterday, seven new Sales Negotiators will be starting with the company next month. It is important that they are able to attend the three day residential Sales Negotiators course as soon as possible. Please give this priority.

ACTIVITY

- **Write a business letter to the customer you spoke to on the telephone in the last activity. Your letter should confirm everything that was said in that telephone conversation. You should choose a name for the business and design your own headed letter paper for your letter.**
- **Write a memo to Mr Peter Taylor, Despatch Manager of the shop, advising him of the delivery to be made, including information about the item to be delivered and the customer's address.**

You should keep your letter and memo in your portfolio of evidence. It will form part of your portfolio assignment for this element.

An advantage of written communications is that they are permanent records of the communication and can be referred to later if required. As they are permanent, they can also be read at leisure, which means that they can contain more information which may take longer to digest and understand. Other types of visual information, such as pictures, tables, graphs and diagrams, can also be included in written communications.

Other forms of written communications are used in business for various purposes. These are often printed or on pre-printed forms. Such communications include:

- customer and product information – such as price lists, specifications, invoices and statements of account (invoices and statements of account are dealt with in detail in Unit 4);
- guarantees and warranties – which explain the rights of customers, and the responsibilities of the supplier after the goods or services have been sold;
- safety notices – which confirm that the product meets statutory safety requirements.

ACTIVITY

Most business organisations have established procedures for dealing with customer complaints. Find out what procedure would be followed in your school or college if either you or your parents or guardians, as customers of the college, wished to make a complaint. Write a summary describing how the complaint would be dealt with and the different stages in the complaints procedure. You should keep your summary in your portfolio of evidence. It will form an important part of your evidence for this element.

CONSUMER LAW

While the high standards of customer service provided by most business organisations ensure that customers can deal confidently with those businesses, there are various laws which protect customers from unsatisfactory or inadequate goods or services. The four main Acts are:

- The Trades Descriptions Act 1968;
- The Sale of Goods Act 1979, extended by the Supply of Goods and Services Act 1982;
- The Consumer Protection Act 1987;
- The Health and Safety at Work Act 1974.

THE TRADES DESCRIPTIONS ACT 1968

This law is intended to protect consumers from misleading and untrue advertisements. It makes it a criminal offence to misrepresent any goods or services offered for sale. Although the Act is mainly concerned with written descriptions in advertisements and labels on products, it does also apply to verbal statements. This is intended to protect customers from false claims for products made by salespeople who might make untrue or exaggerated claims for a product or service in order to make a sale.

Examples of offences under the Trades Descriptions Act are:

- false claims about the facilities of hotels in holiday brochures;

- turning back the recorded mileage of a secondhand car and so falsifying the mileometer reading;
- making false claims about the ability of a health food to cure an illness.

THE SALE OF GOODS ACT 1979

The Sale of Goods Act imposes three important conditions on goods that are offered for sale.

- They must be of 'merchantable quality' – that is, they should be in good condition and have no known defects. For example, it is an offence under the Act to sell as perfect a dress which has a flaw in the material.
- Goods offered for sale must be fit for the purpose for which they are intended and have been sold. For example, it would be an offence under the Act to sell a dish described – verbally or in writing – as suitable for microwave cooking if it is made of a material which warps when used in a microwave.
- Goods sold must be as described. For example, a hair dryer described as suitable for use throughout Europe must be fitted with an adapter which will enable it to be connected to electric sockets in Britain and continental European countries.

While the Sale of Goods Act only applies to goods offered for sale, in 1982 the Supply of Goods and Services Act was passed, extending the terms of the earlier Act to cover services. The Sale of Goods and Services Act introduced the concept of 'merchantable quality' to services, and also required anybody offering a service, such as a car repairer, to provide that service with reasonable care, in reasonable time and at a reasonable cost.

THE CONSUMER PROTECTION ACT 1987

The Consumer Protection Act 1987 was introduced to bring Britain in line with the rest of the European Union. It deals with two important aspects of consumer protection.

- The Consumer Protection Act makes it an offence to supply goods which do not meet general safety standards. For example, if you buy a food mixer and receive an electric shock when you switch it on, you can take legal action against the business which supplied you with the mixer. The Government has the power to prohibit the sale of goods which are considered to be unsafe or dangerous.

- The Consumer Protection Act makes it a criminal offence to give misleading price indications about goods and services. Goods which are offered at reduced prices in a sale, for example, must display the reduced price and the last price at which the goods were offered for sale and available to customers for at least 28 consecutive days in the previous six months.

THE HEALTH AND SAFETY AT WORK ACT 1974 (HASAWA)

The aim of this Act is to improve the safety of employees and others in workplaces. Business organisations must have a written health and safety policy which is made available to all employees. Training must be provided in health and safety matters. Employers have a responsibility to provide a safe environment for their employees to work in. Employees also have a responsibility to work in accordance with health and safety practice and not to behave in any way that could put themselves or others in danger.

The Health and Safety at Work Act is important in protecting the safety of customers on business premises. For example, when floors are being cleaned in shops and supermarkets, and may be slippery and thus cause an accident, signs must be displayed warning customers of the danger.

ACTIVITY

Consider the following cases and identify which Act applies.

- **You have just bought a rather expensive fountain pen from a stationers in town. When you arrive home, you take the pen out of its box and clip it in the top pocket of your jacket. As you do so the clip breaks.**
  When you return the pen to the shop where you bought it, the sales assistant denies responsibility. 'It's obviously a fault in manufacture,' she says. 'If you like, I can give you the address of the manufacturer. I suppose they might repair it for you.'
- **Maria DaCosta is annoyed. She has just taken delivery of a new watch which she bought from a catalogue. 'I'm sorry,' she tells the customer services clerk who answers her telephone call, 'but this isn't what I ordered. I want a gold watch.'**
  'That's what we sent you,' the customer service clerk explains. 'When it's described in the catalogue as gold, we mean gold colour – not made of gold.'

PORTFOLIO ASSIGNMENT

For this portfolio assignment you will look at customer research and protection in a business organisation. Advice on finding information about business was given on p x in the Introduction. You may wish to refer to this again before starting this assignment. An essential part of your evidence for this element is the work you produced for the activities on pp 216, 217 and 220. You should keep this in your Portfolio of Evidence together with work produced for this assignment.

TASK 1

Choose a business organisation to investigate. This may be an organisation you are familiar with, such as your school or college, where you have done work experience, or where you work part-time in the evenings or at weekends. Write an informal report which identifies the organisation's customers and describe the customer services it provides. You should give examples of at least one oral and one written business communication within the organisation and describe the organisation's procedures for dealing with customer complaints.

TASK 2

Write a summary of the following:

- The Trades Descriptions Act;
- The Sale of Goods Act;
- The Consumer Protection Act;
- The Health and Safety at Work Act.

This portfolio assignment also presents an opportunity to gather evidence for the following core skills:

- Communication – take part in discussions; produce written material; read and respond to written material.

Improving Customer Service

The importance of customer service

You have seen that when they are buying goods and services customers expect more from a business organisation than just a quality product which meets their needs. They look for a high level of customer service from the business.

ACTIVITY

Suggest reasons why business organisations must strive to give high levels of customer service.

In today's competitive world, no business organisation can afford to neglect the wishes and expectations of its customers. Many other organisations are chasing those same customers and will respect their wishes and expectations. Providing good customer service is vitally important for business organisations. There are several reasons for this.

- **To gain and retain customers**: A business which gives good customer service will soon find that it is attracting new customers and keeping its existing customers. This will lead to increased sales and profit for the business.
- **To gain customer satisfaction**: Customers are more likely to continue to buy from a business they are satisfied with rather than take their custom elsewhere. In this way a business will obtain repeat sales. Receiving good customer service is an important element in customer satisfaction.
- **To gain customer loyalty**: Satisfied customers of a business will remain customers of that business, and are likely to be loyal to the

business. This means they are less likely to be swayed by the promotional material of competitors.

- **To enhance the organisation's image**: When a business provides good customer service, this becomes known to other customers of the type of goods and services provided by the business. The image of the business is therefore enhanced as one which provides good service. Marks and Spencer, for example, have enhanced their reputation and image by the customer service they give. When the image of a business is enhanced in the eyes of customers in this way, attracting new customers and increasing sales to existing customers are likely results.

MONITORING CUSTOMER SERVICE

As satisfied customers are so important, businesses must monitor, or measure, how satisfied their own customers are with the level of customer service they give. They do this in several ways.

- **Numbers of customers**: Monitoring numbers of customers will tell a business whether these are increasing or decreasing. Increasing numbers of customers are likely to indicate a high level of customer satisfaction with the service the business provides.
- **Level of sales**: Monitoring the level of sales will provide a measure of the uptake by customers of the goods or services provided by a business. An increasing level of sales is likely to indicate a high level of customer satisfaction.

ACTIVITY

Why do you think it is important for a business to monitor numbers of customers and level of sales?

- **Feedback**: Feedback from customers can be obtained in several ways. Information can be gathered either formally or informally. For example, a high level of repeat orders shows that customers are satisfied with the level of customer service a business provides. If a business receives many complaints, however, this shows that customers are not satisfied with the level of customer service provided by the business.

- **Marketing research**: Marketing research involves gathering information in a structured way from a target audience. There are five stages in marketing research.

  1 Identify the type of information required.

  2 Decide the method of collecting the information.

  3 Select the target audience from whom to collect the information.

  4 Collect the information.

  5 Analyse the results obtained.

Fig. 3.12 shows different methods that can be used to monitor customer satisfaction, how they can be carried out and the type of information they obtain.

Method	Type of information obtained	Procedure
Observation	Numbers of customers Level of sales The behaviour of customers and their reactions to customer service given	Watching customers and recording their behaviour, for example in a store, to find out how many customers visit the store, how many actually buy, and what they buy. It is often possible to observe how customers react to levels of customer service provided.
Researching existing records	Numbers of customers Level of sales Repeat business Complaints	Obtaining the required information from records already held by the organisation. Such records may be sales orders and records, customer records, sales reports, and so on. They may be paper records, or held on computer.
Survey	Specific information about customer service and satisfaction	This method involves actually asking customers and potential customers for their views. Surveys may be carried out face to face, perhaps in an interview, over the telephone, or by post. Frequently, surveys are conducted using a questionnaire to obtain quite specific information which can then be easily analysed.

FIGURE 3.12 Methods of monitoring customer satisfaction.

DESIGNING A QUESTIONNAIRE

Some methods of monitoring customer satisfaction use a questionnaire, or list of questions, to obtain the specific information required. When you are constructing a questionnaire, you must make sure that the questions really ask what you intend. **Closed questions**, which call for a specific response, are easier to analyse later, while **open questions**, which may have a wide range of answers, can be difficult to analyse. Examples of closed questions are:

- 'How old are you?'

- 'Have you ever bought X brand dog food?'
- 'On a scale of 1 to 5, where 1 is very dissatisfied and 5 is very satisfied, how satisfied were you with your holiday overall? Tick as appropriate': 1.... 2.... 3.... 4.... 5....

QUICK response

Why is it better to include closed questions in a questionnaire rather than open questions?

Examples of open questions are:

- 'Why did you shop at Riley's?'
- 'What is important to you as a customer?'

You should draft and redraft each question you include on a questionnaire carefully. Try them out on people like those for whom the questionnaire is intended. Ask yourself:

- Who is the questionnaire for?
- What information am I trying to obtain?
- Is there any other information which might be useful?
- Is each question really necessary?
- Does it ask what I want to know?
- Is it easy to understand or might it be misunderstood?
- Is it a leading question – that is, does it imply that a particular answer is right?

ACTIVITY

Design a questionnaire which you can use to find out the types of leisure facilities students would like to see provided by your school or college. Try your questionnaire out on students at your school or college who are not in your class.

IDENTIFYING IMPROVEMENTS TO CUSTOMER SERVICE

The purpose of monitoring customer satisfaction is for businesses to be able to identify areas where they can improve the customer service they give. Areas in which businesses can typically identify improvements which could be made to customer service include the following.

- **Reliability**: A reputation for reliability will help a business to increase sales by retaining existing customers and attracting new ones.
- **Friendliness**: Most customers appreciate being made to feel welcome and that the business, represented by the person serving them, values them as a customer. A smile and a friendly word cost nothing but, as many businesses have found out, friendliness is an aspect of customer service which many customers rate highly. Many businesses, such as major supermarkets and restaurants, give staff who have direct contact with customers special training in greeting and serving customers.
- **Availability of goods and services**: Customers are more likely to go to a business where they know that the goods or services they require will be easily available – either now or when they require them.
- **Speed of delivery**: In the same way, customers expect goods which they have purchased, but may be too heavy or bulky for them to take away themselves, to be delivered without having to wait too long. If you buy a new computer system, you want it delivered in a few days so that you can start using it. If a retailer is unable to deliver it until next month, you will probably buy it somewhere else. You also want it delivered on the day it is promised.

DHL offer a specialist delivery service.

- **Published policy for exchanges or refunds**: Many businesses have a published policy for exchanging goods or services supplied if they are faulty or do not meet the needs of the customer. Many customers are encouraged to buy from a particular organisation, confident in the knowledge that if their purchase turns out to be unsatisfactory in

any way, they can exchange it or obtain a refund. Marks and Spencer is one chain of stores whose policy of exchanging goods or giving refunds is well known. Obviously, the policy is open to abuse, with, for example, people taking back Christmas and birthday presents they have received and obtaining the money for them. However, the option of being able to return goods for exchange or refund encourages more sales, which more than offsets the number of people who do return the goods.

- **Access to buildings**: Ease of access to buildings is an aspect of customer service which businesses often overlook. People in wheelchairs, and parents with children in pushchairs, in particular, need ease of access. Steps can be difficult to negotiate for many customers, and handrails can provide ease of access for the elderly or infirm, while business premises are increasingly being provided with ramps for customers in wheelchairs or with pushchairs. Wide doors and lifts also enable people in wheelchairs to use them. Many supermarkets now have specially widened checkouts for customers in wheelchairs or pushing prams.

QUICK response

Besides providing access to buildings, in what other ways can a business provide customer service for customers with special needs?

- **Care for the environment**: There is increasing public concern for the environment. Customers expect manufacturers and suppliers to help to maintain the environment by avoiding pollution and waste. When McDonalds began a programme of rapid expansion during the 1960s and 1970s, there was a considerable public outcry about the amount of rubbish dropped outside and left to litter the roads and pavements. McDonalds soon responded by employing people to clear up the rubbish and keep the environment around their restaurants litter-free – even though the rubbish was dropped by McDonalds' customers and not McDonalds themselves. McDonalds now has clear environmental policies which are well publicised and are considered to contribute to their success.

- **Customer safety**: Customer safety must be paramount. All customers have a right to expect any business organisation supplying them with goods or services to take all reasonable precautions to ensure their safety and well-being. This is so whether on the premises of the business, of the customer or elsewhere. Even when there is an element of danger involved, a business must take all reasonable measures to safeguard the customer. For example, many sports, such as motor racing, are inevitably dangerous and this is often part of their attraction. However, the organisers of a motor racing meeting have a duty to take reasonable precautions to ensure the safety of spectators.

ACTIVITY

In groups of three or four, discuss the areas of customer service described above. How important do you think they are in attracting and keeping customers. Are there any other areas of customer service where business organisations should try to improve? Discuss your findings as a class.

IDENTIFYING AND PRESENTING PROPOSALS FOR IMPROVEMENTS TO CUSTOMER SERVICE

The reason an organisation monitors its customer service and identifies areas for improvement is so that proposals for improvements in customer service can be made. Such proposals are, in fact, recommendations for improving customer satisfaction with the organisation and the products or services it supplies.

Recommendations for future improvements can be drawn from observation or from more thorough investigation and research. Suggestions should be specific and show how they would result in improved customer satisfaction. Proposals for improvements may be made in many ways. Some organisations have a 'suggestion box', into which individual employees may put their own suggestions for improvements. Any suggestions acted upon may earn the employee a reward.

Proposals based on more detailed research may be made in the form of a formal report. This should explain the suggested improvement and give the results of the research on which the proposal is based. The report should show how the recommended improvements to customer service will help the organisation to attract customers, secure customer satisfaction and loyalty, and enhance the organisation's image. Sometimes the proposal will also be given in a presentation to an audience, particularly when specific individuals are involved in implementing the improvement to customer service.

You have an opportunity of giving a presentation proposing improvements to customer service in the portfolio assignment for this element.

PORTFOLIO ASSIGNMENT

For this portfolio assignment you will investigate and make a presentation on the customer service provided by a business organisation. Advice on finding information about business is given on p x in the Introduction. You may wish to refer to this again before starting this assignment.

TASK 1

Choose a business organisation with which you are familiar. You may, if you wish, choose the organisation you investigated for the portfolio assignment for Unit 3.3 (p 224). Investigate the customer service provided by the organisation and prepare detailed notes on:

- the customer service offered by the organisation;
- the methods used by the organisation to measure customer satisfaction.

Also outline proposals for improvements to the customer service provided by the organisation in three of the following areas:

- friendliness;
- availability of goods or services;
- speed of delivery;
- policies for making exchanges or refunds;
- access to buildings;
- customer safety;
- care for the environment.

TASK 2

Using the notes you have produced for Task 1 as a basis, prepare a presentation proposing the improvements to customer service you outlined in your notes. Make your presentation, using appropriate visual aids, as if you were presenting your ideas to an audience consisting of the directors or senior management of the organisation. In particular, your presentation should show how improved customer service in the areas identified will:

- attract customers;
- gain customer satisfaction;
- secure customer loyalty;
- enhance the image of the organisation.

Your tutor should make a record or observation of your presentation, which you should keep in your Portfolio of Evidence, together with work produced for Task 1 and any other notes for your presentation, such as visual aids used etc.

This portfolio assignment also presents an opportunity to gather evidence for the following core skills:

- Communication – produce written material; use images.

4

UNIT

Financial and administrative support

CONTENTS

OUTLINE

In this unit you will look at different types of financial transactions in business. We will demonstrate the importance of processing and recording these accurately and examine how they are recorded. You will also see how business documents, such as letters, memos, invitations, notices and messages, are produced and stored. Unit 4 provides an introduction to money management and can lead on to employment or higher level studies in accounting and finance. In working through this unit you will develop valuable transferable skills which are important in the world of business.

After completing this unit you will be able to:

1 identify and explain financial transactions and documents;

2 complete financial documents and explain financial recording;

3 produce, evaluate and store business documents.

FINANCIAL TRANSACTIONS AND DOCUMENTS

Whether a business is profit-making, non-profit-making or charitable, it must ensure that its income is equal to, or more than, its expenditure. If the income of a business is less than its expenditure, the business will make a loss. A business which continues to make a loss will not survive.

It is vital for the future planning and management of a business organisation that the senior managers of the organisation monitor the financial health of the organisation – in other words, that they continually check that the income of the organisation equals or exceeds its expenditure. To do this, all financial transactions must be accurately recorded.

ACTIVITY

As a class, discuss what might happen if an organisation did not record its financial transactions accurately – or did not record them at all. Individually, write out and justify your conclusions.

TYPES OF FINANCIAL TRANSACTIONS AND RECORDS OF TRANSACTIONS

A **financial transaction** is an exchange of money between a buyer and a seller.

- The buyer may be a business organisation or an individual customer.
- The seller is normally a business organisation.
- The money is given by the buyer in exchange for goods or services supplied by the seller.

For example, when you go into a shop to buy a can of Coke, you give some money in payment to the person at the till. You can then take the can of Coke away and drink it. You have entered into a financial transaction with the shop.

Further examples of financial transactions are as follows.

- When a business organisation pays another business for materials it has bought, it enters into a financial transaction with the other business.
- A local or national government enters into a financial transaction with organisations such as schools and libraries when it gives them funds to provide a service to the public.
- When you make a donation to a charity, perhaps by putting some money into an envelope that came through the door, or by giving to a collector in the street, you enter into a financial transaction with the charity

In all of the above examples, the transaction is two-way. It is:

- **outward** from the person or organisation making the payment;
- **inward** to the organisation receiving the payment.

The payment you made to the sales assistant in the shop in exchange for the can of Coke was an outward transaction for you, but an inward transaction for the shop.

Normally, a financial transaction between an individual consumer and a business such as a shop involves the minimum of documents. The consumer pays for the goods and may be given a receipt for the money. (Receipts are discussed on p 260.) If payment is made by credit card or debit card, a sales voucher is produced for the consumer to sign (see p 258).

QUICK response

When you pay for something you have bought in a shop, you make an __________ payment. The shop receives an __________ payment.

Individual consumers also receive money in the form of wages and salaries, loans, interest and dividends on savings. These are inward transactions to the individual consumer.

In business, outward transactions pay for the costs of the business, and inward transactions are the income received as payment for goods and services supplied by the business. A company such as Ford will enter into:

- outward transactions to pay for the raw materials it uses in the manufacture of vehicles, wages and salaries for its employees, and overheads such as factory and office costs;

- inward transactions to receive income from the sale of vehicles which the company has manufactured.

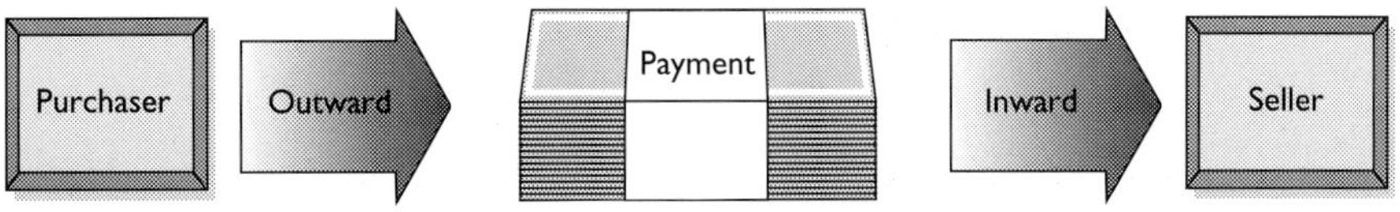

FIGURE 4.1 Inward and outward payments.

In addition, inward transactions may be in respect of money received from other sources, such as loans or government grants.

Many financial transactions in business take place regularly. Business organisations often make payments each month for costs such as:

- raw materials;
- wages and salaries;
- overheads, which include the costs of running the factories and offices of the business:
  - rent and rates;
  - electricity and gas for heating, lighting and running machinery and equipment;
  - telephone and postal charges;
  - other costs connected with carrying out the activities of the business.

The business must keep records of all inward and outward financial transactions for several reasons.

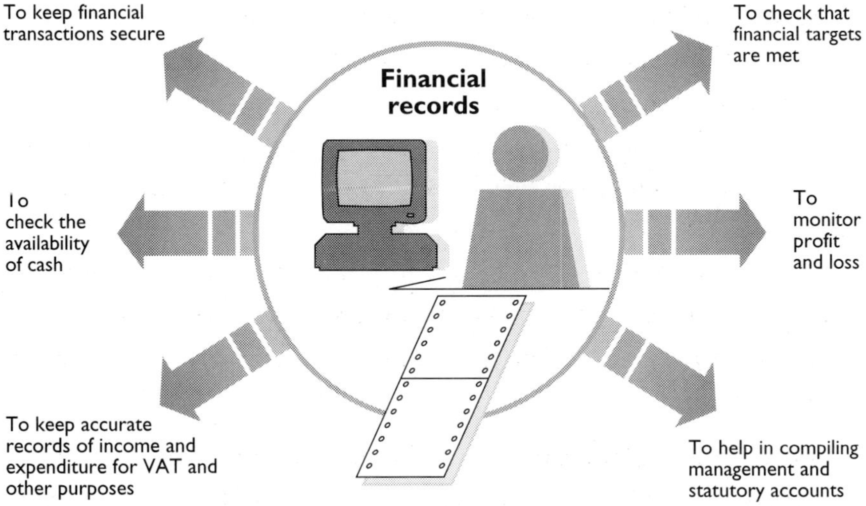

FIGURE 4.2 The purpose of financial records.

- To check that it is meeting its financial targets in terms of income and expenditure.
- To make sure it has enough cash available to pay its costs as they become due.
- To monitor its performance – that is, whether it is making a profit or a loss.
- To ensure security and make sure that all its financial transactions are carried out correctly, accurately and honestly.
- So that accurate records of income and expenditure can be passed to Customs and Excise for the payment of VAT.
- To produce accounts for both internal and external use. Accounts are, in effect, summaries of the financial transactions of a business over a period.

MANAGEMENT ACCOUNTS

Management accounts are produced at the end of each month or quarter. They show a detailed breakdown of the income and expenditure of the business during that month or quarter (known as the accounting period). An examination of the management accounts of the business will enable senior management to see whether the business is making a profit or loss, and whether targets set for income and expenditure are being met. *Fig. 4.3* shows a simple income and expenditure account for a small social club. Larger business organisations will prepare more complex management accounts.

ACTIVITY

Study the income and expenditure account in *Fig. 4.3* carefully. Has the company made a profit or a loss during the period covered by the figures? Give reasons for your answer.

As you can see, income is more than expenditure, and this means that the business has made a profit during the accounting period.

FIGURE 4.3 An income and expenditure account for a small social club.

WILLOWBROOK SOCIAL CLUB
Income and Expenditure Account for the month ended 31 March 1996

	£	£
Income		
Bar sales		5,600
Restaurant sales		1,756
Sale of tickets for disco		175
Sale of raffle-tickets		239
		7,770
Less Cost of Sales		
Bar stock and restaurant supplies	3,800	
Hire of disco equipment	230	
Purchase of raffle prizes	80	
	4,110	4,110
		3,660
Less Other Expenditure		
Personnel costs		
(Wages and Salaries, National Insurance etc)	1,000	
Rates	325	
Telephone and postage	48	
Advertising	30	
Other expenses	968	
	2,371	2,371
		1,289

However, normally a business sells goods or services in one month, but does not receive the money for them until the following month – or even later. Similarly, the business may buy goods or services one month but not pay for them until later. In the management accounts of the business these sales and purchases will be shown in the month in which they were **incurred** – that is, in the month when the goods were received or supplied, not when payment was made for them. For this reason, management accounts are not a guide to the actual money a business has available to spend. To find out how much money it has available to spend, a business must prepare a **cash flow** statement. This records income and expenditure on the date payment is actually received or sent out, regardless of when the goods were received or supplied. A cash flow statement shows the amount of money the business has available to pay bills that are due, including wages and salaries.

Targets for income and expenditure are set at the beginning of the business's financial year in a document called a **budget**. These are the levels of income and expenditure (and therefore profit) that the business hopes or expects to achieve in a given period.

QUICK response

How does the way income and expenditure are recorded in a cash flow statement differ from the way they are recorded in management accounts?

ACTIVITY

You can produce a simple budget for your own income and expenditure for next month. First, list everything you expect to have to pay, including housekeeping or living expenses, fares, the cost of going out in the evenings, books and stationery, food, drinks, sweets, and so on. This will give your total budgeted expenditure for the month. Next, list all the money you expect to receive for the month. Include any grant for the month, wages from part-time work and any other money you expect to receive. This will give you your total budgeted income for the month. If your expenditure is higher than your income, you are in trouble! You will either have to reduce your expenditure or get more income from somewhere – unless you have some extra money hidden away that is not included in your calculations. As you go through the month covered by your budget, keep a check on your actual income and expenditure and see how close you are to your budget.

Management accounts normally show budgeted targets as well as the actual figures achieved in the accounting period for comparison. They usually also show **cumulative totals**, which are totals from the start of the financial year to the end of the accounting period. These enable the management of the business to see how well the business has performed during the year up to the date of the accounts, as well as during the accounting period covered by the accounts.

Besides management accounts, a business must prepare **statutory accounts** once a year. The Inland Revenue requires these for taxation purposes (business organisations have to pay tax on any profits they make, and may have to pay other taxes as well).

PURCHASES AND PURCHASE DOCUMENTS

The expenditure of a business is largely made up of purchases of goods, materials and services. A business must also pay wages and salaries to its employees for the work they do. In order that accurate records of purchases can be kept for management accounting and other purposes, most business organisations use an established system of documents to be produced at various stages in the purchasing process. These help to ensure that the required goods or services are purchased and delivered in the right quantity, and that the correct payment is made when it is due.

Different organisations produce different documents according to their own needs. However, some types of documents are common to all organisations, although the format varies according to the requirements of specific organisations. The examples of documents in this section are those of Trojan Horse Toys. You will need to take photocopies of these documents for activities later in this unit. Alternatively, you may produce your own documents using a computer package.

Once the need for a particular product or service has been identified, the first stage in the purchasing process is to place an order. For example, Willows Bank plc is running out of headed letter paper and must purchase some more. The paper is supplied by Eastfield Printers Limited. To purchase more headed letter paper, Willows Bank must order the paper from Eastfield Printers.

To do this they complete an **order form** by entering details of the product they require. The order form can then be sent to Eastfield Printers by post or by fax. If necessary, they can give an order over the telephone, but in this case the order number (from the order form) and the date of the order must be quoted. This is done so that, when they receive the goods, they can identify the order form covering the order. Often, when an order is telephoned to a supplier for reasons of speed, the order form is still sent to the supplier later, as confirmation. The organisation which places the order keeps a copy for checking and accounting purposes.

QUICK response

If you had the choice of placing an urgent order by telephone or fax, which method would you choose? Why?

An example of an order form is shown in *Fig. 4.4*.

Goods and services requested on an order form may either be delivered by the supplier or collected from the supplier by the customer. In the case of the headed letter paper ordered by Willows Bank, this is to be delivered by Eastfield Printers. When the paper is delivered, it is accompanied by a **delivery note** giving details of the items delivered. The person who receives the delivery on behalf of Willows Bank signs the delivery note. A copy of the delivery note, called a **goods received note**, is left with the delivery. Many businesses also produce their own goods received notes on which they enter details of the delivery. Willows Bank will check the details on the goods received note:

- against the goods actually delivered, to ensure that the details on the delivery note or goods received note are correct;

TROJAN HORSE TOYS LTD.

Willowbrook Road Birmingham B15 7AR

PURCHASE ORDER

Order No

Supplier	This order is CONFIRMATION of	Job No	Order Date

Delivery address if different from above	Any queries with this order contact	Delivery Date

Quantity	Description	Price

OUR ORDER NUMBER MUST BE QUOTED, OTHERWISE INVOICES WILL BE RETURNED UNPAID
Under COSHH Regulations Safety Literature covering all products on this order MUST be supplied

Signed for and on behalf of TROJAN HORSE TOYS LTD.. Date...

NOTE: OTHER CONDITIONS OF PURCHASE SEE OVER

FIGURE 4.4 An order form.

- against the order form which refers to the goods delivered to ensure that Eastfield Printers have delivered the right quantity of the correct goods.

Any discrepancies must be notified to the supplier at once by telephone, and confirmed in writing. The order number and the delivery note or goods received note number must be quoted when informing the supplier of any discrepancy.

An example of a goods received note is shown in *Fig. 4.5*.

TROJAN HORSE TOYS LTD.
Willowbrook Road Birmingham B15 7AR

No 123/

GOODS RECEIVED NOTE

Supplier	Received from

Description	Quantity	Order Number	Checked

Received by (signature).. Date..

FIGURE 4.5 A goods received note.

Obviously, once the goods have been received and checked, they must be paid for. The supplier sends the purchaser a request for payment in the form of an **invoice**. An invoice for goods or services received (that is, purchased) is called a **purchase invoice**. The purchase invoice gives full details of the goods or services for which payment is requested, including the order number and delivery note number. The invoice also shows the amount to be paid and how this has been calculated, including any VAT to be paid or discounts allowed, for example for prompt payment.

The purchase invoice must be carefully checked:

- against the order form to ensure that it is for the correct goods and services and that the quantity, price and any discount shown on the order form are correct;

- against the delivery note or goods received note to ensure that the goods and quantity on the invoice are those that were delivered;
- the calculations on the invoice must be carefully checked to ensure that the invoice total is correct and that the purchaser is not overcharged (or undercharged).

ACTIVITY

The current rate of VAT, which is charged on the basic cost of most goods and services, is 17.5%. The amount of VAT which should be charged on the basic cost (that is the cost excluding VAT) of the goods or service is therefore found by:
basic cost of goods × 17.5 ÷ 100 = VAT
Using this formula, calculate the amount of VAT which should be charged on the following:

- **10 items at a cost excluding VAT of £1.00 each;**
- **3 items at a cost excluding VAT of £7.99 each;**
- **goods totalling £19.27 excluding VAT.**

A purchaser should notify the supplier of any discrepancies as soon as possible. The numbers of the appropriate invoice, delivery note, goods received note and order should be quoted. If the purchase invoice is correct and agrees with both the order form and the delivery or goods received note, it will be authorised and passed as correct by a senior employee in the purchasing organisation, who will sign the document. The purchaser uses the checked purchase invoice:

- as authority to pay the supplier the amount shown on the invoice for the goods or services detailed on the invoice;
- as a record of the outward financial transaction;

An example of an invoice is shown in *Fig. 4.6*. You should note that, to the seller, this is a sales invoice (see p 251).

There are occasions when a purchase invoice is incorrect. For example:

- the goods or quantities on the invoice may not agree with those ordered or delivered;
- the calculations on the invoice may be incorrect;
- VAT may be charged incorrectly or at the wrong rate;
- the amount of discount allowed may be incorrect.

TROJAN HORSE TOYS LTD.

Willowbrook Road Birmingham B15 7AR

SALES INVOICE

Customer	Invoice No	File Ref.	Invoice Date	
Delivery address if different from above	Customer Order No	Prod. Code	Despatch Date/s	Route

Quantity	Description	Price	Per	Goods Value	VAT Rate

Total Goods	
Total VAT	
Invoice Total	

TERMS STRICTLY NETT ONE MONTH

FIGURE 4.6 An invoice.

TROJAN HORSE TOYS LTD.

Willowbrook Road Birmingham B15 7AR

DELIVERY NOTE

Order Date	Job No

Customer	Customer Contact	Tel No	Customer Order No

Delivery address if different from above	Any queries with this order contact	Route	Delivery Date

Quantity	Description

Received by (signature).. Date..

Name in capitals..

NOTE: CONDITIONS OF PURCHASE SEE OVER

FIGURE 4.7 A delivery note.

If the purchaser notifies the supplier that an invoice is incorrect, the supplier will send either a **credit note**, which has the effect of reducing the amount due if the total on the invoice is too high, or an additional invoice if the total on the original invoice is too low. Some organisations prefer to cancel an incorrect invoice completely by issuing a credit note for the full amount of the invoice, and then to issue a new invoice for the correct amount. An example of a credit note is shown in *Fig. 4.8* on p 250.

SALES TRANSACTIONS AND SALES DOCUMENTS

The income of a business is mainly generated by sales of the goods or services it produces. In order that the business can keep accurate records of sales for management accounting and other purposes, most business organisations use established systems of documents which must be produced at various stages in the sales process. These enable a business to make sure the required goods or services are delivered in the right quantity, and that the correct payment is received when due.

As with purchase documents, the actual sales documents produced vary from organisation to organisation. Many sales documents are, in fact, the same as purchase documents, the difference being that they are processed and recorded by the seller or supplier, rather than the purchaser or customer.

The first stage in the sales process is when an order is received from a customer. The supplier may receive the order through the post, by fax or by telephone. If the order is received by telephone, the person taking it should obtain an order number and the name of an authorised person who can confirm the order. Confirmation of the order in writing should be requested. Sometimes, especially when the customer is another business organisation, the order is obtained by a sales executive while visiting the customer.

QUICK response

Why should a person taking a telephone order ask for an order number?

ACTIVITY

Suggest reasons why written confirmation of a telephone order should be requested.

TROJAN HORSE TOYS LTD.

Willowbrook Road Birmingham B15 7AR

CREDIT NOTE

Customer	Credit Note No	File Ref.	Credit Date	

Delivery address if different from above	Customer Order No	Prod. Code	Despatch Date/s	Route

Quantity	Description	Price	Per	Goods Value	VAT Rate

Total Goods	
Total VAT	
Invoice Total	

FIGURE 4.8 A credit note.

Once an order is received, the supplier checks whether the goods ordered can be supplied from stock or have to be made specially. If the goods have to be made, or if the order is for a service to be supplied, a date for delivery of the goods, or providing the service, is established.

When goods which have been ordered are ready to be delivered to the customer, the supplier produces a **delivery note** to send with the goods. The delivery note contains details of the goods being delivered, including the quantity, and also the customer's order number. Before the goods are sent, the supplier should check the delivery note carefully against the order received to ensure that the correct goods are delivered. An example of a delivery note is shown in *Fig. 4.7*.

The delivery note is usually produced in duplicate. One copy must be signed by the person who receives the goods. This confirms that the goods detailed on the delivery note have been received in good condition. The duplicate copy of the delivery note, sometimes called a goods received note (see p 243), is left with the customer for their records.

The supplier usually produces a **sales invoice** at the same time as the delivery note. A sales invoice is the same document as a purchase invoice. To the supplier it is a sales invoice because it is in respect of goods or services sold by them; to the customer it is a purchase invoice because it is in respect of goods or services purchased by them. The invoice for the headed letter paper is therefore Willows Bank's purchase invoice and Eastfield Printers' sales invoice. The supplier sends the sales invoice to the customer, requesting payment for the goods or services supplied.

The supplier should check each sales invoice thoroughly before sending it to the customer.

- The goods or quantities on the invoice must agree with those ordered or delivered.
- The calculations on the invoice must be correct.
- VAT must be charged correctly and at the right rate.
- The amount of any discount allowed must be correct.

> **QUICK response**
>
> **Which document can a sales invoice be checked against to confirm that the quantity shown on the invoice is the quantity that was delivered?**

Any errors found on the invoice by the customer (see p 246) will cause delays in payment of the invoice and in the supplier receiving the money for the goods supplied.

If an invoice is found to contain an error after it has been received

TROJAN HORSE TOYS LTD.

Willowbrook Road Birmingham B15 7AR

STATEMENT OF ACCOUNT

Any queries regarding items on this statement should be addressed to CREDIT CONTROL

Date	Item Reference	Debit	Credit	Balance	

Total Due

Please note that if no instalment dates are shown on invoices, payment is due within 30 days from invoice date.
If you have made any recent payment(s) which are not shown above, such payment(s) will be shown on your next statement.
All values shown are pounds sterling.

FIGURE 4.9 A statement of account.

by the customer, the supplier must produce a **sales credit note** which corrects the error. For example, if an invoice states that 100 items were supplied at £1.25 each, but only 75 items were, in fact, delivered, the supplier must issue a credit note for 25 items at £1.25 each. An example of a credit note is shown in *Fig. 4.8*. If the sales invoice contains an error that results in the customer being *undercharged*, the supplier will issue an additional invoice for the amount of the undercharge.

A sales invoice is a request for payment for goods or services supplied. Most customers pay all the invoices they receive during a month at the end of that month. A supplier may deliver goods and services to a customer at any time and often several times during a month. The supplier may therefore issue several invoices to a customer in the course of any one month.

To help their customers to check that all the invoices they have issued for goods or services supplied during a particular month have been received and are paid at the end of the month, most suppliers send a monthly **statement of account** to each customer. This lists all invoices the supplier has issued to the customer during the course of the month. The statement of account also shows any invoices issued during previous months which have not yet been paid by the customer and are still outstanding on their account. The statement of account serves not only as a means of checking that all invoices have been received by a purchaser, but also as a reminder to the purchaser of what is owed to the supplier.

A **remittance advice** is often attached to the statement of account. This contains details relating to the customer and lists the invoices shown on the statement. The customer indicates the invoices being paid and returns the remittance advice to the supplier, together with the payment. In this way the supplier can make sure that the payment is correctly **allocated**, or set against the appropriate customer and invoices. Many customers who operate computerised payment systems prefer, however, to produce their own remittance advices. These contain similar details and serve the same purpose.

PAYMENT METHODS AND RECEIPT DOCUMENTS

Goods and services can be paid for by a variety of methods. Many are suitable for both individual consumers and businesses. Some, however, are more frequently used by individual consumers, while others are only suitable for business organisations. The principal methods of making payments are:

> **QUICK response**
> **Which payment methods are frequently used by individuals?**

- cheque;
- cash;
- bankers automated clearing system (BACS);
- electronic data interchange (EDI);
- credit card;
- debit card;
- credit.

Despite the many new methods of paying for purchases which have been made possible by developments in the banking system and computer technology, cash is still the most common method of paying for goods and services generally. It is more commonly used by individual customers buying from shops and small traders, however, than by businesses. Business organisations normally keep only a small amount of cash, called **petty cash**, available to pay for small purchases and items which must be paid for in cash. Such items may include postage stamps, window cleaning, fares and other travelling expenses, and so on. The main disadvantages of using cash are:

- large amounts of cash are bulky and heavy to carry around;
- cash is difficult and expensive to send through the post;
- cash that is lost or stolen can be used by anybody who finds or steals it.

An alternative method of paying for goods and services, which does not have these disadvantages, is by cheque. Any individual or business with a current bank account can pay by cheque, and certain building society accounts also provide this facility.

ACTIVITY

Visit one or more local branches of high street banks in your area and obtain literature on their current or cheque accounts for private customers and also for business customers. Make a list of the advantages of having a cheque account. What are the disadvantages? Are there any differences in the cheque accounts the banks offer to private customers and those they offer to business customers?

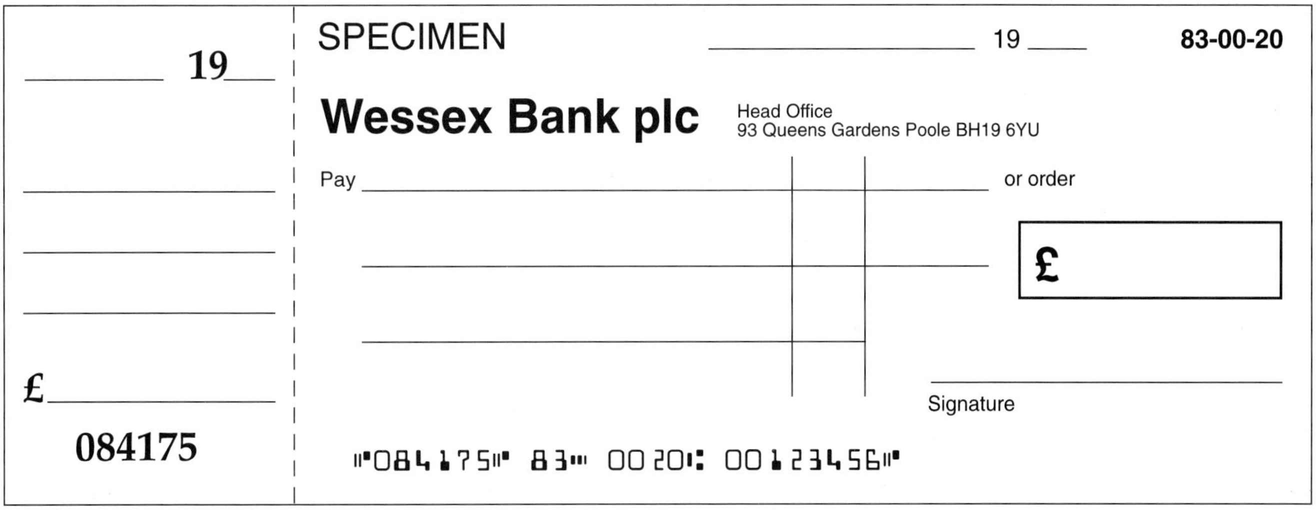

FIGURE 4.10 A cheque.

A cheque is a form which is completed by the purchaser. The purchaser completes the cheque, signs it and gives it to the supplier. The cheque instructs the purchaser's bank to transfer a stated amount of money from their account into the account of the supplier, which may be at a different bank. In this way, a person or business has access to all the money in their bank account – and sometimes more if they have arranged an **overdraft** facility with their bank.

The person or business who receives the cheque pays the cheque into their bank account using a paying-in slip. The transaction is then cleared through a central clearing house, and the money **debited to** (that is, taken out of) the purchaser's bank account and **credited to** (that is, put into) the supplier's bank account. If there is not enough money in the account of the purchaser to cover the cheque, the cheque will be returned unpaid to the supplier's bank and then to the supplier. In order to help to prevent fraud, many retail businesses only accept cheques which are presented with a **cheque guarantee**

card. This guarantees that the bank of a person or business who writes a cheque will honour the cheque and pay the amount shown into the account of the person or business receiving it, up to the limit of the card (normally £50 or £100).

For businesses which make many payments, however, writing a large number of cheques can be inconvenient and time consuming, while sending them individually through the post is expensive. The **bankers' automated clearing system** (BACS) is a system whereby the business making the payments records details of each payment to be made on magnetic tape. Included must be the amount of each payment, and the name, bank and bank account number of the individual or business to whom the payment is to be made. The organisation making the payments gives the tape to its bank which sends it to the BACS computer centre. The appropriate payments are then made automatically by debiting the bank account of the business making the payments and crediting the bank accounts of the individuals or businesses to whom the payments are being made, which may be at different banks.

If regular payments are to be made to the same bank account, a **standing order** can be set up. To set up a standing order, an individual or business instructs their bank, in writing, to transfer a fixed sum from their account to the bank account of the individual or business to whom payment is to be made on a regular basis. For example, a standing order may be set up to pay a fixed amount on the 28th of each month or on the 1st January each year. Standing orders may be for a set or indefinite period.

QUICK response

Which would be the most suitable method of paying a quarterly telephone bill:
a) standing order:
b) direct debit?

Unlike standing orders, which are originated by the payer's bank, **direct debits** are collected by the bank of the business receiving the payment. In this way it is possible for regular payments of varying amounts to be made. For example, if you wanted to pay your gas bill by direct transfer from your bank account each quarter, you could not do this by standing order as the amount of the bill would be different each quarter. By setting up a direct debit, however, you would authorise the gas company to collect the amount of each quarterly bill from your bank account, and your bank to make the payments requested. Standing orders and direct debits are methods of making payments that can be used by individuals or businesses.

An increasingly common method of making payments is **electronic data interchange**. Electronic data interchange, or EDI, is made possible by modern developments in computer technology whereby computers can exchange information and carry out transactions using the so-called information superhighway.

STANDING ORDER MANDATE

To ______________________________ Bank

Address ______________________________

	Bank	Branch Title (not address)	Code Number
Please Pay			

	Beneficiary	Account Number
for the credit of		

†the sum of		

	Date and amount of 1st payment			Date and frequency
commencing	*now		and thereafter every	

	Date and amount of last payment	
*until		
quoting the reference		

and debit my/our account accordingly

*This instruction cancels any previous order in favour of the beneficiary named above, under this reference
†If the amount of the periodic payments vary they should be incorporated in a schedule overleaf

Special instructions

Signature(s) ______________________________ Date ______________

Title and number of account to be debited ______________________________

*Delete if not applicable

Note :The Bank will not undertake to
- (i) make any reference to Value Added Tax or pay a stated sum "plus VAT"
- (ii) advise payer's address to beneficiary
- (iii) advise beneficiary of inability to pay
- (iv) request beneficiary's banker to advise beneficiary of receipt

FIGURE 4.11 A standing order mandate.

One application of EDI can be seen in many supermarkets, department stores and other retail outlets with electronic tills. When a customer in a supermarket takes a basket of shopping to the till, the cashier scans a barcode printed on each item the customer is buying. This records both the item and the price in the computer memory of the till. When all items have been scanned in this way, the total to be paid is automatically calculated and printed out on a till roll, together with a list of items purchased, their prices and any discounts.

If the customer wants to pay by **credit card** or **debit card**, their card is pushed through a guide past a magnetic 'eye' which 'reads' information contained in a magnetic strip on the back of the card. This information includes details of the customer and the customer's bank account or credit card account number. The electronic till is connected to the banking system and if there is sufficient money available the payment is automatically debited to the customer's bank or credit card account and credited to the bank account of the supermarket.

QUICK response

What types of information about its customers do you think Tesco can gather through EDI?

In addition to carrying out financial transactions, EDI can be used with computers within the business, and in different businesses, automatically to update stock records, request deliveries of goods from suppliers, and generate payments. Tesco, for example, is using EDI in conjunction with customer 'club cards' to gather information about its regular customers and the products they purchase. This information will help Tesco in its marketing and in providing a better service for customers.

Credit cards and debit cards have already been mentioned as methods of making payments in conjunction with EDI. Both can, however, be used to pay businesses which will accept them but may not have the appropriate technology for EDI. In these cases, a manual sales voucher is completed in respect of the goods or services sold. This voucher must be signed by the purchaser as authorisation. The voucher is then paid into the supplier's bank account in the same way as a cheque.

When a customer who is a credit card holder makes a payment by **credit card**, the amount of the payment is credited to the bank account of the business receiving the payment by the company which issued the credit card. Once a month, the credit card company sends its card holders a statement showing the payments they have made using the credit card during that month. Card holders do not actually pay for goods and services they have purchased using their credit card until they pay the balance shown on their statement. In addition, they normally have a choice of paying this either with a single payment or in instalments. Any balance left outstanding for more than a specified number of days, however, normally incurs interest which must be paid in addition to the balance outstanding. Credit card interest charges are often very high.

ACTIVITY

Your friend has just bought an electric guitar costing £500. She paid for this using her credit card. As your friend cannot afford to pay off the credit card bill in full, she intends to repay £25 per month. The rate of interest charged is 2% per month on the amount outstanding at the end of each month. This is added to the amount outstanding at the beginning of the next month, so that the payments your friend makes pay off the interest charged plus some of the original debt.

Calculate:

- **How long it will take your friend to pay off her credit card in full, assuming she makes no further purchases and continues to pay £25 per month.**
- **How much interest she will have paid.**
- **How much she will pay in total for the guitar.**

Debit cards are issued by banks and building societies to their current or cheque account holders. A debit card is used to make purchases in the same way as a credit card. However, in this case, the payment is debited directly to the bank or building society account of the cardholder. There is, therefore, no element of credit in paying by debit card.

In addition to paying by credit card, many retailers offer **credit terms** for more expensive items, which allow customers to pay for them in instalments, normally weekly or monthly. Sometimes, in order to attract customers, payment of the first instalment may be delayed for several months. There is normally a charge for paying on credit terms, based on a percentage interest rate on the full cost of the goods purchased. Goods bought on credit terms become the property of the purchaser as soon as the first instalment is paid.

Goods bought on **hire purchase**, on the other hand, remain the property of the seller until the last instalment is paid, at which time they become the property of the purchaser. This means that should the purchaser fail to make payments as agreed, the goods can be taken back, or repossessed, by the seller. Where the goods are not covered by a hire purchase agreement, the seller must take action for the recovery of unpaid money through the courts.

Credit and hire purchase can both be arranged and financed by larger retailers and manufacturers. They are, however, often financed by banks and finance companies who make a profit out of the interest they charge. All agreements for the purchase of goods on credit terms or hire purchase are governed by the Consumer Credit Act 1974.

RECEIPT DOCUMENTS

A receipt is a written statement confirming that a payment has been made. Many types of document can serve as receipts. It is important that some form of receipt is obtained so that it can be referred to later if there is any query about the payment or the goods purchased. The following documents can all be used as receipts to show that a particular payment has been made.

> **QUICK response**
> **When you buy clothes from a clothes shop, what form of receipt are you usually given?**

- **Receipts**, such as till rolls and printed forms, are completed to confirm that a certain payment has been received. Printed receipt forms should be signed by the person who received the payment. When a customer pays an invoice, an acceptable receipt is given by the person writing 'received with thanks', or similar wording, on the invoice and appending their signature and the date.
- **Cheques** do not need separate forms of receipt as a record of the date of the cheque, the amount and to whom it was made out is kept on the cheque counterfoil. Once the cheque is banked by the payee, it will go through the banking system and a record of the payment will appear on both the drawer's and payee's bank accounts as proof of payment.
- **Paying-in slips** are used to pay money into a bank account. Some suppliers, such as British Telecom, British Gas and mail order catalogue companies, also issue their customers with paying-in slips to enable them to make payments directly into a bank or post office. Paying-in slips have counterfoils similar to those attached to cheques. The counterfoil is stamped and initialled by the cashier at the bank or post office who accepts the payment and this acts as a receipt for the payment.
- **Bank statements** also act as proof of payment of cheques and cash paid into the bank account, and cheques drawn on the bank account.

THE IMPORTANCE OF SECURITY AND SECURITY CHECKS FOR RECEIPTS AND PAYMENTS

The financial performance of a business is vital to its success and security is an important aspect of the financial administration of a business. All businesses must carry out checks to ensure that their finances are managed correctly. This means that there must be an established system for checking receipts, to ensure that money received is handled correctly, and for checking payments, to ensure that the correct money is paid out in respect of goods and services ordered and received.

The purposes of such a system of security checks are to:

- prevent fraud, within the business or outside;
- prevent theft, by employees of the business or its suppliers;
- ensure high standards of honesty among those handling the financial transactions of the business.

A typical system of security checks involves authorising and checking financial transactions and documents at all stages.

- All purchase orders placed must be authorised by an official of the purchasing organisation, who can ensure that only goods and services needed by the purchasing organisation are ordered and that the most advantageous price is obtained.
- Goods delivered should be checked against orders and delivery notes to ensure that the correct items and quantity have been delivered as ordered and stated on the delivery note or goods received note.
- When the invoice is received by the purchasing organisation, this should be checked against the original order and delivery or goods received note to ensure that only those goods ordered and delivered are paid for.
- Cheques should only be drawn against invoices or other payment requests which have been checked and passed according to the set procedure. Cheques should be signed by authorised signatories. Similarly, if other methods of payment are used, they must be duly authorised.

PORTFOLIO ASSIGNMENT

SCENARIO

Mary Stellar and Joe Dube run a small catering business, called M&J Catering. The largest part of their trade is catering at executive luncheons and other functions on the premises of local businesses but they also do weddings and some private parties. As they operate from their own homes, doing the basic preparation, cooking and so on in their own kitchens, they are able to keep their expenses to a minimum. They employ one full-time assistant and for larger events they hire waitresses to help them.

Mary and Joe have been in business for just over three months and have spent their time building up a list of more or less regular clients. Wedding and private party business comes through responses to their regular advertisements in local papers. During the first month, their income from catering for businesses was £1,892, and they also made £568 catering at a wedding. Expenditure on supplies for the catering was £1,230. They also had to pay £642 in personnel costs for their assistant, £84 in telephone and postal charges, and £175 in advertising, including a leaflet drop. Other expenses amounted to £1,024 for the month.

During their second month, their business started to develop. Income from catering for businesses amounted to £2,376 and weddings £1,023. Expenditure on supplies for catering was £1,720, personnel costs were the same as the first month, telephone and postal charges were £102, advertising costs £120 and other expenses £815.

In their third month of operation, revenue from catering for businesses was £2,560 and from weddings and private parties £1,189. The cost of catering supplies amounted to £1,807. Personnel costs were the same as before, telephone and post £98, advertising £410 and other expenses £743.

TASK 1

Construct a simple income and expenditure account for each of the three months Mary and Joe have been in business. Write notes explaining what the accounts show and why it is important for Mary and Joe to maintain information about the financial transactions of their business.

TASK 2

Provide examples of each type of financial document that M&J Caterers may receive or produce. Write notes explaining the purpose of each document.

TASK 3

Construct a table showing at least four payment methods used in business, giving examples of when M&J Caterers may use each method.

TASK 4

List the security checks that M&J Caterers should carry out on their financial transactions and documents and explain their importance to the business.

COMPLETING FINANCIAL DOCUMENTS AND RECORDS

This section gives you an opportunity of completing financial documents and recording income and expenditure over a time period yourself. You will also investigate the different computer software applications that are used in business to record financial transactions.

You should keep all work produced for the activities in this section in your Portfolio of Evidence. This will form an essential part of your portfolio assignment for Element 4.2.

In this section you will investigate some of the financial transactions of Trojan Horse Toys Limited. Trojan Horse Toys is a small private limited company which makes wooden toys which it sells to retail outlets throughout the Midlands. It also sells some toys to private customers.

In carrying out the activities in this section, you will be using photocopies of documents used by Trojan Horse Toys or received by them from their suppliers and customers. Documents used by other business organisations may look different, but they serve the same purpose and contain the same basic information. You can therefore transfer the knowledge and experience you have gained in completing Trojan Horse Toys' documents to documents of other organisations in the real world.

Although Trojan Horse Toys is a small business, it is busy. We shall look at some of the financial transactions which took place during March this year. You may also have an opportunity to complete financial documents during any period of work experience you undertake during this course.

When completing financial documents, you must always check the following details carefully, as appropriate:

- customer details;
- delivery details;
- quantities;

QUICK response

Before reading this section, make a list of all the different types of financial document you have encountered so far on this course.

- unit prices;
- VAT;
- discounts;
- carried forward figures;
- totals.

COMPLETING PURCHASE AND SALES DOCUMENTS

PURCHASE DOCUMENTS

You have seen that the purchase documents used in business are:

- orders;
- purchase invoices;
- credit notes;
- goods received notes.

These are described on pp 242–9.

In any purchasing system, once the need for an item has been established, the first step is to place an order with a supplier. For this, an official order form should be completed and sent to the supplier. For reasons of speed, the purchaser may want to place an order over the telephone. However, completing an order form beforehand is still advisable, so that all appropriate information is to hand when making the telephone call. The order form should then be sent to the supplier in confirmation of the telephone order, to avoid mistakes and misunderstandings.

ACTIVITY

Take six photocopies of the blank purchase order in *Fig. 4.4* on p 244. Complete them in respect of the following orders placed during February by Trojan Horse Toys. Do not forget to give your orders order numbers. These should be consecutive, following on from the last order used, which was 1932. Your first order should therefore be numbered 1933. Alternatively, you can produce your own purchase order using a computer package.

2 Feb	**10 cubic metres of treated pine costing £180 + VAT per cu.m. from Pine Distributors Limited of 16 Trentham Way, Nottingham NG16 1YQ**
7 Feb	**1 set of integrated computer software @ £349 + VAT from R & J Computer Consultancy of 27 Back House Street, Birmingham B4 7AJ**
9 Feb	**1 25 litre drum of clear varnish costing £24.00 + VAT from Craft Supplies Limited, 235 West Dudley Road, Birmingham B3 2AW**
16 Feb	**1 box of 12 inkjet cartridges for computer printer @ £130 + VAT per box from Dudley Home and Office Limited, Station Road, Coventry CV2 1AB**
23 Feb	**5 reams photocopier paper @ £2.50 per ream + VAT from Quality Paper Mills Limited of 1 Sheldon Way, Nottingham NG16 1YQ. There is a 5% discount for quantity on this order.**
28 Feb	**1 new typist's chair @ £69.00 + VAT from Think Big Limited, 79 Dover Street, Dudley, West Midlands**

Keep these orders in your Portfolio of Evidence. You will need them for future activities.

Once an order for goods has been placed, the supplier will arrange for the goods to be delivered. This may be on a prearranged date or as soon as possible, especially if the supplier has to make the goods.

When the goods are delivered, they will be accompanied by a delivery note detailing the goods delivered. The customer signs this in confirmation that the delivery has been received. Obviously, the customer must check the delivery note before signing it, to ensure that the goods and quantity shown on the note are the goods and quantity actually received. The delivery note should also be checked against the original order placed, to see that the goods received are those which the customer wants.

A copy of the delivery note, called a goods received note, is often left with the goods for the customer's own records. The customer returns the delivery note to the supplier, and passes the goods received note to their own accounts department. This is to advise the accounts department that goods have been received and an invoice for the goods will follow. As you saw on p 243, some businesses complete their own goods received notes in respect of goods they have received.

ACTIVITY

The goods you placed orders for in the last activity have now been delivered as follows:

4 March	**1 × 25 litre drum of Clear Varnish from Craft Supplies Limited**
7 March	**4 reams photocopier paper from Quality Paper Mills Limited**
11 March	**9 cu.m. treated pine from Pine Distributors Limited**
18 March	**1 typist's chair from Think Big Limited**
27 March	**1 box of 12 ink jet cartridges from Dudley Home and Office Limited**
29 March	**1 set integrated computer software from R & J Computer Consultancy**

Trojan Horse Toys Limited has its own goods received note, to be completed in respect of goods received by the company. This is shown in *Fig. 4.12*. Take copies of this and complete your copies in respect of the above deliveries. Alternatively, you may produce your own goods received note using a computer. Do not forget to save your work. When you have completed your goods received notes, check these carefully against the original orders you made out and make a note of any discrepancies.

Any discrepancies between the goods ordered and those delivered should be notified to the supplier immediately. Similarly, the customer should notify the supplier of any damaged or unusable goods. Notification should be by telephone, and always followed up in writing as telephone messages can get forgotten. With a letter, you always have proof of the communication and the date on which you sent it.

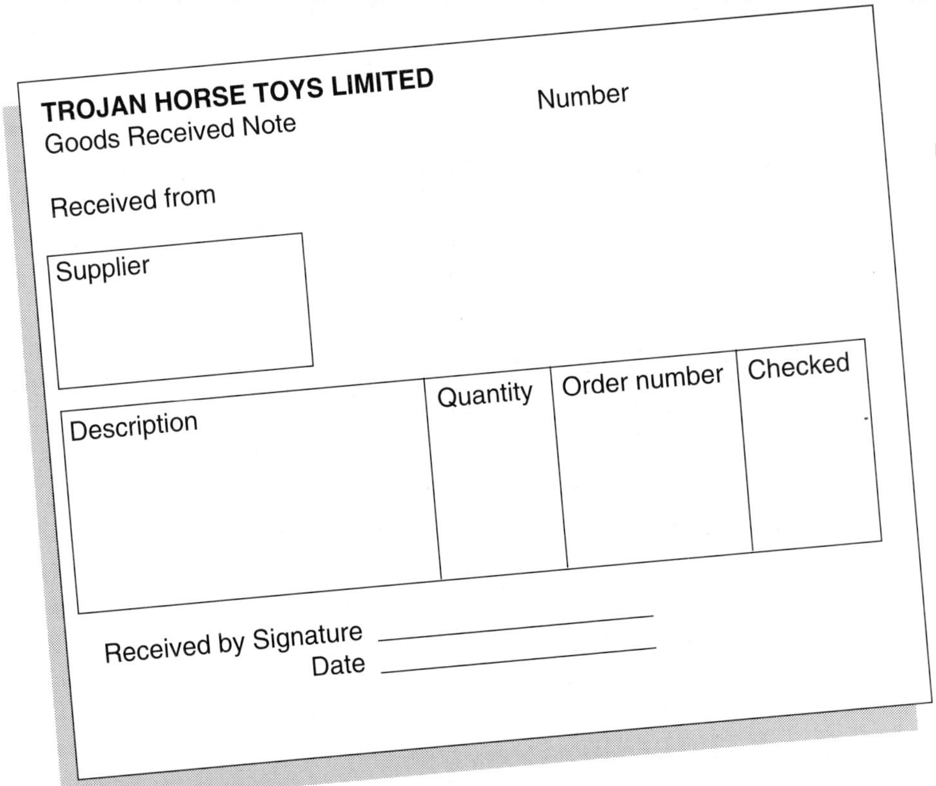

TROJAN HORSE TOYS LIMITED
Goods Received Note

Number

Received from

Supplier

Description	Quantity	Order number	Checked

Received by Signature ____________
Date ____________

FIGURE 4.12 A goods received note.

ACTIVITY

If you found any discrepancies between the orders you made out and the deliveries received by Trojan Horse Toys Limited, draft a letter to the company which made the delivery, pointing out the discrepancy.

When the purchase invoice is received, it should be checked carefully. It should be checked against the goods received note to see that the correct goods and quantity are shown on the invoice. All calculations on the invoice should also be checked.

ACTIVITY

Fig. 4.13 **shows a blank invoice. Take copies of this and complete them in respect of the deliveries received by Trojan Horse Toys Limited. Enter the name and address of the supplier in the box marked 'from'. Invoices for the deliveries on 7 and 11 March have been completed for you and are shown in** ***Figs 4.14*** **and** ***4.15*****. Check these invoices carefully against the goods received notes. When you have completed the other invoices, check them carefully against the original orders and the goods received notes. Initial those invoices which are correct to show that you have checked them and that they are ready for payment. Write notes describing the checks you have made, and any discrepancies you have found.**

Invoice

Number:
Date:

From:

To:	Shipped to (if different address):

ORDER NO		DATE SHIPPED			

QTY		DESCRIPTION		UNIT PRICE	TOTAL
					0.00
					0.00
					0.00
					0.00
					0.00
					0.00
					0.00
				SUBTOTAL	0.00
				VAT RATE %	
				VAT	0.00
				TOTAL	£0.00

THANK YOU FOR YOUR ORDER

FIGURE 4.13 A blank invoice.

Quality Paper Mills Ltd.
1 Sheldon Way
Nottingham NG16 1YQ

SALES INVOICE

To	Ship to (if different address)
TROJAN HORSE TOYS LTD Willowbrook Road Birmingham B15 7AR	

Customer Order	No	Date Shipped	Invoice date	Invoice no
1937		7 March	7 March	768

Quantity	Description	Unit Price	Total
5	Reams photocopier paper	£2.50	£12.50

Sub Total	£12.50
VAT Rate %	17.50%
VAT	£2.19
Total Due	£14.69

THANK YOU FOR YOUR ORDER!

FIGURE 4.14 A completed invoice for photocopier paper.

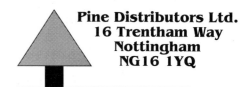

SALES INVOICE

Pine Distributors Ltd.
16 Trentham Way
Nottingham
NG16 1YQ

Customer
Trojan Horse Toys Ltd
Willowbrook Road
Birmingham
B15 7AR

Ship to if different from above

Customer Order No	Date Shipped	Invoice Date	Invoice No
1933	11 March 19xx	11 March 19xx	5678

Code	Description	Quantity	Unit Price	Total
3097	Treated Pine	10 cu m	£180.00	£1,800.00

Sub Total	£1,800.00
VAT Rate%	17.50%
VAT	£315.00
Invoice Total	£2,115.00

FIGURE 4.15 A completed invoice for treated pine.

The customer should notify the supplier immediately concerning any discrepancies between the invoice and the goods received. They should also notify the supplier of any calculation errors on the invoice.

If an invoice is correct, it may be passed for payment after it has been authorised. If, however, there is an error on the invoice, the supplier should send a credit note to correct this. The invoice should only be passed for payment once the credit note has been received and checked to ensure that the error has been corrected and the amount the supplier is charging for the goods delivered is correct.

ACTIVITY

Using copies of the credit note in *Fig. 4.16*, make out credit notes to correct any invoices on which you found discrepancies. Enter the name and address of the supplier in the box marked 'from'.

SALES DOCUMENTS

Sales documents used in business are:

- orders received;
- sales invoices;
- delivery notes;
- sales credit notes;
- statements of account;
- remittance advices.

These are described on pp 249–53.

The first stage in any sales system is when a supplier receives an order for goods or services from a customer. They should obtain an official order form for this, even if the order has initially been placed by telephone. This helps to avoid mistakes and misunderstandings.

Credit Note

From:

Credit Note Number:
Date:

To:	Shipped to (if different address):

ORDER NO		DATE SHIPPED			

QTY		DESCRIPTION		UNIT PRICE	TOTAL
					0.00
					0.00
					0.00
					0.00
					0.00
					0.00
					0.00
				SUBTOTAL	0.00
				VAT RATE %	
				VAT	0.00
				TOTAL	£0.00

FIGURE 4.16 A credit note.

ACTIVITY

You have received the following orders for Trojan Horse Toys Limited by telephone. Make a copy of the list and keep it to use with the next activity.

Telephone Orders Received

Date	Customer	Qty	Product	Job no
1 March	Hammonds Department Store Broadmarsh Centre Nottingham NG1 1BM	100	Rocking Horses	392/96
4 March	The Willows Nursery and Play Group Willowbrook Road Birmingham B15 9AX	1	Special Order Toys (confirmation – as quoted)	393/96
8 March	Wellers Emporium Toy Shop Severns Avenue Sutton Coldfield B76 1XY	25	Dolls Houses	394/96
12 March	Hughes County Secondary School Thorpe Road Hockley Heath Birmingham B94 7CJ	1	Climbing Equipment (confirmation – as quoted)	395/96
15 March	Leicester Craft Centre High Street Hinckley Leicestershire LE10 7HN	15	Rocking Horses	396/96
19 March	Leicester Craft Centre High Street Hinckley Leicestershire LE10 7HN	50 sets	Wooden Soldiers	397/96

When the Sales Department receives an order, they pass it to the Production Department at Trojan Horse Toys so that the order can be made up. When it is ready for despatch, the Production Department makes out a delivery note (see p 248). This gives details of the goods being delivered.

ACTIVITY

Make six photocopies of the blank delivery note shown in *Fig. 4.7* on p 248. Complete them in respect of the list of telephone orders in the last activity. Each order is despatched on the day it was received, except for the order from The Willows Nursery and Playgroup, which was despatched on 11 March and the order from Hughes County Secondary School which was delivered on 19 March.

A copy of the delivery note is sent to the Accounts Department so that they can produce a sales invoice (see p 251), charging the customer for the goods delivered. When producing the invoice, this should be checked carefully for:

- customer and delivery details (from the order received and the delivery note);
- quantities;
- unit prices (against the price list);
- VAT;
- discounts;
- any figures and totals carried forward.

ACTIVITY

Take six photocopies of the Trojan Horse Toys invoice in *Fig. 4.13* on p 268 and complete them in respect of the deliveries for which you completed delivery notes in the last activity. Alternatively, you may wish to produce your own sales invoices using a computer package.

- **The unit prices are:**
  - **Rocking Horses – £69.20 each + VAT;**
  - **Dolls Houses – £118.00 each + VAT;**
  - **Wooden Soldiers – £20.48 per set + VAT;**
  - **the climbing equipment for Hughes County Secondary School is at a special price of £5269.95 plus VAT, less 5% educational discount;**
  - **the toys for The Willows Nursery and Play Group are a special order at £4336.50 plus VAT, less 5% educational discount.**
- **VAT is charged at 17.5%.**

ACTIVITY

As you have seen, if the customer advises the supplier of any errors on the invoice, the supplier should produce a credit note to correct this. One item in the delivery to Hammonds Department Store was damaged. It has been charged on the invoice you prepared in the last activity. Take a copy of the Trojan Horse Toys credit note in *Fig. 4.16* on p 272, or produce your own credit note using a computer, and complete it to correct this.

At the end of each month, Trojan Horse Toys sends each of its customers a statement of account. This details the numbers and totals of invoices and credit notes which they have sent to the customer during that month. The statement also shows any unpaid balance from previous months and the total amount the customer owes. Part of the statement of account may be a tear-off section which also lists details of the invoices and amounts outstanding to be paid. Customers can use this tear-off section as a remittance advice when making payment. This ensures that, when the payment is received, Trojan Horse Toys know who it is from and what invoices it is settling.

ACTIVITY

Take six photocopies of the blank statement of account in *Fig. 4.9* on p 252, or one produced by yourself on a computer. Complete these for the month of March for those customers for whom you produced invoices or credit notes in the previous two activities. The balances outstanding for February are nil, except in the case of Leicester Craft Centre which has an unpaid balance of £257.30 outstanding.

COMPLETING PAYMENT AND RECEIPT DOCUMENTS

PAYMENTS

When a purchaser has received and checked a purchase invoice, they can pass it for payment. You have seen that there are many ways in which a payment may be made (p 254). The most common way of making payments in business, however, is by cheque. Cheques are described on p 255.

ACTIVITY

***Fig. 4.10* on p 255 shows a blank cheque, with counterfoil attached. Take photocopies and complete them to pay the purchase invoices and credit notes received and checked by you in the activities on pp 274 and 275. You must complete a separate cheque for each supplier, and the amount should be the total of the invoice, less any credit note received.**

Businesses do not only make payments in respect of invoices they have received. Payments are also made:

- to employees, in respect of salaries and wages;
- to suppliers in respect of small items paid for out of petty cash (see p 254).

When an employee is paid their salary or wages, they are given a statement of earnings, often called a **pay slip**. This shows details of the payment being made to the employee, including:

- total amount earned by the employee during the period, including overtime and other payments (gross wage or salary);
- total amount earned by the employee during the financial year so far, including overtime and other payments;
- the amount deducted in respect of National Insurance;
- the amount deducted in respect of income tax;
- any other deductions, for example in respect of a company pension scheme;
- the actual amount being paid to the employee (net wage or salary).

Employees' remuneration, and how this is made up, was described on p 115.

A pay slip is given to an employee either with their wages or salary, if they are paid in cash or by cheque, or, more usually, in a separate envelope if the wages or salaries are paid by BACS (see p 256).

National Insurance and income tax are normally calculated from tables issued by the Department of Social Security and the Inland Revenue. These are updated following changes announced in the Chancellor's budget.

ACTIVITY

Fig. 4.17 shows a pay slip issued to employees by Trojan Horse Toys. Pay slips are normally produced by computer, and all calculations made automatically. However, during the week ending 31 March, they have not entered a new employee, Marc Johnson, who started work that week, on to the computer. You must now produce a manual pay slip for him. Marc's wages are £6.97 per hour and he has worked 40 hours at his basic rate plus five hours' overtime at time and a half. National Insurance deductions are £7.60 and income tax deducted is £70.00. Because Marc is a new employee, his tax code is not known to the company. In addition, Marc pays £16.72 per week into the company pension scheme. Using a photocopy of the pay slip in _Fig. 4.17_, prepare a pay slip for Marc, showing his wages for the week ending 31 March.

<table>
<tr><td colspan="5">Employee Name</td><td colspan="2">Pay Period</td></tr>
<tr><td colspan="5">National Insurance Number</td><td colspan="2">Tax Code</td></tr>
<tr><td>Hours</td><td>Rate</td><td>Total</td><td>Deductions</td><td>Amount</td><td>Year to date</td><td></td></tr>
<tr><td></td><td></td><td></td><td>Tax
N I
Pension
Other</td><td></td><td>Gross Pay
Tax
N I</td><td>Amount</td></tr>
<tr><td colspan="2">Gross Pay</td><td></td><td>Total Deductions</td><td></td><td colspan="2">Net Pay</td></tr>
</table>

FIGURE 4.17 A pay slip.

When a business pays in cash for goods or services, the cash is taken from a cash 'float' which is normally kept in a cash box in the office. This is called 'petty cash'. There are many small items which a business may pay for in cash, such as:

- small items purchased from retailers;
- services, such as window cleaning, purchased from small businesses who often prefer to deal in cash;
- bus and taxi fares which are normally paid for in cash.

Cash can only be obtained from the petty cash box with special authorisation. A form, called a petty cash voucher, must be completed for this. The completed petty cash voucher shows:

- the name of the person taking the cash;
- the amount of cash taken;
- the purpose for which the cash has been taken;
- the date.

Both the person withdrawing the petty cash from the cash box and the person authorising the withdrawal sign the petty cash voucher. Where possible, a receipt for the goods or service purchased, showing the VAT registration number of the supplier and the amount of VAT paid, must

PETTY CASH VOUCHER

Description	Amount	VAT	Amount excl VAT
Totals			

Cash received by ______________

Authorised by ______________ Date ______________

FIGURE 4.18 A petty cash voucher.

be obtained and attached to the petty cash voucher. This is done so that the VAT paid can be reclaimed from Customs and Excise.

ACTIVITY

***Fig. 4.18* shows a petty cash voucher. Take a photocopy of this and complete it in respect of £2.50 petty cash taken for postage stamps purchased at your local post office. There is no VAT on postage stamps. Get your tutor to authorise the petty cash voucher for you – although you are unlikely to get the money!**

RECEIPTS

A receipt is given by a supplier to a purchaser as an acknowledgement that the supplier has received payment for the goods supplied. Receipt documents were described on p 260. Business organisations and individual customers often require a receipt for a payment as this provides proof that they have made the payment. This is important in case there is any query regarding the payment, or the goods have to be returned to the supplier at a future date.

The principal forms of receipt used in business are:

- Receipts, such as till rolls and printed forms signed by the person who received the payment. Sometimes writing 'received with thanks', or similar wording, on the invoice serves as a receipt. A supplier normally gives this type of receipt to a purchaser who pays in cash. It is, however, sometimes given when the purchaser pays by another method, such as cheque, debit card or credit card. Many retail outlets, in particular, give a till receipt to purchasers when they make a payment, whatever method is used.

ACTIVITY

Some businesses also provide a retail service for the goods they supply. Trojan Horse Toys operates a counter in its showroom, where customers can purchase its products. When a customer pays for stationery at this counter, they are given a receipt on a preprinted form. This is shown in *Fig. 4.19*. Take a photocopy of this and complete it in respect of a payment for a rocking horse costing £125.00, which includes £18.61 VAT, bought on 18 March by John Richards of 29 Hope Gardens, Coventry.

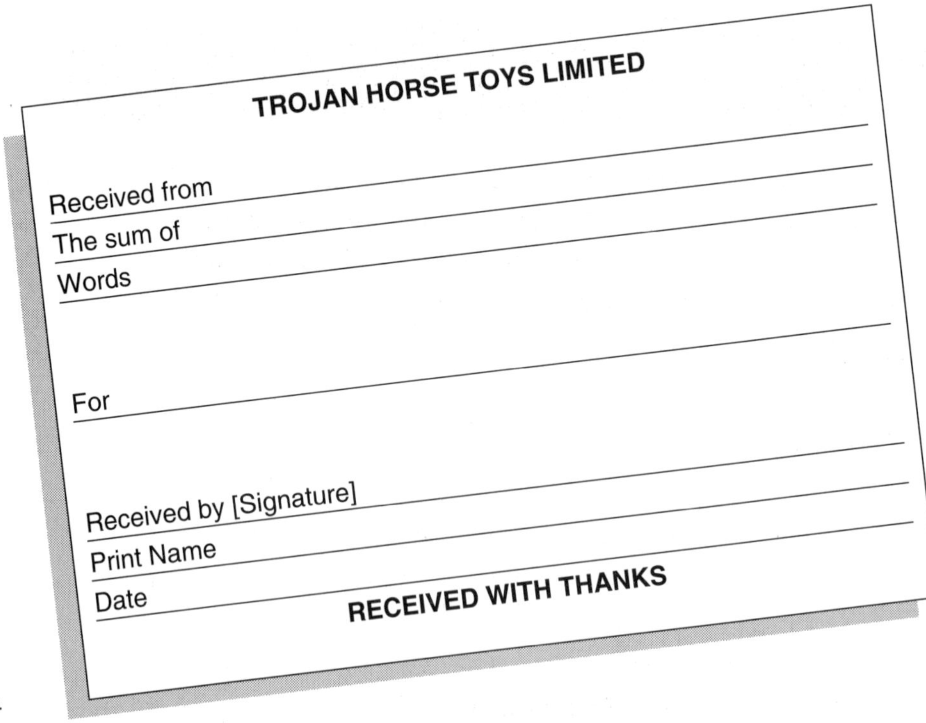
TROJAN HORSE TOYS LIMITED

Received from

The sum of

Words

For

Received by [Signature]

Print Name

Date

RECEIVED WITH THANKS

FIGURE 4.19 A simple receipt.

- Normally, payments by cheque do not need separate forms of receipt, although, as you have seen above, retail outlets often give receipts for payments by cheque. This is because a record of the date and amount of the cheque, and to whom it was made payable, is kept on the cheque counterfoil. Also, once the cheque is banked by the payee, it will go through the banking system. A record of the payment will appear on both the drawer's and payee's bank accounts as proof of payment.

ACTIVITY

In the activity on p 276 you completed several cheques to pay invoices received by Trojan Horse Toys. Write notes explaining how the cheques can provide proof of payment.

- You have seen that paying-in slips are used to pay money into a bank and to some suppliers, such as British Telecom, British Gas, and mail order catalogue companies. Paying-in slips have counterfoils which the cashier at the bank or post office accepting the payment stamps and initials as a receipt for the payment.

RECORDING INCOME AND EXPENDITURE OVER TIME PERIODS

Records of income and expenditure may be kept manually in a handwritten ledger, or on a computer using a spreadsheet or accounting software package. The recording of income and expenditure is an ongoing process. However, businesses work to different accounting periods. These may be:

- monthly;
- quarterly.

QUICK response

What advantages do you think a business would gain from working to monthly rather than quarterly time periods?

Often, to aid financial management, each item of income or expenditure is analysed into the type of goods and services involved. For example, a business may want to know how much income it has received in respect of different types of goods or services which it supplies, or how much expenditure it has incurred in respect of raw materials, wages and salaries, overheads, and so on.

This type of information will help the business to concentrate on supplying those goods and services which are most profitable, while controlling costs in areas of high expenditure. When income and expenditure are recorded in this way over a time period, this information can be used in compiling a simple income and expenditure account, such as that shown in *Fig. 4.3* on p 241.

Some items, however, are not covered by purchase or sales invoices. In addition, they may relate, at least in part, to different time periods. For example, the insurance premium of a business may be £12,000. This sum is paid to the insurance company in January. However, the insurance covers the business for the full year, and so it is fair to say that, for profit and loss purposes, the cost of insurance is £1,000 per month. In this case the business would show an amount of £1,000 as expenditure under insurance in its income and expenditure accounts each month.

ACTIVITY

How much would the business show as expenditure under insurance if it compiled quarterly income and expenditure accounts?

Although it covers the full year, the insurance premium is said to be prepaid, and is called **a prepayment** in accounting terminology. Types of expenditure which may be prepaid include:

- insurance – which is paid at the beginning of each year;
- electricity, gas and telephone bills, which are paid quarterly, but relate to services supplied throughout the quarter;
- rent and rates which may be paid annually, half-yearly or quarterly and relate to property which is occupied throughout the year.

Another type of prepayment is in respect of the purchase of plant (machinery and equipment) and buildings. These items are often very expensive but have to be paid for when they are first purchased (even if a loan is taken out). However, they tend to last a long time and it is not fair, therefore, to take the full cost into the month or quarter in which they are paid for. Indeed, by following this method, a company which bought a new factory for several million pounds could find its profits more than wiped out for many accounting periods.

In order to spread the cost of the item in the accounts, and therefore not adversely affect profits, the item is **depreciated** over its expected life. A new factory, for example, may be expected to last for 20 years or more, while a business may expect to get four years' use out of a company car. The cost of the factory would therefore be spread over 20 years, and the cost of the car over four years. In the income and expenditure record for each month an expenditure for depreciation would be entered until the full cost had been covered. In simple terms, this would be calculated as:

- cost of factory ÷ 20 years ÷ 12 months = monthly depreciation of factory;
- cost of car ÷ 4 years ÷ 12 months = monthly depreciation of car.

ACTIVITY

In previous activities, you produced six sales invoices and six purchase invoices for Trojan Horse Toys Limited. In addition you completed a receipt for one cash sale. These items are part of the income and expenditure for the company for March. Other items of expenditure, which include prepayments, depreciation, goods purchased on invoice and goods purchased for cash, are:

- **wages and salaries £10,000.98**
- **consumables £1225.00**
- **rates and insurance £2,500.00**
- **telephone, post, etc. £450.26**
- **general expenses £35.00**
- **depreciation £3,900.00**

Compile a simple income and expenditure account for the March accounting period for Trojan Horse Toys. Income and expenditure accounts were described on p 240. You should use the format on the right for your account:

	£	£
Income		
	———	———
Less Expenditure		
Timber		
Varnish		
Consumables		
Wages and salaries		
Rates and insurance		
Office expenses		
Telephone and post		
General expenses		
Depreciation	———	
Profit/loss		———

WHY RECORD FINANCIAL INFORMATION?

You will see that financial records can be used to monitor income and expenditure and to check whether income is greater than expenditure.

ACTIVITY

Check the totals of your income and expenditure account for Trojan Horse Toys. Did income during March exceed expenditure during the same period? What do you think are the implications of this? What might be the implications if the reverse had been the case? Write out your answers.

Other reasons for recording financial information are:

- for security – to guard against fraud;
- to keep customer accounts up to date – to enable the business to know which invoices a customer has paid and which remain outstanding;
- to keep the business accounts up to date – by providing information about financial transactions;
- to monitor performance – by ensuring that the up-to-date financial position of the business is known and can be compared with targets set in the budget.

ACTIVITY

Write notes explaining what you think might happen if a business did not keep up-to-date financial records.

USING IT TO RECORD AND MONITOR FINANCIAL INFORMATION

The examples of financial records you have looked at so far have been manual – that is, they have been produced by hand. However, the development of information technology and, in particular, computer technology, has meant that most businesses nowadays record and monitor financial information using computers. This is so even with quite small businesses, and many sole traders find it most convenient to keep all their financial records on a computer.

The use of computers in recording and monitoring financial information depends on the software package used. Software applications range from spreadsheets, which may be used to keep simple records of financial transactions, to complex integrated accounting software packages for recording and monitoring information. Sophisticated accounting software can be used to:

- record sales orders received;
- make out and record purchase orders;
- record stock movements and purchases;
- produce delivery documentation;
- produce invoices;
- prepare payment documentation;
- keep records of income and expenditure;
- produce management and statutory accounts;
- monitor performance.

QUICK response

What advantages would you expect a computerised accounting system to have over a manual system?

A simple application of information technology in recording and monitoring financial information is using a spreadsheet to produce simple income and expenditure accounts.

A spreadsheet is like a sheet of paper. It is divided into boxes or 'cells' into which information can be entered as it would be in a manual cash book. Each cell has a reference number which is used to identify where information should be entered on the spreadsheet. For example, the cell with the reference number A:1 is at the top left-hand corner of the spreadsheet; cell reference number C:7 is the third cell from the left on the seventh row of the spreadsheet.

Fig. 4.20 shows a computer spreadsheet of the income and expenditure account for Willowbrook Social Club (see *Fig. 4.3* on p 241).

Columns

A	A	B	C	D	E	F	G
1	Willowbrook Social Club						
2	Income and Expenditure Account						
3	March 1996						
4	£					£	£
5	Income						
6		Bar Sales				5600	
7		Restaurant Sales				1756	
8		Sales of Disco Tickets				1765	
9		Sales of Raffle Tickets				239	
10							7770
11	Less Cost of Sales						
12		Bar Stock and Restaurant Supplies				3800	
13		Hire of Disco Equipment				230	
14		Purchase of Raffle Prizes				80	
15							4110
16							
17	Sub Total						3660
18							
19	Less Other Expenditure						
20		Personnel Costs				1000	
21		Rates				325	
22		Telephone and Postage				48	
23		Advertising				30	
24		Other Expenses				968	
25							2371
26							
27	Total						1289

Rows

FIGURE 4.20 A computer-generated spreadsheet for Willowbrook Social Club.

ACTIVITY

Use a computer spreadsheet software package to produce the income and expenditure account you produced manually in the activity on p 241. Do not enter any totals at this stage. Remember to save your work – you will need it for the next activity.

Once information has been entered on to a spreadsheet, the computer can do all the calculations for you. This is one of the benefits of using computers to record and monitor financial information. If you require a calculation to be made (for example, a total of a column in a cash book), the first step is to identify the cell in which you want the result of the calculation to appear. You then enter a special formula into this cell which tells the computer what calculation you require.

Different spreadsheet software packages require different formulae. It is important that you check the correct formulae with your tutor or the software information manual. However, to add the figures in a column, for example cells C:7 to J:7, and enter the total in cell K:7, you will probably have to enter one of the following formulae in cell K:7:

=SUM(C7..J7)

or

@SUM(C7..J7)

ACTIVITY

Enter the totals on your spreadsheet by entering the appropriate formula and letting the computer do the calculation. Don't forget to save your work.

Many computer software manufacturers produce spreadsheet software. Some of these packages are part of integrated applications suites. For example, Quattro is a spreadsheet package produced by Novell which forms part of the Perfect Office suite. Excel, produced by Microsoft, is a spreadsheet package which forms part of the Microsoft Office Suite. Both of these suites include word processing, presentation and other applications. Both spreadsheet packages are also available on their own.

As well as spreadsheet software, many accounting software packages are available. Some of these are specifically designed for small businesses and are readily available from stores such as Dixons, Escom and Computer World. Other, more sophisticated and specialised accounting and financial management software systems are available from businesses which specialise in computer systems for use by other businesses. Sometimes a large or complex business organisation will employ a firm of computer consultants to develop and install computer systems, including accounting and other software, which meet the specific needs of the business.

PORTFOLIO ASSIGNMENT

TASK 1

You have already completed the work for Task 1 of this portfolio assignment in the activities for this element. You should check that you have the following documents in your Portfolio of Evidence.

- six completed order forms for orders placed by Trojan Horse Toys (activity p 264)
- six completed goods received notes (activity p 266)
- six completed purchase invoices (activity p 267)
- credit notes as appropriate (activity p 271)
- list of six telephone orders received by Trojan Horse Toys (activity p 273)
- six completed delivery notes (activity p 274 top)
- six completed sales invoices (activity p 274 bottom)
- one completed credit note (activity p 275)
- six statements of account (activity p 276 top)
- six completed cheques in payment (activity p 276 bottom)
- one completed pay slip (activity p 277)
- one completed petty cash voucher (activity p 279)
- one completed receipt (activity p 280)
- Trojan Horse Toys' manual income and expenditure account for March (activity p 283)
- Trojan Horse Toys' computerised income and expenditure account (activity p 287)

TASK 2

Find out what different types and makes of spreadsheet and accounting software are available on the market, who supplies it, what it can do and how much it costs. Construct a table like this:

Name of software	Type of software	Features	Manufacturer	Supplier	Cost

Obtain sales literature and any other information you can (such as reviews in computer or business magazines) about the software on your table. Write notes evaluating the software. Justify your conclusions.

Producing, Evaluating and Storing Business Documents

The purpose of routine business documents, and producing draft and final versions

Many other documents are used in business besides those used for recording financial transactions or monitoring income and expenditure. The most common documents are:

- letters;
- memos;
- invitations;
- notices;
- messages.

The purpose of these documents is to communicate with people. They may be used to communicate with customers, with colleagues in the same business organisation or with other businesses.

The appearance and quality of the documents produced by an organisation are very important, whether they are for use within the organisation itself or outside. An organisation's documents reflect the image of the organisation itself: shoddy documents give the impression of a shoddy organisation. Most organisations have specially designed headed paper for letters, and the same design may be used on other printed documents. This gives an instantly recognisable identity and house style.

You must take care with any business documents you produce and check that each one is as attractive and easy to read as possible, paying particular attention to spelling, grammar and punctuation. Good documents should be:

- **accurate** – everything in the document should be checked, including all facts; a dictionary or computer spellcheck should be used to check spelling if necessary;

- **clear** – the person reading the document should be able to understand its content immediately; the person writing the document must have the message they want to send clear in their mind before they begin to write it down;
- **simple** – short words and sentences are more effective and have more impact than long ones; they also save time and are easily understood;
- **complete** – a document which leaves a message unfinished or leaves out a vital piece of information will fail in its purpose.

It is a good idea always to do a draft (rough copy) of a business document you are producing so that you can check this carefully before you produce the final copy. A second copy should also be made of every business document produced so that it can be filed and retrieved later in case of any query or further action having to be taken. Filing and retrieving documents is described on p 299.

LETTERS

> **QUICK response**
> **Why are business letters typed or word-processed rather than handwritten?**

Letters are sent to people outside the organisation you work for. They may be used, for example, to confirm a meeting with a client, answer an enquiry from a prospective supplier, or deal with a complaint from a customer.

Most business letters are typed or printed by a computer word-processing package on the organisation's headed letter paper. The headed paper shows basic details of the organisation including:

- business name;
- address;
- telephone and fax numbers;
- names of the proprietor, partners or directors of the business;
- name and address of the parent company if the business is part of a group of companies.

Letter heads frequently also contain a company logo which identifies the business and links the letter head with other documents produced by the business bearing the same logo. They may also show the VAT number if the business is registered for VAT. Sometimes, some of this information is put at the bottom of the headed letter paper, where it is called a footer.

All business letters should follow certain conventions of layout and structure. This will help to ensure that the letter contains all the basic

Westfield Printers Ltd
Westfield House
Derby Road
Sheffield
S3 8TY

Telephone 01742 639944

S Osborne Esq
Midshire Bank plc
1 Bruton Street
Derby
DEl 3XY

27 October 1997

Dear Mr Osborne

Re: Brochure

Please find enclosed a first proof copy of the new brochure for Midshire Bank plc.

Would you please check this and return it in the enclosed stamped addressed envelope with any amendments. We hope that the look of the brochure meets with your approval, but if you wish to make any alterations with regard to style or layout, please let us know as soon as possible.

With thanks for your valued custom.

Yours sincerely

Paul Taylor
General Manager

FIGURE 4.21 A business letter to a customer.

Westfield Printers Ltd
Westfield House
Derby Road
Sheffield
S3 8TY

Telephone 01742 639944

R & J Computer Consultancy
27 Back House Street
Birmingham
B4 7AJ

9 January 1996

Dear Sir or Madam

We are currently looking into the possibility of updating our computer systems, and would be obliged if you would advise us of the different types of accounting software packages suitable for a medium sized company such as ours.

In due course we will be looking for quotations for the supply and installation of the software, and will ask you to give a full quotation at that time.

We look forward to hearing from you at an early date.

Yours faithfully

J Rowley (Mrs)
Financial Director

FIGURE 4.22 A business letter to another business.

information necessary for the reader, and also make it easier to write, read and understand. *Fig. 4.21* shows a business letter to a customer, where the name of the person to whom the letter is to be sent (the addressee) is known. *Fig. 4.22* shows a letter from one business organisation to another, where the name of the addressee is not known.

ACTIVITY

You work from home as a self-employed advisor to small businesses on types of computer software. You have received an enquiry from Gardenia Nurseries Limited, of 17 Needham Rise, London NW3 1AW, about different types of accounting software. Write a letter to Gardenia Nurseries, answering their enquiry, based on the information you obtained for the activity on p 288. You should design your own letter head and use your own address as your business address. Date your letter today. Produce a draft and final version of your letter.

Westfield Printers Ltd

MEMO

To Paul Taylor, General Manager
Date 27 March 1996
From Jane Rowley, Financial Director
Subject 1996/97 Budget

Paul, just a note to remind you that the new computer software will be installed by R & J Computer Consultancy within the next two months. This means that the budget will be delayed, but if you can have your figures ready for inputting onto the computer by the end of May, we should be able to get the budget out by mid-June.

Thanks for your help.

FIGURE 4.23 An informal memo.

Westfield Printers Ltd

MEMO

To Paul Taylor, General Manager
Date 18 November 1996
From Hussein Pareich, Print Room Supervisor
Subject Brochure for Midshire Bank plc

I am pleased to advise you that we are now ready to go ahead with producing the above brochure. Will you please confirm the exact size of the first print run. This will cover an initial supply to the customer, plus stock to be held in our warehouse.

FIGURE 4.24 A more formal memo.

MEMOS

Memos (short for memoranda – singular memorandum) are used to communicate with colleagues inside the organisation. They are used for giving instructions and information, making requests, asking for information or guidance and so on. As with letters, memos should follow certain conventions of layout and structure, in order to help the reader. Memos are usually written or typed on printed forms headed Memo. As they are communications between colleagues within the same organisation, they are written with less formality of style and language than business letters. However, the status of the person to whom the memo is addressed must be taken into consideration. A memo to the managing director should be more formal than a memo to a junior clerk in another department. *Figs 4.23* and *4.24* show memos to two people in the same organisation.

ACTIVITY

Your partner in your business is Kamal Parmar who looks after the sales side of the business. Write a memo to Kamal asking him to let you have last week's sales figures together with an estimate for the current week. Produce a draft and final version of your memo.

INVITATIONS

Many types of invitations are sent in business. An individual in one organisation may invite an individual in another to a meeting, perhaps to discuss a new contract. An organisation may invite a business or individual customer to the launch of a new product, for example a new car. An organisation may invite a valued customer to a sporting or other event as a 'thank you' for past business, and to encourage the customer to remain loyal to the business. Depending on the purpose of the invitation, it may be made in a letter or memo. Some invitations, especially to the launch of a new product, or to a sporting or other event, are specially printed to look impressive and persuade the person receiving the invitation to attend.

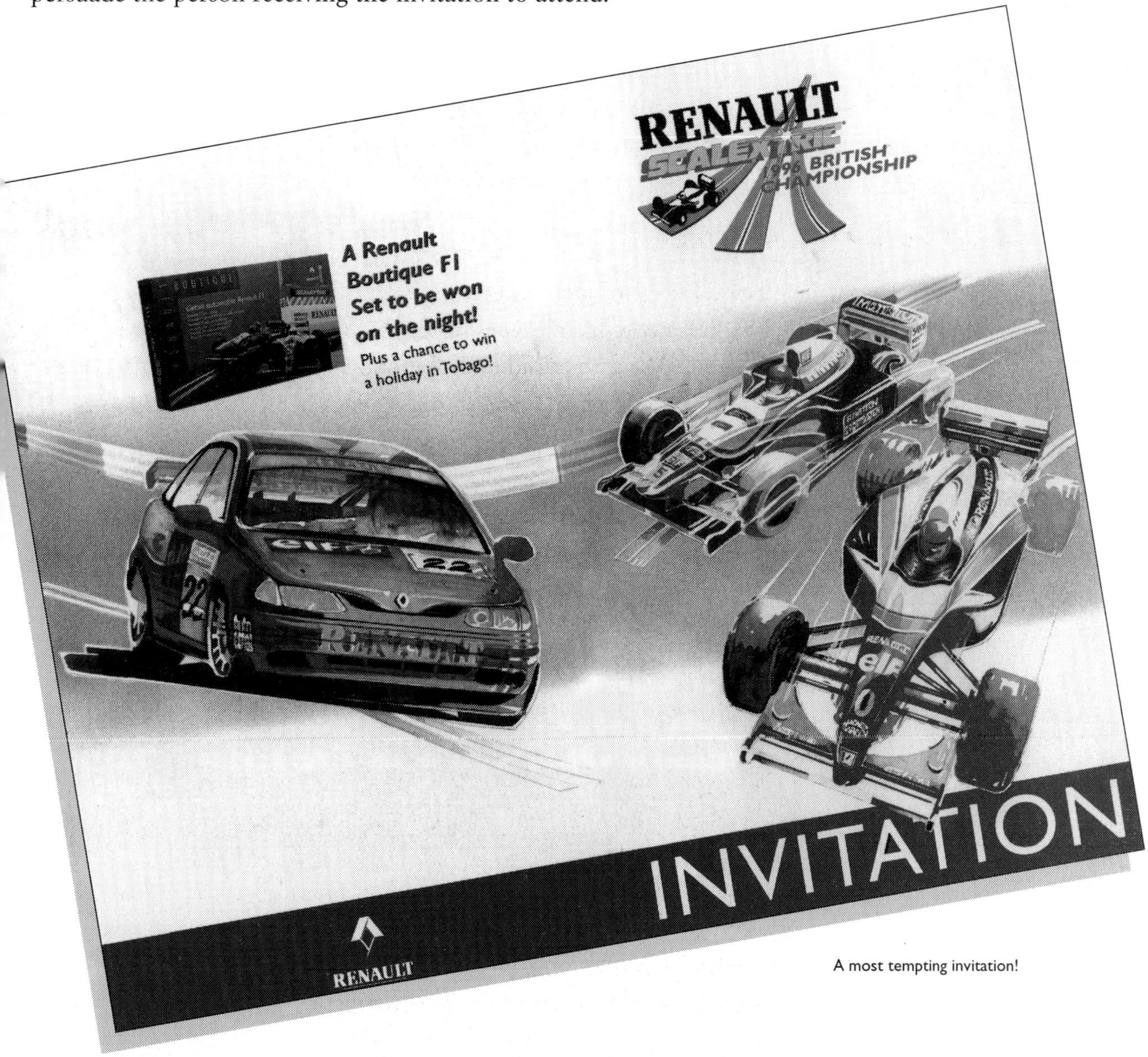

A most tempting invitation!

ACTIVITY

Micropore Computer Systems are planning the launch of a new integrated software package for small businesses, comprising word processing, spreadsheet, accounting and presentations software. The launch is to be on 23 August at 7.00 for 7.30 pm at The Savoy Hotel, Strand, London WC2, and you can invite some of your clients to the launch. Design and produce an invitation to this event to send to selected clients. Keep your original designs together with the final version.

DANGER
PROTECT YOUR HEAD
Always wear a hard hat in this area

A typical safety notice.

NOTICES

Unlike letters and memos, notices are not addressed to a particular person, but are used to communicate with groups of people. They are used to give general information, warnings of possible hazards, instructions and so on. To be effective, a notice should attract the attention of the people at whom it is aimed, convey the desired message, and persuade them to take appropriate action. Notices which apply generally should be placed on a notice board or other site where everybody they concern will see them. If a notice board is used to display notices, it must be kept tidy and up to date. A notice board which is crammed with dogeared notices, many of which are old and no longer applicable, will be ignored and important new notices may be unread.

Other notices may be sent to individuals, if they apply to a small, identifiable group, or placed on or near a product if they give information or warnings about the use of that product.

ACTIVITY

Look round your school or college and make a list of all the notices you can find, together with their purpose. Evaluate the effectiveness of the notices. Design your own notice to warn people of a possible fire or other hazard.

MESSAGES

There will be many occasions when you will have to take a message for somebody else. For example, if you answer the telephone and the caller wants to speak to somebody who is not there at the moment, or if someone calls in person and wants to see one of your colleagues who is not available, you may be asked to take and pass on a message.

When taking a message it is important that you write it down clearly. The message should contain:

- the name, title, and, if appropriate, the department of the person for whom the message is intended;
- the name, title, and, if appropriate, the department of the person who gave the message;
- the date and time the person leaving the message called or telephoned;
- the telephone number or address of the person who left the message;
- the content of the message;
- details of how the person receiving the message is to respond to the message – for example, phone back at two o'clock, or send a brochure in the post.

Always check the details of the message with the person leaving it to ensure there are no mistakes.

QUICK response

Why, in business, is it usually better to take a message and pass it to the person for whom it is intended, rather than to ask a caller to call back?

EVALUATING BUSINESS DOCUMENTS

All business documents reflect the organisation which produces them. A document which is poorly constructed, looks untidy and is difficult to read will give the reader the impression that the organisation which produced it is inefficient and unprofessional – and one to be avoided. A document which is well constructed, looks impressive and is a pleasure to read will give the reader the impression that the organisation which produced it is efficient and professional in its approach to business – an organisation with which it is a pleasure to do business. When you produce a business document, you must evaluate it in terms of:

- appearance, both style and format – is the document a pleasure to look at, does it look professional and efficient?
- language, including spelling and grammar – is the language appropriate to the reader and written concisely and unambiguously so that the message will be easily understood?

ACTIVITY

Look critically at the business documents you have produced for activities in this section, and also at business documents shown in the figures. Make notes about each document, evaluating it in terms of appearance and language, as above.

HOW BUSINESS DOCUMENTS ARE PROCESSED

The development of modern information technology has radically changed the way in which business documents are produced. There are many different methods of producing and distributing documents, which are appropriate in different situations. Business documents may be:

- handwritten;
- typed;
- word processed;
- printed;
- photocopied.

Before deciding which method to use for a particular document, the different methods must be compared in terms of:

- legibility – which method is easiest to read?
- cost – which is the cheapest method which will produce a document of the required standard?
- time taken to produce – will a particular method produce the required document in the time available?
- ability to make changes – if alterations to the document are

required, can these be made easily and without the need to redo the document completely?

- storage – can the document be easily stored and retrieved when necessary?

Handwritten documents

Everybody's handwriting is different. Some people's is neat and clear, while others' is untidy and difficult to read. Although handwritten documents can be quick to produce, handwriting is mainly used in business for taking messages and filling in some forms. Handwritten documents look untidy and unprofessional. They can be difficult to read and, if a mistake is made, the whole document must be rewritten to produce a document without errors. Handwritten documents can be easily copied and stored in a paper-based filing system (see p 302).

Typed documents

Typed documents are easy to read and can be produced in about the same time as handwritten documents. A typewritten document looks more professional than a handwritten document. Some electronic typewriters have limited memories which allow changes to be made in the last line of typing, but any major revisions to a document will require the document to be completely retyped. As with handwritten documents, copies of typed documents can easily be stored in a paper-based filing system.

A stand-alone word processor.

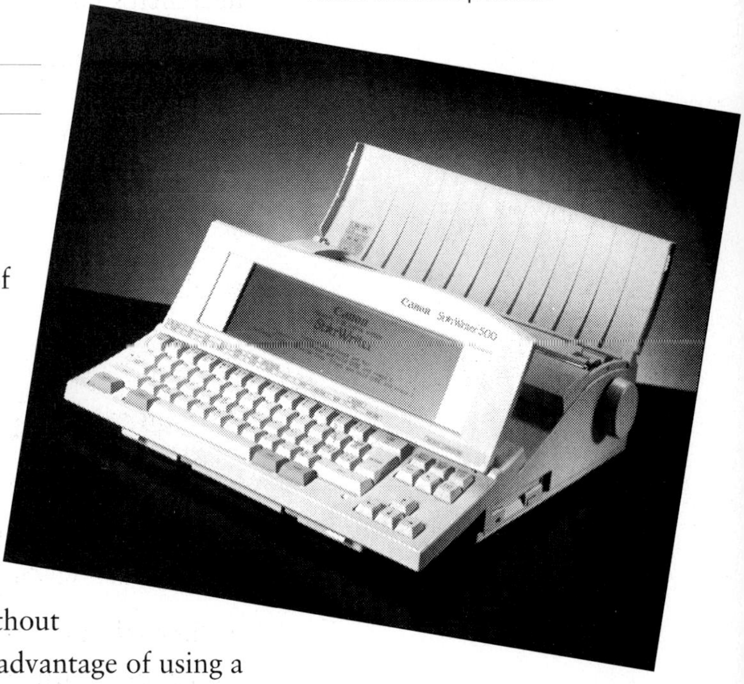

Word-processed documents

Word-processed documents may be produced on stand-alone word processors, or on computers using word-processing software packages. A computer word-processing package may be part of a full desk-top publishing software package, enabling a wide range of business documents to be produced. It is usually possible to use different fonts (styles of lettering) and even incorporate drawings, graphics and photographs into the document.

Any alterations to a word-processed document, no matter how major, can be made without retyping the entire document, and this is a major advantage of using a word-processing package. In addition, word-processing packages usually have spell checks which check and correct spelling. Modern word-processing packages also check for errors in grammar, and suggest alternative words if the writer feels that a word has been used too often in a document, or does not convey the exact meaning intended.

Word-processed documents look professional and efficient. They can easily be formatted to give the right appearance and to read well. However, word processors and computers with word-processing packages are very expensive when compared with typewriters and this must be taken into consideration when choosing new equipment. Documents produced on a word processor or computer can be stored electronically in the computer's memory or on a 'floppy' disk. A great number of documents can therefore be stored in a very small space. In addition, it is possible to retrieve a document, alter it to suit current needs and store both versions of the document.

Printed documents

Printed documents are normally produced by outside printing firms. They are expensive and take a long time to prepare and produce. They are only suitable where a large number of good quality copies of the document is required, for example:

- brochures and other promotional material;
- headed letter paper and memo forms (but not the actual letter or memo);
- invitations to events and product launches, etc.;
- forms of which a large number is required, to be filled in individually.

Because printed documents are expensive and take time to produce, they must be prepared carefully in draft form – often several times – before the final version is sent to the printer.

Photocopied documents

Photocopying is a quick and easy method of producing extra copies of documents however the original was produced. The quality of photocopies can vary, however, and unless the original is of an acceptable standard it may be preferable to produce a copy by another means – even producing another original if necessary. Obviously, it is impossible to make alterations to a photocopy, although alterations may be made to the original before it is copied.

REFERENCING BUSINESS DOCUMENTS FOR FILING AND RETRIEVING

Many documents have to be referred to some time after they have been issued or received. For example, when a reply to a letter sent out the previous week is received, it is usually necessary to refer to a copy of the original letter when considering the reply. To enable this to be done, the original document must be given a **reference**. The copy of the document can then be filed in accordance with its reference so that it can easily be retrieved when required.

There are several ways of referencing documents, and the method chosen should be the one most appropriate to the type and subject matter of the document. It is also important that the person responsible for filing and retrieving the document should feel that the system of referencing is logical, simple and easy to understand. The most common ways of referencing documents are:

- **Alphabetically**, usually by subject matter or name: This system of referencing is common in business, as it is easy to understand and operate. For example, a letter enquiring about new computer software may be referenced computer/JAL/AW. Here, computer is the subject matter of the letter, JAL are the writer's initials, and AW are the initials of the person who produced the letter. The copy of the letter will then be filed alphabetically under C for computer in the filing system of the writer, JAL.
- **Numerically**: Numerical systems of referencing are mainly used either when account numbers are used, for example to identify customers, or where confidentiality is important, so that the identity of the person or subject covered by a document in a filing system is kept secret. An advantage is that each individual or subject can be allocated a unique reference number, which may be in random rather than alphabetic or any other order. The major disadvantage is that a key or index is required in order to be able to file and retrieve documents.
- **By subject**: Many businesses reference and file documents in subject order. This is normally combined with an alphabetical system. It is important, however, to be consistent as documents can easily be considered to fall into more than one subject area. For example, a report on sales in Germany may be given a reference 'sales', or 'Germany', and filed accordingly. If there is likely to be any confusion, then two copies of the document should be produced,

> **QUICK response**
>
> **Out of alphabetical, numerical and subject methods of referencing documents, which two can easily be used in conjunction with each other?**

one of which should be filed under 'sales', and the second under 'Germany'. Alternatively, a system of cross referencing could be used where, if the document is filed under 'sales', a reference to the document is filed under 'Germany', instructing anyone wanting to retrieve the document to look under 'sales'.

- **By date**: This system is most commonly used for filing documents within sub-files. For example, an individual file for Johnson Brothers, a major customer, may be placed alphabetically within the filing system but, within the file itself, documents such as letters may be placed in date order.

ACTIVITY

In previous activities in this element, you have produced a variety of business documents on a range of topics. Review each document now, and decide on the most appropriate way of referencing it for ease of filing and retrieving the document. Put the reference in pencil in the top right-hand corner of the document.

A recorded delivery form.

SENDING AND STORING BUSINESS DOCUMENTS

SENDING DOCUMENTS

Modern technology has also had a considerable affect on how business documents can be sent. The method used depends on the type, content, value and urgency of the document. In addition, the cost of using different methods varies considerably. It may be cheaper to send a bulky A4 document by courier service than through the post.

The most common method for sending letters, however, is still through the **post**. Letters sent by first-class post normally arrive at their destination on the first working day after posting, provided they are put in a post box or delivered to a post office before the last collection of the day. Letters sent by second-class post usually arrive at their destination on the second working day after posting. A **guaranteed next day delivery** is available by paying a fee in addition to the normal postage. If the sender of a letter requires proof that the letter has been received, it can be sent by **recorded delivery**, in which case the postman will obtain a signature from the recipient of the letter as proof of delivery. Letters with valuable enclosures can be sent by **registered post**. A certificate confirming that an item has been posted can also be obtained from a post office.

Documents which are required urgently can be sent by **special delivery**. As well as the special delivery service provided by the Post Office, many private delivery companies provide special delivery and courier services which guarantee delivery of letters and other packages within a stated time, often on the same day or overnight. Some companies, such as DHL, provide a world wide delivery service and operate their own fleets of vehicles and even aeroplanes.

Fax, or facsimile, machines are now widely used to transmit copies of documents through telephone lines. Both the sender and the recipient must have fax machines. The original document is scanned by the sender's machine and transcribed into digital electrical impulses. The impulses are transmitted through the telephone line to the receiving fax machine. The receiving machine transcribes the electrical impulses and reproduces a copy of the original document on paper. In this way it is possible to send a copy of a form, drawing or signed document in the time it takes to make a telephone call.

Electronic mail, or **e-mail**, is a method of sending documents electronically from one computer terminal to another. The computers must be linked to a network. Many large business organisations use e-mail to transmit documents between colleagues. The document is produced on the computer terminal of the sender and transmitted to

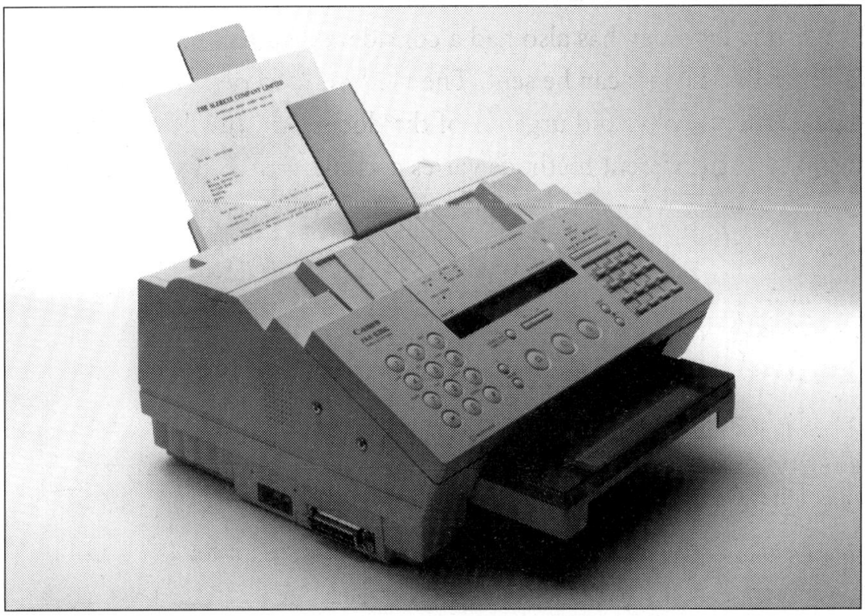

A fax machine.

the computer terminal of the receiver, where it is called up on screen and can be printed out if required. If a computer is linked to the telephone system through a **modem**, it is possible to transmit e-mail to other computers. It is therefore possible to transmit information and documents between the computers in one business organisation and another, between a business and a private individual, and even to computers in other countries. In order to transmit to computers outside the organisation, the sender and the recipient must be members of a computer network such as Internet.

STORING DOCUMENTS

You have seen that businesses produce many different types of documents, each of which has to be stored in a system which will allow it to be easily retrieved when required.

An effective storage and retrieval system should:

- be secure from hazards such as fire, unauthorised access and industrial espionage;
- provide for easy retrieval of documents by authorised personnel;
- keep documents and information in good condition;
- be capable of being added to as necessary;
- be cost-effective.

QUICK response

Why is it important to make a back-up copy of everything you produce on a computer?

Document-storage or filing systems can be paper-based or computer-based. The type of system used will depend on the type of document stored. The principal methods of storing documents and information are shown in *Fig. 4.25*.

If documents and records are kept on computer, it is important that back-up copies are kept on 'floppy' disk. This ensures that files and documents are not lost should there be a failure of the computer system. Making back-up copies of your work may seem time-consuming and unnecessary – until disaster strikes and you have lost all your work! Never cut corners by not bothering to make back-up copies of your work.

Method	Advantages	Disadvantages
Hard copy of original document, held in filing cabinets, rotary filing systems, registries and other filing systems	Documents and files can be easily handled and read; affords quick access if the system is efficient and files are to hand; classified documents can be held by prescribed individuals; suitable for storing all types of documents, drawings, diagrams, legal documents, maps, etc.	Takes up space; files and papers can be borrowed and not returned, misplaced or filed in the wrong place; classified documents require special procedures with regard to authorisation.
Microfilm filing systems: microcopy or microfiche	Saves space: requires only about 2 per cent of the space of a hard copy filing system; photographic hard copy can be made when required; suitable for various types of documents.	Requires a special microfilm reader; documents must be photographed on to microfilm first, requiring a special camera; to get a readable copy, the original document must be good.
Floppy disk	Large capacity; can be stored in a small space; files and documents can be easily updated and overwritten; confidential documents can be protected by password access; hard copy can easily be printed out.	Index of file names on disk is required; not useful for incoming documents unless transmitted by e-mail; inappropriate for signed or handwritten documents, photographs, diagrams, etc. unless produced on computer.
Hard disk	Very large capacity; files and documents can be easily updated and overwritten; confidential documents can be protected by password access; can be downloaded on to individual floppy disks; hard copy can easily be printed out.	Index of file names on disk is required; not useful for incoming documents unless transmitted by e-mail; inappropriate for signed or handwritten documents, photographs, diagrams, etc. unless produced on computer; can be corrupted or wiped clean in the event of an operator error or a failure in the computer system.

FIGURE 4.25 The principal methods of storing documents and information.

PORTFOLIO ASSIGNMENT

TASK 1

You work in the Administration Department of AK Engineering Limited at AK House, Clarkia Avenue, London NW1. During the course of one Monday, you carry out the following tasks. You should produce draft and final versions of each document.

9.00 am: You arrive at your desk. Your first task is to design an invitation to the launch of a new luxury car which contains several parts manufactured by AK Engineering. The launch is to take place at The Hilton Hotel, Park Lane, London W1A 2HH on the 28th of next month. The invitation will be sent to customers of AK Engineering.

9.30 am: David Johnson, the Sales Manager, hands you three letters from customers, which have arrived in this morning's post and asks you to reply to them.

The first letter is from Hayden Products plc, Invicta Trading Estate, Cardiff CF7 9TY, asking for a copy of your brochure. You must reply to the letter, explaining that the brochure is being revised. You will send a copy when it is printed.

The second letter is from John Newcombe of Aitcheson and Tofts, Broad Street, Stamford, Lincolnshire PE9 1IT. He is complaining that an alternator which should have been delivered last week has not arrived. You must reply, promising to look into the matter. David tells you that the alternator will definitely be delivered the day after tomorrow.

The third letter is from Diksha Saehania of Software Solutions, a computer consultancy based at Bank Chambers, 39 Holt Street, London NW1. You have asked her to show you some computer accounting software and she wishes to arrange a meeting at AK Engineering on Tuesday of next week at 2.30 pm. You are to reply, confirming this date and time.

12.30 pm: Sara Piercy, who has just been offered a job as a computer operator with your company, telephones and asks to speak to Jill Bryant, the Personnel Manager. Jill is at lunch so you ask if you can take a message. Sara tells you that she wants to accept the offer of the job and will put a letter confirming this in the post. She just wanted to let Mrs Bryant know by telephone first. You make a note of the message and promise to give it to Jill as soon as she returns.

2.30 pm: Amrish Kotecha, the Managing Director of AK Engineering, telephones you. He wants to put up a notice in the staff canteen to let employees know that AK Engineering has won a major contract to supply components to Japan, and asks you to design a suitable notice. Design the notice and write a covering memo enclosing your design.

TASK 2

Give examples of three different methods of processing the business documents included in Task 1. Compare each method in terms of legibility, cost, time taken to produce, ease of making changes and storage.

TASK 3

For this task you will need access to a manual or computer filing system and at least 36 documents and six files. Your tutor should be able to arrange this, or you may be able to obtain evidence for this part of the assignment during a period of work experience. Your tutor or work experience supervisor should make a record of you accurately referencing, filing and retrieving the documents and files.

Index

Acknowledgements

Thanks to Trish for unfailing patience, support and love.
Chris Nuttall

To Martha, Dominique, Norma, Mark, Mary, Rosalind, Katharine, Helen and Gregg for the quality time they missed.
Tony Pitt, David Knight, Malcolm Meerabux and Barrie Birch

The authors and publisher would like to thank the following for permission to reproduce material:

ACAS (p 111 top)
Alfred Marks (p 153)
Allsport (p 41 right)
Anchor (p 33)
ASA (p 195)
Axiom (p199 left)
Brighton Resort Services (p 170)
Canon (pp 297, 301)
Club 18-30 (p 168 left)
DHL (p 229)
European Parliament (p 111 bottom)
HMSO (pp 38, 65, 66, 70-1, 73, 171, 173, 183)
ICI (p 23)
JCB (p22)
Legal & General (p 23)
Midland Bank (p 22)
Nissan (p 36)
Pizza Hut (p 24)
Post Office (p 300)
Powerstock (p 22)
Press Association (p 110, David Giles)
The Prince's Business Trust (p 154)
Puma (p 193)
Renault (p 293)
Rex Features (p 165)
Rover (pp 22, 52, 105)
Saga (p 168 right)
St John's Ambulance (p 145)
SM Hudson (p 199 right)
TCL Stock Directory (pp 50 left, 132)
Tony Stone (pp 3, Frank Siteman; 49, Ian O'Leary; 61, Craig Schmittman; 88, Walter Hodges; 89, Donald Johnston; 95, Walter Hodges; 122, Charles Thatcher; 128, Michael Rosenfeld; 130, Jean Y Ruszniewski; 137, Walter Hodges; 155, Kurt Henseler)
TSB (p 9)
Virgin (p 22)
Waitrose (p 211)

Photographs by Jay Ward (pp 26, 35, 41 left, 44, 47, 50 right, 57, 146, 213).
Illustrations were drawn by Julia Osorno.
Cartoons were drawn by Daniel Betts (pp 39, 73, 103, 107, 116, 120, 184, 215) and Nathan Betts (pp 18, 44, 101, 109, 118, 152, 158, 228, 230).